Choosing a Sustainable Future

Most of us want to be part of the solution. Thank you, Liz Walker and Ithaca, for showing us how — with verve, clarity, and just enough detail to make it all real. *Choosing a Sustainable Future* proves that we don't have to give in to fear. We can use today's horrific threats to propel us into common action, creating communities that are more beautiful in every way. Let Ithaca's story be spread far and wide.

> — FRANCES MOORE LAPPÉ, author of *Diet for a Small Planet* and *Getting a Grip2: Clarity, Creativity and Courage for the World We Really Want*

An economy based on ingenuity, thrift, competence, full-cost accounting, and grounded in its place! What an idea! *Choosing a Sustainable Future* is radical — in the right sense of the word — but practical. Liz Walker and her colleagues are demonstrating in Ithaca a blueprint for economic resilience, fairness, and honest prosperity everywhere.

> — DAVID W. ORR, Paul Sears Distinguished Professor and Senior adviser to the President, Oberlin College, author of *Hope is an Imperative: the Essential David Orr*

Ithaca is one of those places showing the way towards a workable future, and Liz Walker is a key guide on that tour. Pay attention!

> — BILL MCKIBBEN, founder 350.org

Buckminster Fuller is famous for saying "The best way to predict the future is to design it." Liz Walker shows us how the citizens of Ithaca, NY and Tompkins County have taken that message to heart, and for the past 20 years have been creating a fair, equitable and sustainable future.

> — KEN ROTHER, President and COO of Treehugger.com

As we awaken to the many trends and injustices that threaten our environmental and social future, and enter this era of reinvention, we need models and mentors of strategies that work, so that we can re-imagine how we might structure our food, water and energy systems, and appreciate indigenous ecological wisdom. *Choosing a Sustainable Future* offers practical and visionary solutions that have been proven and work, to re-orient our children, ourselves and our communities toward just and regenerative life ways. This is a vital resource for anyone seeking to engage with neighbors and community members to co-create a healthy, resilient, peaceful and just future.

— NINA SIMONS, Cofounder, Bioneers and editor,
Moonrise: The Power of Women Leading from the Heart

In this fascinating description of one community's efforts to design and implement more sustainable living, learning and work environments, Liz Walker strikes just the right balance between successes achieved and the challenges that remain. I highly recommend the book to all who are interested in this urgent issue.

— DAVID J. SKORTON, President, Cornell University

Liz Walker's voice should resonate all over the world. Ithaca is no longer a "utopia," but an outstanding achievement of sustainable living in the US, and a great model and inspiration for change anywhere in this planet.

— CARLOS FRESNEDA, author of *La Vida Simple*,
and US correspondent with *El Mundo*

Liz Walker chronicles the stories of those struggling happily (for the most part) to make our cities healthy and sustainable into the deep future. This is an adventure with dozens of real people's experiences, and in the first person of the explorer.

— RICHARD REGISTER, author, *Ecocities: Rebuilding Cities in Balance with Nature*, President of Ecocity Builders and founder of the International Ecocity Conferences series

Choosing a Sustainable Future

Choosing a Sustainable Future

IDEAS AND INSPIRATION FROM ITHACA, NY

Liz Walker

NEW SOCIETY PUBLISHERS

Cover design by Diane McIntosh.
Cover images: Water image: Harmony © Helena Cooper, www.helenaart.com
Top inset photos: Jim Bosjolie / © iStock Plainview (stamp)
David Schrader (handmade paper).

Printed in Canada. First printing September 2010.

Inquiries regarding requests to reprint all or part of *Choosing a Sustainable Future*
should be addressed to New Society Publishers at the address below.

To order directly from the publishers, please call toll-free (North America)
1-800-567-6772, or order online at www.newsociety.com

Any other inquiries can be directed by mail to:
New Society Publishers
P.O. Box 189, Gabriola Island, BC V0R 1X0, Canada
(250) 247-9737

New Society Publishers' mission is to publish books that contribute in fundamental
ways to building an ecologically sustainable and just society, and to do so with the
least possible impact on the environment, in a manner that models this vision.
We are committed to doing this not just through education, but through action.
Our printed, bound books are printed on Forest Stewardship Council-certified
acid-free paper that is **100% post-consumer recycled** (100% old growth forest-
free), processed chlorine free, and printed with vegetable-based, low-VOC inks,
with covers produced using FSC-certified stock. New Society also works to reduce
its carbon footprint, and purchases carbon offsets based on an annual audit to
ensure a carbon neutral footprint. For further information, or to browse our full
list of books and purchase securely, visit our website at: www.newsociety.com

LIBRARY AND ARCHIVES CANADA CATALOGUING IN PUBLICATION

Walker, Liz
Choosing a sustainable future : ideas and inspiration from Ithaca, NY / Liz Walker.

Includes bibliographical references and index.
ISBN 978-0-86571-675-9
eISBN: 978-1-55092-464-0

1. Sustainable development—New York (State)—Ithaca.   2. Community
development—New York (State)—Ithaca.   3. Environmental
management—New York (State)—Ithaca.   4. Sustainable living—New
York (State)—Ithaca.   I. Title.

HC79.E5W2678 2010   333.7   C2010-905766-X

NEW SOCIETY PUBLISHERS
www.newsociety.com

Mixed Sources
Product group from well-managed forests,
controlled sources and recycled wood or fiber
www.fsc.org   Cert no. SW-COC-000952
© 1996 Forest Stewardship Council

FSC

Contents

Acknowledgments

It is a rare occurrence to observe the unfolding of a powerful social movement from within, and a privilege to take part in both helping to catalyze the growth of that movement and to document its rapid evolution. I have been deeply inspired by the hundreds of creative, dedicated individuals and dozens of local organizations that together are working to bring about a remarkable cultural shift towards social justice and long-term sustainability.

I want to thank my colleagues in this movement, particularly those who offered support, granted interviews, joined in focus groups, edited drafts or organized the events mentioned in these pages. I hope this book will help your collective work to reach an even broader audience. And for those whose work is not mentioned, please understand that while it is still deeply appreciated there has been simply too much to capture in one book.

Special thanks go to my friends Joanna Green, Arthur Godin, Larry Hershberger and Saoirse McClory for encouraging me to take the necessary leap of faith to write *Choosing a Sustainable Future*, to the EcoVillage at Ithaca board of directors for granting me a six-month sabbatical to write (and for their patience when it took a year), to the Park Foundation for assisting with a grant, to Kurt Pipa for helping to organize focus groups and to Teal Arcadi, a high school student who provided me with a much-needed personal clipping service. Thanks to members of my family for their encouragement and review of chapters, especially Margery Walker, Daniel Katz and Rachel Cogbill. Thanks also to the following friends and colleagues who reviewed one or more chapters: Sharon Anderson, Peter Bardaglio, Katie Borgella, Marian Brown, Kirby Edmonds, Marcia Fort, Dick Franke, Jeff Gilmore, Bill Goodman, Joanna Green, Brooke Hansen, David Kay, Kat McCarthy, Steve Nicholson, Tina Nilsen-Hodges, Jan Norman, Krishna Ramanujan, Dan Roth,

Monica Roth, Elan Shapiro, Fred Shoeps, Bethany Schroeder, Jeanne Shenandoah and Sara Silverstone. Your comments were invaluable. Any mistakes are entirely my responsibility.

Many professional photographers donated or discounted their work. Special thanks to Jim Bosjolie, Helena Cooper, Tony Ingraham, Jon Reis, Sheryl Sinkow, Bill Truslow, Toba Pato Tucker and the organizations who shared great images. Also thanks to Rob Morache for sharing his design of the Aurora Street Dwelling Circle.

I also want to thank Chris and Judith Plant and Ingrid Witvoet from New Society Publishers for encouraging me to begin writing this book and Betsy Nuse, my editor, for helping to polish it for publication.

For ongoing emotional support when the way got tough I am deeply grateful to Betsy Crane, my women's group and various friends, especially Jalaja Bonheim, Elan and Rachael Shapiro and Krishna Ramanujan, who all believed in my writing abilities, even when I had doubts. Most important of all, this book would not have become a reality without the ongoing love and support of my wonderful life partner Jared Jones.

Preface—Why I Wrote This Book

*In our every deliberation we must consider the impact
of our decisions on the next seven generations.*

FROM THE GREAT LAW OF THE IROQUOIS CONFEDERACY

Writing a book is a lot like the process of gestation and childbirth,
only it often takes longer. First there is the flicker of an idea, a creative flash and an intention to write. It may take a while for this intention to grow—to become pregnant with an idea that is so strong and
palpable that it must be shared. Although one may choose to birth
a child or a book, there is some point at which natural forces seem
to take over from human will. Momentum builds, and the creative
process must be followed through to its conclusion despite any obstacles or discomforts along the way. As the body of the book grows,
one becomes obsessed with it. Will it be grow to be healthy and
strong? Will it be smart and beautiful? Will people like it? There may
be pangs of midnight doubt—who am I to bring this baby into the
world? Surely someone else would be a better qualified parent!

Choosing a Sustainable Future had a long gestation period. The
idea came to me in 2007, a full two years before I was able to carve
out the time to write it. During that time, the world situation de-
teriorated: the devastating effects of climate change became widely
recognized, the US went into a national recession, the world followed and *peak oil*, that time when demand for oil outstrips world
supply, became a term used by the mainstream. Every day brought
worse news: collapse of global fisheries, worsening drought from
the Central Valley of California to the deserts of Sudan, high unemployment, sharply escalating food prices and countries torn apart
by wars over scarce natural resources. The problems continue to
worsen and often seem completely overwhelming.

During the same time, my conviction grew: there was something happening in our town that was simply too big to ignore. Ithaca, New York was bubbling with innovation. I was witnessing the birth of a powerful movement, one that included old and young, women and men, local government officials, businesses and grassroots activists alike. There often seemed to be a racial divide — one that I wanted to understand better. The overall momentum and growth of this movement was simply astonishing, and I felt that someone had to document it. Looking around, I was surprised to find that person seemed to be me. No one else was taking it on.

Immediately self-doubt started to kick in. While in some ways I felt well qualified — I had been working as an environmental activist all my adult life and had co-founded a successful ecovillage — in other ways I felt woefully inadequate. I was neither trained as a writer nor as a researcher, I was not an expert in any of the subject matter that I wanted to cover and I was certainly not an academic (although I was surrounded by scholars in this college town). But I found that I wanted to share the excitement, the discovery, the growing pains and the challenges with others who are actively engaged in the search for a better, more sustainable way of living on this planet. This conviction has carried me through the process of exploring, researching, interviewing dozens of people and writing *Choosing a Sustainable Future*. And perhaps this experience is emblematic of the way that all of us are compelled to grow, to reach beyond our comfort zones and across disciplines if we want to create a more positive future. There is no more time for hiding away — now is the time for all of us to build our individual and collective capacity for action.

The biggest challenge has been that there is simply so much activity going on in Ithaca in the areas of social justice and sustainability that it is hard to even begin to capture it. It is rather like describing the flowering of a garden in the spring — every day brings new sprouts, new tendrils of connection between the plants and brilliant new colors. There is too much richness to include in one small book, and by the time it was written it was already out of date — some flowers had faded and new ones had bloomed.

I owe an apology in advance to my fellow Ithacans: *Choosing a Sustainable Future* is not comprehensive, and for the sake of readability and brevity I have chosen to include some (but by no means all) of the very worthy sustainability oriented projects that are burgeoning in this city, town and county. I have tried to include examples of both small and large efforts — from the grassroots to the institutional, from the rural hamlets of Tompkins County to the city of Ithaca. Although many people think of sustainability in purely environmental terms, the concept encompasses far more. Most chapters include examples of social justice and equity issues and of community-building cultural efforts. I have attempted to draw a quick watercolor portrait of the garden in bloom, yet by describing it, I have captured just one moment in time.

Because I think people respond well to the personal and storytelling approach, I have concentrated on the examples that I know best, including ones from my home community of EcoVillage at Ithaca, as well as many other organizations that have touched my life. This approach necessarily leaves out many, many valuable organizations and pioneering individuals. Although they aren't mentioned they are still worthy of acknowledgment — it just reinforces how much vigorous growth is going on. To include every example would take an encyclopedia!

Finally, a word about what *sustainability* means to me. When figuring out a title for this book, my publisher urged me to stay away from this term. "Everyone is using it, and it has lost its meaning," the marketing staff told me. I beg to differ. I think the term sustainability is becoming increasingly popular precisely because it beckons us to a deeper understanding which cannot be described in a clear, concise way. The most widely used definition of sustainability comes from the Brundtland Commission (named after the Norwegian Prime Minister and Environmental Minister who headed the Commission): "Sustainable development is development that meets the needs of the present without compromising the ability of future generations to meet their own needs."[1] This definition directs our attention to our children and grandchildren who will inherit the earth from us. It therefore implies a sense of intergenerational solidarity. It further implies that we should not have to sacrifice the present: the tools of modern science and the knowledge that we can derive from ancient cultures should be enough to create a sustainable way of life.

Ultimately, a sustainable future comes through a paradigm shift — social, environmental, economical and cultural — that a growing percentage of the human population knows we need to make. Deep in our hearts, we know that there is a positive alternative future at stake — one that promises a stronger connection with nature and beckons with the warmth of community. But to reach this positive future, we must act on this choice today! I feel blessed to live in Ithaca, one of many bright spots around the world which are making practical headway developing this vision.

INTRODUCTION

Another World Is Possible

Another world is not only possible, she is on her way.
On a quiet day I can hear her breathing.

ARUNDHATI ROY

This is a remarkable time to be alive. We are in the midst of the most widespread, rapid changes that have ever happened in human history, and not surprisingly, no one seems to know quite how to react. The threats to human survival are real. We are facing what some call the *triple crisis*: global climate change, reaching the limits of easily accessible key natural resources such as oil and water, and increasing economic chaos. The devastation that humans are wreaking on the lifeways of planet Earth are also well documented: the unprecedented rate of species extinction and the toxic pollution of air, water and soil.

In addition to these critical environmental problems, there are equally pressing social and economic issues, such as massive cultural disruption caused by wars over scarce natural resources, increased urbanization and terrible inequities between the impoverished majority and the powerful super rich.

This book is about the unfolding of a compassionate human response to these dilemmas—about choosing a very different future based on social justice, wise use of natural resources and a greener, more satisfying way of living at a local level. Just as the problems are so deeply rooted in the dominant culture and so intertwined

1

as to often seem insoluble, the solutions have even deeper roots in the values of indigenous cultures and in appropriate uses of modern technology. Interestingly, the solutions are also remarkably intertwined, so that a solution in one area may have cascading positive effects in others. Between facing the problems and their possible solutions, I do not think it is an exaggeration to say that we are at the most important choice point in human history.

In 2008, our species made a quiet but remarkable transition into new territory. For the first time in human history, over one half of our population now lives in cities. Many of the city dwellers are rural, often indigenous people who have been pushed off their land and can no longer make a subsistence living farming or fishing. While cities can provide an oasis of cultural, intellectual and economic vitality, the world's largest cities often include slum districts that are cesspools of vast human poverty and suffering. These megacities also produce most of the world's pollution.[1]

As the global economy makes inroads into the most remote corners of the earth, local cultures suffer. These cultures, previously sustainable over hundreds of years and frequently in careful balance with their ecosystems, are often seriously damaged within decades of exposure to corporate media and the dominant industrial worldview. Helena Norberg-Hodge described her firsthand experience seeing these changes happen in Ladakh, a high-altitude desert in northernmost India that until recently was isolated from modern society. She observed that the local economy was traditionally based on self-sufficiency, cooperation and trade and that when the area was opened to tourists, media and public education, the Ladakhis began to lose their sense of pride and feel instead a cultural inferiority complex.

In 1975, I was shown around the remote village of Hemis Shukpachan by a young Ladakh named Tsewang. It seemed to me that all the houses we saw were especially large and beautiful. I asked Tsewang to show me the houses where the poor people lived. Tsewang looked perplexed a moment, then responded, "We don't have any poor people here." Eight years later I overheard Tsewang talking to some tourists. "If you could only help us Ladakhis," he was saying, "we're so poor."[2]

Norberg-Hodge further pointed out that "Media images focus on the rich, the beautiful and the brave, whose lives are endless action and glamour... In contrast to these utopian images from another culture, village life seems primitive, silly and inefficient."[3] Increasing alienation, often violent frustration and an exodus to cities should be no surprise in a world in which three quarters of the human family lives on a real income of US$4 per day or less,[4] and in which the disparity between this lifestyle and that of the affluent minority is glaringly obvious through movies, television and the Internet.

Humans are an intensely social species. Our babies are born with no ability to survive on their own, and we learn almost everything through interacting with other humans. Until recently we never lived alone, but like our primate ancestors, lived in small groups which helped one another. This is no longer the case, especially in developed countries such as the US, as the growing number of households of single people and single parents testifies.[5] Our modern lives make it hard to find a sense of community. In many cases, people in the US live fragmented lives: we sleep in bedroom communities and commute long distances to work, to school, to shopping and to recreation. There is very little time for civic engagement or for getting together with friends. "Community is perhaps the most valuable and most essential resource on this planet," said Michael Brownlee, head of Boulder Relocalization, "Community has also become our scarcest and most threatened resource."[6]

Not only are we starved for community, we are also rapidly losing our connection to nature. In his bestseller, *Last Child in the Woods*, author Richard Louv wrote about the staggering divide between modern children and the outdoors, and directly linked the lack of nature in the lives of today's wired generation to some of the most disturbing childhood trends, such as the rises in obesity, attention disorders and depression.[7]

As a human species we are very rapidly hurtling towards a cliff — from an environmental, economic, social and spiritual perspective.

Will we, like the hypothetical mad lemmings, rush off this cliff into a freefall of chaos and destruction? Or are we capable, as an amazingly adaptive species, of learning how to fly? We may not know the answer for several more decades. What we do know is that if we want to survive and thrive as a species it will take all of us, working together, to turn around the predominant industrial, exploitative paradigm of a globalized economy and culture.

A New Worldview

There is a new, emerging worldview that is almost the opposite of our current experience. It values cooperation between people and respect for all life. It holds community as a sacred trust, and values equal access to resources such as food, shelter, meaningful work and healthcare. This worldview believes in providing nurturing support for the old, young and sick. It celebrates diversity. It focuses on place-based identity and honors ecosystem health. It takes care to clean up and maintain our precious natural resources of earth, water and air.

There are seeds of the new culture springing up wherever we look. In Paul Hawken's book, *Blessed Unrest*, he estimated that the largest citizen movement on the planet is emerging, consisting of over a million grassroots organizations, working towards ecological sustainability and social justice.[8]

In the United States, this movement is growing rapidly. Duane Elgin, a well-known futurist, said,

> Based upon three decades of research, I estimate that as of 2009, roughly 20 percent of the US adult population, or approximately forty million people, are consciously crafting Earth-friendly or green ways of living. These lifeway pioneers are providing the critical mass of invention at the grassroots level that could enable the larger society to swiftly develop alternative ways and approaches to living.[9]

In addition to individual actions, the immediacy of global climate change has begun to jog us into collective action. Where national policy is lagging, the initiative of some local and state governments is beginning to pick up the slack. Around the US, 1,042 mayors have now signed the Mayors' Climate Protection Agreement to reduce greenhouse gases.[10] Higher education has followed suit, with 673 colleges committed to the American College and University Presidents' Climate Commitment.[11]

At the same time, grassroots groups have created popular educational and political campaigns, such as 350.org, a campaign started by environmental writer Bill McKibben to awaken the public to the scientific understanding that we must reduce the carbon dioxide in the atmosphere from a current level of 387 parts per million (ppm) to no more than 350 ppm — or face a catastrophic tipping point of climate change. This movement, largely organized online, spread virally in 2009. October 24th, 2009 was called "the most widespread day of political action in the planet's history," with more than 5,200 events in 181 countries.[12] The citizens' movement it unleashed had a real impact on the 2009 United Nations climate negotiations in Copenhagen, with admiration acknowledged by many leaders, despite the fact that their governments were only able to reach a weak agreement. The organizers planned even more activity in 2010.

Another online organization, MoveOn.org, has mobilized 4.2 million progressive Americans to speak up strongly on a variety of environmental and social justice issues.[13] There is a growing relocalization movement, which seeks to consciously revitalize local economies and cultures.[14] And the rapidly growing Transition Town movement, which started in a small English town in 2005, has already garnered official commitments from 265 cities and towns around the world to create "energy descent plans," community-based endeavors to plan for the effects of climate change and peak oil.[15]

All of this activity — from the global to the local — is exactly what needs to be happening. We need both top-down and bottom-up strategies, and we need to affect change on all levels — from the personal to the community to state and federal levels in the US. And we need to do it now!

The Power of Real, Living Examples

This new movement is infusing new values. As values change, there are places where the new paradigm begins to shine through the detritus of the rotten old one. In some places there are pockets of new growth that are growing like mats of deep green moss. In these areas the new, cooperative culture is clearly visible. It is inviting and appealing. In fact, living on one of these green islands, it is hard to imagine another way of life, because it is so deeply soul-satisfying.

Ithaca, New York is one of these mossy patches where the new, green culture is beginning to shine through. Ithaca has become a kind of gathering place for people who are ecologically minded. Despite its small size (about 30,000 permanent residents, with another 26,000 students) it has often been singled out for its quality of life. *Mother Earth News* named it the first of "Twelve Great Places You've Never Heard of" in their August 2006 issue. Ithaca ranked second in "Best Green Places to Live" by *Country Home* magazine in April 2007 and third in Relocate America's "Top 100 Places to Live in 2007."[16] It's amazing that such a small metropolis could garner such acclaim!

This is not to say that Ithaca does not have its share of problems — like cities anywhere it faces racial tension, deep-seated poverty and the uneasy juxtaposition of rural, traditional values with an urban, cosmopolitan outlook, sometimes leading to a volatile mix of cultures. Despite its cloudy climate (second only to Seattle, Washington), steep hills, harsh winters and the dismal economy of upstate New York, what makes this small city work so well? Certainly if people can create a wonderful quality of life here, there is hope that they can do it in many other places.

Choosing a Sustainable Future looks at what makes Ithaca an exciting place to live and its efforts to create a thriving, sustainable community. It examines all aspects of the emerging new green culture, introduces successful innovators and looks at examples of great ideas that can be replicated elsewhere. It describes what works and what doesn't work. But most of all, it offers a taste of another possible future — the inspiration and the tools to build sustainable communities anywhere.

Perhaps more than anything else, the world needs inspiration. We need to know that a different way of life is not only possible, but that it already exists and that it works. There is a tremendous power in working models, especially when these examples combine to form a whole system.

I have seen this power at work during my 19 years as co-founder and executive director of EcoVillage at Ithaca (EVI) — an educational nonprofit that has developed a living laboratory of a socially and environmentally sustainable community — one whose residents enjoy an exceptionally high quality of life while using 40% less resources than typical US citizens. Our nonprofit project owns 176 acres of land just two miles from downtown Ithaca. Ninety percent of the land is preserved as open space for organic agriculture, wildlife habitat, recreation and beauty. Two, soon to be three, cohousing neighborhoods form a small, densely clustered village. Homes are modest duplexes built with environmentally friendly materials. They are all passive solar and superinsulated, and many generate their own electricity from the sun. Two on-site organic farms supply vegetables, fruit and berries to EcoVillagers and the surrounding community alike. EVI's educational partnerships with Cornell University and Ithaca College allow a forum for reaching hundreds of students a year, and over a thousand people come from around the US and other countries for tours every year.

Like any human endeavor, EVI is not perfect, and our project is filled with contradictions. While we aim to be part of the broader Ithaca community, we are somewhat isolated on a steep hill two miles out of town. As environmentalists we are still largely dependent on our cars. While we try to live simpler lives, living in community is quite complex. We often struggle with interpersonal conflicts, some of which take many meetings to resolve and can leave bruised feelings. Some people do more work for the community than others, and there is often resentment of those who do less. Despite longstanding efforts to keep our housing affordable, our newly constructed homes carry price tags that reflect the relatively affluent Ithaca housing market. We strive to be a diverse community, yet most of us are white and middle-class.

Our saving grace is that we keep trying. When we have conflicts, we encourage each other to talk things through, with a mediator if needed. To keep houses affordable in the short and long-term, our planned third neighborhood is building small homes that will use very little energy, and almost no fossil fuels. Over time, we are becoming an increasingly diverse community which welcomes the differently abled, people of all ages, races, sexual preference and in-come levels. We are constantly engaged in trying practical measures to solve our problems, and our efforts have largely succeeded. The level of community camaraderie and ecologically friendly lifestyles is something that we as residents take for granted, but it is often a welcome surprise to visitors.

As someone who leads group tours of EVI on a weekly basis, I've noticed a magical moment that often happens. At some point, after walking down the winding, pedestrian street, visiting passive solar homes and talking with a resident, the energy of the group shifts, people relax and their eyes brighten. One woman expressed it beautifully. She said, "You are showing us the future."

Like EcoVillage at Ithaca, the greater Ithaca area is filled with amaz-ing, on-the-ground examples of one possible future. I hope this book conveys both the joys and the challenges of these working models and gives you a glimpse of the transformative power of people tak-ing action based on their deepest values.

1

Learning from the First Nations

Thanksgiving Address:
Greetings to the Natural World

The People
Today we have gathered and we see that the cycles of life continue.
We have been given the duty to live in balance and harmony with
each other and all living things. So now, we bring our minds together
as one as we give greetings and thanks to each other as People.
Now our minds are one.

The Earth Mother
We are all thankful to our Mother, the Earth, for she gives us all that
we need for life. She supports our feet as we walk about upon her.
It gives us joy that she continues to care for us as she has from the
beginning of time. To our Mother, we send greetings and thanks.
Now our minds are one.[1]

Our story begins here—this was once a land in which six sovereign nations who lived in constant warfare with each other eventually learned to bridge their cultural divides and live in peace—and more extraordinary still, maintain that peace between themselves for centuries. This was a land in which some of the primary values were respect of Mother Earth and all of Creation. The people who lived here understood that there was a living spirit in all things—animals, plants, minerals, water and winds. An important role for

9

humans was to give thanks for this bounty on a daily basis. In this culture, thinking collectively and considering future generations (intergenerational sustainability) were essential. Work was meant to be shared, as well as the benefits of that work. Each person was considered important. Men and women had separate but equal roles. Elders and young were valued. Each person was expected to develop a strong sense of self-worth, accumulated through spiritual growth and life experiences. Everyone had a special gift to contribute to the benefit of the larger community. In this land, living in harmony with Nature and other people was considered a spiritual path. Women chose the chiefs and decided when to go to war. Men sat in Council where listening was valued as much as speaking.

This is not a fantasy. This is a description of a way of life of the very well developed culture of the Haudenosaunee[2] also known as the Six Nations or the Iroquois, that thrived here in the Finger Lakes region of upstate New York for over 1,000 years before European settlement. Stretching from Lake Erie on the west to Albany on the east, and from Lake Ontario in the north to Pennsylvania on the south, these people forged a way of life that left a profound legacy for Turtle Island (North America). It is only fitting that a book about long-term sustainability in this region should focus first on the culture that was already in place for centuries.

Lighting the Commemoration Fire

Tutelo Park is a small park that was established in 1996 by the Town of Ithaca. It commemorates the Tutelo people who once lived here, a nation of Siouan people from the Virginia-Carolinas Piedmont, who, while originally persecuted by raids from the Iroquois, came under even greater danger from the encroachment of European settlers by the 1740s. The Tutelo decided to ask the Iroquois, an enemy, for their protection. They initially settled along the Susquehanna River in Pennsylvania, then gradually moved into New York State on the Chemung River and then to Coreogonal (now Ithaca) by 1753.[3] That year the Cayuga adopted the Tutelo. How remarkable — that former enemies should choose to treat each other as family members!

The Cayuga Nation, one of the Six Nations, is also known as the People of the Great Swamp, or the People of the Large Pipe. Their original territory extended from Lake Ontario, down both sides of Cayuga Lake into Pennsylvania, and over into what is now Sandusky, Ohio. In 1779, just 26 years after peacefully adopting the Tutelo, the Cayuga were driven from their homeland by the brutal Sullivan-Clinton campaign. Under orders from George Washington to eliminate anyone who had presumably supported the British during the Revolutionary War,[4] continental soldiers killed the inhabitants of Coreogonal and 42 other Iroquois villages and burned their homes and crops to the ground. It was right before the cold of winter set in, and the newly homeless survivors were deprived of their winter food supply. They fled west to shelter near Niagara Falls. The Cayuga and the Tutelo are now scattered throughout the US, although many have made their homes on other Native territories in Western New York, Oklahoma and Grand River, Canada.

Tutelo Park is modest — it consists of an open field with a playing field on one side, and a covered gathering area with a concrete slab and a metal roof. A path leads into the woods, which shelters two of the oldest trees in Tompkins County. On the Sunday of the Fall Equinox in 2007 I walked along the narrow wooded path to a clearing in the woods on top of a knoll. A circle of fifty people surrounded the fire ring in the middle. At least half of the people were Native Americans, most of them dressed in traditional dress, including silver and turquoise pendants, beaded necklaces and long, beaded earrings. One of the Native elders opened the ceremony by lighting the central fire. Another elder, Heriberto Dixon, eloquently set the scene and told us that this was the ninth time the community had come together for a homecoming ceremony for the Tutelo. This time a group of Tutelo have come down from Canada to join in the ceremony. "We are not guests," one woman said, her voice breaking, "This is our home."

Dan Little Eagle Rivera, a Cherokee who had recently moved to Ithaca, sang a haunting song, accompanying himself with the beat of a frame drum. As his voice rose, singing the loss of a culture, the heat waves from the bonfire wavered over his face and the elders sitting beside him. Looking through the wavering heat, I sensed the presence of many ghosts…native people who once lived peacefully on this land, growing corn, gathering water from the creek and children pantomiming a deer hunt. They were still here, both in spirit and in the remnants of their nation gathered here in flesh.

For me, this ceremony also brought up profound feelings about my own heritage. My father loved genealogy and researched our family tree back to the 1600s. It turns out that seven generations ago, in the late 1700s, one of my great-great-great-great-grandfathers married an "Iroquois squaw." While she was not given a name in our family's written history, I am proud to be related to her. I have tried to picture her life — she grew up where I live now, and she lived at a tumultuous time when the world was rapidly changing. The US Revolutionary War was the backdrop of her childhood. As she raised her children, how did she teach them her own cultural traditions? How did she live the Great Law — "in our every deliberation we must consider the effects on the seventh generation?"

On this day, seven generations later, I searched back with tears in my eyes to feel her presence. As I stared into the red and gold flames of the fire, I pictured her, first as a young, graceful woman with a child in her arms, later as a white-haired elder. My heart formed a prayer:

> Dear Grandmother, please help me to live my life in accordance with the values that your people so eloquently taught. Help me to remember and to teach these values of living in harmony with the natural world and in peace with her peoples. Help me to live so that there will be a seventh generation.

The Great Law of Peace

Hundreds of years ago, a man called the Peacemaker traveled among the Iroquois, spreading his message of peace, unity and the power of the good mind. According to oral history, it took him 40 years to reach everyone, and he was met with a lot of skepticism. Along the way he also developed some powerful allies: Hiawatha and Jingosaseh, a powerful female leader also called the Mother of

Nations, insisted that women be given important rights. Finally, in approximately 1142 AD,[5] Peacemaker eventually prevailed and gathered together 50 leaders to receive his message. He recited the passages of the Great Law of Peace, which became the founding constitution of the Iroquois Confederacy, recorded on a series of wampum belts which are now held by the Onondaga Nation. The passages define how the Grand Council of the five (and later, six) nations would function. The Peacemaker assigned duties to each of the leaders. He selected women as the Clan Mothers to lead the family clans, maintain social harmony and select male chiefs. A clan is a group of families that share common female ancestry. Clans are named after animals that give special assistance to the people — water (turtle, eel, beaver); land (bear, deer, wolf); sky (snipe, heron, hawk). This identity is very important to the Haudenosaunee people.

The chiefs were charged with thinking about the welfare of the people. "We are to view the chiefs like a circle of standing trees, supporting the Tree of Peace that grows in the middle. They help to keep it from falling over," explains the official website of the Haudenosaunee Confederacy.[6]

Not only is peace the absence of a state of war; it is viewed as a state of mind. "Each individual has a base spiritual power. As you go through life as Haudenosaunee, experience different things, learn more, comprehend more and tap into other forms of spiritual power, your own spirit grows as well. The old timers called it *orenda*. Everyone is thought to have it to some degree. It affects how we do things. Good minds have strong *orenda*."[7]

The Great Law of Peace, then, is powerful to the extent that individuals also develop their own spiritual power and sense of self. Part of the teaching is that this sense of self is interrelated with the well-being of the others in the clan, the village, the nation and in the Confederacy of Six Nations. This is the foundational principle of sustainability: we are all interrelated.

What a remarkable feat — for the visionary Peacemaker to forge a new way of governance that respected individual nations while bringing them together as a confederacy, and to do so with the aim of creating peace not only among nations but also spiritual peace within éach person. This would be like Jefferson teaming up with Gandhi! But not only did this vision catch hold, it also profoundly influenced the course of the history of North America — not only for the Confederacy of Six Nations, but also for the European settlers who came hundreds of years later.

The Two Row Wampum, *Guswenta*

In the 17th century, the Haudenosaunee Confederacy made a seminal treaty with the Dutch colonists. This treaty became the basis for all subsequent treaties, and was also seen as a model of the relationship between diverse peoples. The Haudenosaunee were very clear that the relationship was not one of father and son, as the Dutch originally proposed, but rather like brothers, as equals.

The treaty was recorded by a wampum belt, made of white shells, with two parallel rows of purple shells. The white background symbolizes peace and friendship, while the purple rows represent separate but equal paths, like two vessels traveling down a river. One is a canoe, for the Indian people and their laws, customs and ways. The other is a ship for the white people and their laws, customs and ways. "We shall each travel the river together, side by side, but in our [own] boat. Neither of us will make compulsory laws or interfere in the internal affairs of the other. Neither of us will try to steer the others' boat."[8] We would do well to follow the wisdom of the Two Row Wampum. In fact, perhaps this is a symbol of what has gone wrong in our western, industrialized world view — the prevailing world view might be characterized by "exploit and colonize," rather than "travel the river together in our own boats." Somehow we descendants of European settlers need to rediscover and learn to respect and celebrate the diversity of all cultures. We need to reclaim the beauty and the colors of the original wampum belt and their symbolism of peaceful coexistence.

Haudenosaunee Influence on US Government

Not only did the Iroquois create treaties with the colonists, they profoundly influenced the whole course of US history. As early as 1736,

Benjamin Franklin, a Philadelphia printer, made copies of Indian treaties which sold surprisingly well. Franklin was a regular visitor to Iroquois councils and saw the Iroquois as a positive example for the early colonies. On July 4th, 1744, the Lancaster Treaty Council brought together a powerful gathering of Iroquois and European colonists. Franklin published the proceedings, including this speech by Canassatego, an Iroquois *sachem* (chief):

> Our wise forefathers established Union and Amity between the Five Nations. This has made us formidable; this has given us great Weight and Authority with our neighboring Nations. We are a powerful Confederacy; and by your observing the same methods our wise forefathers have taken, you will acquire such Strength and power. Therefore whatever befalls you, never fall out with one another.[9]

This idea of federalism — of uniting nations together under certain principles (such as the Great Law of Peace) while leaving them to still have their own internal governance — was entirely new to the colonists. This was an enormous gift from the Iroquois! It was Franklin's exposure to the Iroquois, and Canassatego's speech in particular, that sparked this radical idea of a new form of governance, "united states." The response at the time of his speech was also recorded. The colonists said their forefathers had rejoiced to hear his words and that they sank:

> Deep into their Hearts, the Advice was good, it was Kind. They said to one another, the Six Nations are a wise people, let us hearken to their Council and teach our children to follow it. Our old Men have done so. They have frequently taken a single Arrow and said, Children, see how easy it is broken, then they have tied twelve together with strong Cords — and our strongest Men could not break them — See said they — this is what the Six Nations mean. Divided a single Man may destroy you — United, you are a match for the whole World.[10]

After the Lancaster Treaty Council, it took a while for this idea to truly catch on. Franklin proposed it to the colonies at a meeting in Albany, NY a decade later. While this Albany Plan failed to gain ratification by the colonies, it did serve as a rough draft for Franklin's later designs for the Articles of Confederation. The newly formed Continental Congress was called "the thirteen fires" by colonists and Iroquois alike. At the Constitutional Convention, John Adams, who favored a stronger central government than Franklin, still used the Iroquois "fifty families" as an example in his *Defence of the Constitutions*, which was used as a type of handbook during the convention.

The Great Law of Peace offered some amazing precedents for the new United States, beyond its profound influence in uniting the colonies as one government.[11] The Great Law also includes provisions for freedom of religion and the right to redress before the Grand Council. It even forbids unlawful entry of homes — all codified in the US Bill of Rights. In addition, it built in checks and balances so the chiefs are not all powerful. Iroquois *sachems* were not allowed to name their own successors or to carry their title to the grave. In fact, the Great Law stipulates that *sachems* can be removed from office if they can no longer function. It also says that *sachems'* skins must be "seven spans thick" to withstand the criticism of their constituents. All of this was fresh thinking to the colonists who were used to religious persecution and the omnipotent reign of kings.

Iroquois Women Inspire 19th-Century Feminists

There is another way in which the Iroquois made their mark on the new nation. In the 1800s some of the early feminists such as Lucretia Mott, Elizabeth Cady Stanton and Matilda Joslyn Gage were profoundly influenced by the example of Iroquois women.[12] The settler culture of the time was characterized by a very subservient role for women. Women could not vote, hold property, control their own wages or have any say over their own bodies or their own children. Unmarried women were under the control of their fathers. Both the church and the laws of the time reinforced a very diminished view of women.

How, then, did the idea that women could have greater power emerge? One very important factor was early feminists' direct observation of Iroquois women. Lucretia Mott visited the Seneca in the summer of 1848 and saw women who had equal responsibilities with men in family, spiritual, government and economic practice. While a portion of the Seneca eventually accepted the constitutional form of governance (rather than the traditional clan system), they refused to accept the element of male dominance. They specified that no treaty would be approved without the consent of three quarters of the "mothers of the nation." Meanwhile, Stanton, who lived in upstate New York and also had a chance to observe Iroquois culture, marveled that "the women were the great power among the clan." Among the Iroquois, the clan mothers had the authority to nominate, hold in office and remove the representative of her clan. Descent of property and children was through the female line. Iroquois women also "ruled the house," Stanton wrote. "The stores were common; but woe to the luckless husband or lover who was too shiftless to do his share of the providing. No matter how many children, or whatever goods he might have in the house, he might at any time be ordered to pick up his blanket and budge; and after such an order it would not be healthful for him to attempt to disobey... and unless saved by the intercession of some aunt or grandmother, he must retreat to his own clan..."[13] This was in direct contrast to the "civilized" women of the time, who had no recourse to divorce, no matter how bad the marriage.

Exposure to these ideas as well as to their own Quaker heritage propelled Mott and Stanton to plan and organize the first women's rights convention in Seneca Falls, New York in 1848. To a large extent, the Iroquois clan mothers helped these early feminists to envision a life in which women had status, authority and dignity.

Three Sisters Agriculture

Corn, beans and squash, otherwise known as the *Three Sisters*, formed the staple diet of native people of the northeast US. These foods were considered part of the spiritual as well as physical sustenance of the people, having been brought as a gift from the Sky

World at the creation of Turtle Island. The Iroquois farmed without the plow and without commercial fertilizers. Instead women planted a few corn seeds at a time in holes set about three feet apart. When the corn sprouted they weeded and mounded up the soil around the stalks. The mounds exposed the soil to the air, helping it warm up in the spring and helping to drain the soil. Two weeks later the women planted beans next to the corn and squash between the mounds. The beans fix nitrogen (which the corn needs) in the soil. The corn stalks provide a support pole for the growing bean vines. The squash leaves provide shade, keep the soil moist and minimize weed growth. The mounds prevent soil erosion and help recycle nutrients, especially at harvest time when plant residues are thrown back on the mounds. Cornell University agricultural scientist Jane Mt.Pleasant discovered that the total caloric output per unit of land from the Three Sisters is 30% greater than on a modern monocrop cornfield that uses commercial fertilizer and pesticides.[14]

Another amazing aspect of the Three Sisters is that they provide complementary proteins, thus creating a healthy diet all by themselves. Corn is high in calories, but low in protein, and beans supply the amino acids lacking in corn protein. Squash is high in calories and the seeds provide protein and oil. This productive and nutritious system of agriculture was freely shared with the early colonists and helped them to stay alive during the first cold winters.

The Iroquois had discovered principles of a truly sustainable agriculture. Today, inspired by the Three Sisters and other indigenous agricultural practices, many people are rediscovering similar *guilds* of plants that grow well together and use nature's processes of providing fertilizer and weed control rather than using pesticides and herbicides...knowledge that the Iroquois have been successfully using for hundreds of years! No-till farming—as in the Iroquois mound system—is spreading rapidly in the US and around the world. An entire school of agricultural thinking called *permaculture* uses principles similar to those of Iroquois farming, including the idea of plant guilds. As defined by one of the founders of permaculture, the practice is designed to promote "consciously designed landscapes which mimic the patterns and relationships in nature while yielding an abundance of food, fiber [and other products] for human needs."[15]

UN Peace Summit

Iroquois values continue to influence the surrounding culture today. Oren Lyons, faithkeeper of the Onondaga Nation, and Audrey Shenandoah, Onondaga Nation clan mother, represented indigenous peoples of North America at the United Nations Millennium World Peace Summit of Religious and Spiritual Leaders in August 2000. They each spoke very powerfully. In a prescient address, long before most people were aware of the problems of global climate change and long before Hurricane Katrina, Lyons said,

> ...the ice is melting in the north. We see the acceleration of the winds. We see the fires that are raging in North America. And, we see that the sun's rays that provide us with light, energy and the very essence of life now are causing cancer in people, blinding animals and killing the plankton and krill of the sea.

He continued:

> There can be no peace as we wage war upon Our Mother, The Earth. Responsible and courageous actions must be taken to realign ourselves with the great laws of nature. We must meet this crisis now, while we still have time. We offer these words as common peoples in support of peace, equity, justice and reconciliation. As we speak, the ice continues to melt in the north.[16]

For Lyons, the primary problem is a moral and spiritual one. For indigenous people, there are natural laws that govern the order of the universe. One of these is to honor all living beings. If this moral code is broken there must be reconciliation "...between people and the natural world, between nation states and the forests that sustain us; between corporations and the resources that they mine, the fish that they catch and the water that they use." He continued, "The human species has become the most voracious and abusive consumer of

Earth's resources. We have tipped the balance of life against our children and we imperil our future as a species."

To bring about peace is a dynamic process that "requires great efforts of spirit and mind to attain unity."[17] This Iroquois interpretation is very similar to the philosophy of the Dalai Lama, who recently made a special visit to Ithaca. His message was that peace begins within oneself...it is a disciplined approach to mastering one's inner state and letting go of hostility, blaming and anger. When one is in harmony with oneself, one can be in harmony with others.

Audrey Shenandoah, in turn, gave the traditional Haudenosaunee thanksgiving greetings to the UN assembly in 2000. She concluded, "Our minds put together as one can be one of great power. Our acknowledgments and thanksgiving reinforce that we all are connected, all related, family. We address the whole universe as such."[18]

We have much to learn from the native peoples and their profound philosophy and practice of sustainable ways of living.

Onondaga and Cayuga Land Claims

Both Audrey Shenandoah and Oren Lyons are members of the Onondaga Nation, part of the Six Nations that comprise the Iroquois Confederacy. In fact, the Onondaga have one of the oldest known participatory democracies in the world, which continues to this day.

Deer Clan Mother Audrey Shenandoah with daughters Jeanne Shenandoah, midwife, and Rochelle Brown, Eel Clan.

The Onondaga are the Fire Keepers of the Iroquois, and it was on the shores of Onondaga Lake, just south of the present city of Syracuse, that the Peacemaker met with the leaders of the original five native nations to give them the Great Law of Peace.

A lot has happened since that time. In 1790, the US federal government passed a set of laws governing conduct with all Indian nations. Called the Non-Intercourse Act, it specified that only the federal government, not states, could regulate and negotiate Indian affairs. In the 1794 Treaty of Canandaigua, signed by George Washington, the federal government promised "We will not disturb your lands forevermore from this point forward." However, these treaties were violated by New York State, which knowingly signed illegal "treaties" that took land away from the Iroquois nations. Now, a number of Iroquois nations are suing New York State to reclaim this stolen land.

The Cayuga Nation has tried to return home for over a hundred years. They won a land claim against New York State in 1980 that caused tremendous local furor in the rural communities surrounding the claim. People were worried that they would be evicted, and that tax revenue would be lost to the local townships. In fact, no one has ever been evicted as a result of a land claim. The Cayuga Nation claim was later dismissed in 2005 on a technicality — that too much time had elapsed since the law was broken.

The Onondaga filed a more recent land claim in March 2005. In this claim, the Onondaga assert their aboriginal rights to two million acres of New York State — a 40–50 mile wide swath ranging from the Saint Lawrence River on the north, down into Pennsylvania. The claim encompasses the cities of Syracuse and Binghamton, as well as many small towns, and it passes within about ten miles of Ithaca. It is a historic claim, since the Onondaga are interested in environmental and cultural healing as much as in ownership of the land.

Because of major corporate polluters such as Honeywell and Trigen Energy, Onondaga Lake has a reputation as the most polluted lake in the country and is a federal Superfund priority site. The Complaint in the Onondaga Land Rights Action names the state, the City of Syracuse, the county and five corporations for illegal land takings and damage inflicted on Central New York's environment. It opens with the following words:

> The Onondaga People wish to bring about a healing between themselves and all others who live in this region that has been the homeland of the Onondaga Nation since the dawn of time. The Nation and its people have a unique spiritual, cultural and historic relationship with the land, which is embodied in

Gayanashagowa, the Great Law of Peace. This relationship goes far beyond federal and state legal concepts of ownership, possession or legal rights. The people are one with the land, and consider themselves stewards of it. It is the duty of the Nation's leaders to work for a healing of this land, to protect it, and to pass it on to future generations. The Onondaga Nation brings this action on behalf of its people in the hope that it may hasten the process of reconciliation and bring lasting justice, peace, and respect among all who inhabit the area.[19]

The Land Claim has helped to set a number of interesting actions in motion. Five months after the suit was filed, Honeywell and the New York State Department of Conservation (NYSDEC) signed an agreement for a cleanup plan for the lake bottom of Onondaga Lake. In addition, the Onondaga have joined with local groups to stop a gravel pit in the town of Tully, and with African-American activists in South Syracuse to stop an ill-conceived sewage plant that would pollute the nearby creek and lake. The Onondaga website explained:

The extraordinary multi-cultural, multi-racial, environmental and political collaboration that exists between the Onondaga Nation and neighboring communities is not only encouraging, but may well become the centerpiece of wholesale economic revival in central New York, a revival based on promoting the natural resources of the area without exploiting them irresponsibly.... The Nation hopes to...[take actions] reversing some of the environmental degradation that has affected everyone in Central New York, and re-establishing the area as one of the most beautiful and important ecological regions in the world.[20]

In November 2009, the Onondaga Nation and its allies won an important legal victory for cleaning up Onondaga Creek and Lake. A US District Judge approved the county using green technology, including planting trees and using vegetated roofs, rain gardens, permeable pavement and rain barrels, rather than building three new sewage plants to handle urban runoff. This is expected to reduce storm runoff into the lake by 95%. Bringing green technology to bear on current problems offers very modern leverage for native values!

Reclaiming Lost Homeland: The SHARE Farm

While the Onondaga seem to be having some success with their land claim, they are more fortunate than their neighbors, the Cayuga, who were left homeless after the devastation of the Sullivan-Clinton campaign. There were further illegal land "treaties" with New York State in 1795 and 1807, which completely dispossessed the Cayuga. That is, until very recently.

In a rather extraordinary move, two very determined Ithaca College anthropology professors, Brooke Hansen and Jack Rossen, teamed up with a local group they helped to found called SHARE (Strengthening Haudenosaunee — American Relations through Education) to purchase a 70 acre organic farm near Union Springs, NY. Putting in their life savings as a down payment on the $240,000 farm, Hansen and Rossen then offered the improved farm several years later to the Cayuga Nation. The Haudenosaunee put up the remaining money needed, and on December 22, 2005, ownership of the farm was officially deeded to the traditional council of the Cayuga Nation.[21] The SHARE Farm has now become a very important cultural gathering place for the Cayuga, a place they can truly call home after 200 years and where they plan to build a longhouse and to perform sacred ceremonies. The site is situated on top of a sacred site adjacent to Cayuga Castle, one of the largest Cayuga towns that used to accommodate 50 longhouses and was surrounded by a log palisade.

Hansen and Rossen's years of fundraising and sacrifice towards helping the Cayugas reclaim a small piece of their home territory is part of a growing trend called public anthropology. Anthropologists use their skills for positive social change which helps a community. "[The] promotion of cultural survival," said Hansen, "is at the heart of my work as a cultural anthropologist. Getting a piece of homeland to the Cayuga represents the greatest achievement an anthropologist can accomplish."[22]

The historic roots of the Haudenosaunee peoples form a strong basis for the current movement for sustainability in this area. They model the profound importance of a values system that is carried out in action—based foremost on a respect for Mother Earth and all living beings. They see the importance of not taking the land and its abundance for granted. Instead their culture emphasizes the importance of gratitude—giving thanks every day for the blessings of creation. They honor individual personal and spiritual growth. Their social system honors women, children and elders. The Haudenosaunee demonstrate a deep connection with the natural world. We all benefit from the immense value of gifts from these Six Nations traditions—women's empowerment and equality, democratic governance, sustainable agriculture and stewardship of the land. The latest native land claims in this area show a remarkable cooperation with neighboring groups who share their environmental values, leading to some historic opportunities for collaboration.

With this rich heritage, it is no wonder that the Finger Lakes region of upstate New York has a strong impulse for regeneration and balance. Within this cradle of ancient culture, a new movement is emerging, one that draws on some of the same values as the Iroquois nations, to create a sustainable future.

2

Growing a Local Food Culture

My son Jason and his wife Shradha, who is from India, are visiting Ithaca for the first time since they've been married. They currently live in the San Francisco Bay Area—a place known for its sophisticated, international palate. I decide to take them to the Ithaca Farmer's Market, always a happening place on a summer weekend. As we arrive, we note how crowded the parking lot is, and we park on a little side street instead. Threading our way through the entrance to the market we enjoy the bustling ambiance of old and young people carrying flowering plants and mesh bags of fresh vegetables. The large, clerestory pavilion housing the market is light and airy, with room for 94 vendors. It overlooks Cayuga Lake, and the cool breeze is welcome on this late August day.

Jen and John Bokaer-Smith at the Farmer's Market.

I pause to say hello to one of the local craftspeople, a friend and colleague who is the owner of Silk Oak, a silk-screen clothing business with whimsical nature-inspired designs for sale. Jan Norman is past president of the board of directors of the Farmer's Market and also serves on the nonprofit board for EcoVillage at Ithaca. I buy a little yellow hat from her, with a silkscreened black and white panda on it, for my nephew's newborn son.

It makes me feel good to support her business, while providing a unique, homemade gift to my newest family member.

We move on, checking out the colorful array of heirloom tomatoes, carrots, fat green cucumbers and onions at another stall. The farmer invites us to take a taste of the heirlooms—strange-looking purple, green or orange tomatoes that offer a welcome surprise. These are traditional varieties that are completely opposite from the tasteless commercial ones—they taste like summer itself. I buy several for a salad I plan to make for dinner. Further down one of the aisles we find a local goat farm that makes feta cheeses. After sampling two or three varieties, I select some tangy feta for the salad. Jason spots a photo gallery, and we pause to enjoy the stunning images of Finger Lakes waterfalls. Now we are getting hungry. The only problem is that it is so hard to choose. Shall we skip lunch and go straight to dessert? There are some marvelous home-made ice creams in unusual flavors—blackberry, green tea, mango. We decide to take the healthier alternative, and wait in the longest line at the Market, for a lunch from Macro Mama's, offering a scrumptious selection of macrobiotic foods. Luckily our long wait is broken up as several friends stop by to chat.

Soon we are seated on massive benches by the water's edge, enjoying our fabulous food. We watch as people cross the dock to board a boat, the Tiohero, for a short tour of the lake. The chattering of families quiets down as two performers step up and begin some lively old-time fiddle music. Behind us on the lake, a family of ducks paddles by. I look at Shradha and smile…between the sun and the cool lake breezes, the delicious vegetarian food and the live music, the friendly atmosphere and the local farm produce, this is some of the best that Ithaca has to offer. I can tell that she loves it just as much as I do.

The Ithaca Farmer's Market is one of the best in the US. Started in 1973, it has come a long way. Initially it was composed of a few farmers who came to town and had a market in the parking lot of Agway, a hardware and gardening supply store. It started as one response to a number of trends—around the country gas prices spiked in the oil embargo, and people did not want to travel out of town to farm stands in the country, so farmers came to them instead. The counterculture movement was also strong, and many people were looking for fresh, local foods instead of the shrink-wrapped, weeks-old produce that was sold in supermarkets. A few local farmers began growing organic produce and fruits, and the trend began to take hold.

After a successful ten year run, the market was forced to find a new location to accommodate more vendors and customers. After much searching, a city council member found a site for the Farmer's Market on the waterfront. The only problem was the site was not very attractive: it was a former construction dump for the city, adjacent to the sewage treatment plant and the Department of Transportation, and across the railroad tracks from a petroleum facility. "It was out of sight, out of mind," recalled Jan Norman. However, the Farmer's Market board, headed by Anna Steinkraus of Littletree Orchards, worked hard to obtain a 20 year lease from the city, and Monika Roth of Cornell Cooperative Extension of Tompkins County helped to secure a grant from the New York State Agriculture Department. A local architect designed the pavilion. "The waterfront was on one side, with enormous NYSEG power lines on the other. There was only room to build it in a long, narrow corridor. It took hundreds of hours of volunteer labor to build. Littletree [Orchards] actually took out a loan against their farm to get it built." Jan went on, "When you think about it, it was pretty awe-inspiring to negotiate the lease and build the pavilion. It took a lot of commitment on their part.... It [the Farmer's Market] really wasn't part of the consciousness of the whole community, the way it is now. It really was like Sisyphus pushing a boulder up the hill."[1] Like many other worthwhile projects, the Ithaca Farmer's Market took a big vision, persistence and a huge amount of work to make it what it is today.

Now, three decades later, the Ithaca Farmer's Market has an international reputation. It provides locally produced agricultural products, prepared food and crafts and attracts thousands of people each week. About a third of its sales are to tourists, but it also provides a wonderful meeting ground for local community people. The market starts in April and ended in December, right before Christmas. In 2009, an experimental indoor market was started in downtown Ithaca during January, which expanded in 2010 to January and February. It became wildly popular and featured not only prepared foods and crafts, but great root vegetables, sauerkraut, micro greens and baked goods, some made with locally grown and milled flour! During the summer there are actually not one, not two, but four markets a week. All-day farmer's markets on weekends are held in the large open-air market on the northern edge of Ithaca. On Tuesday mornings and Thursday evenings, there is a market in DeWitt Park in downtown Ithaca. At either of these places, customers are treated to a wide variety of delicious seasonal fruits and vegetables, flowers, baked goods, cheeses and more. The markets are lively meeting grounds for people of all ages as well as tourist destinations. Jan told me "It's a fabulous three-ring circus…something for everyone." She noted that "there are different flavors to different market days." Saturdays, the participation is "off the charts." Sundays were somewhat quieter, although that has recently changed, and it has gotten so crowded that dogs are no longer allowed inside the pavilion. "We're bursting at the seams and looking for ways to grow our market and continue incubating new businesses," Jan said.[2] The downtown Tuesday markets are especially oriented towards families and children. In fact this Farmer's Market hosts a special storytelling hour in the park. The Ithaca Farmer's Market is also a zero-waste facility: customers and vendors alike are asked to compost food scraps, compostable plates and tableware are required and what can't be composted is recycled.

Fast Food Nation: We Are What We Eat

Things have changed dramatically since my grandmother's time. In 1900, the US was largely a rural, agrarian nation, and nearly 40% of the population made its living as farmers. Today that has shrunk to close to 1%. There are now more prisoners than farmers in the USA.

In addition, the average age of farmers has risen to close to 60 years old. It makes you wonder who will grow our food in 20 years!

Not only the farmers themselves, but the way we grow, produce and eat food in this country has also shifted dramatically in the last several generations; these changes have profound repercussions on the health-care crisis, energy independence and climate change. After cars, the food system uses more fossil fuel than any sector of the economy — 19% — and produces more than one third of all greenhouse gases. Fossil fuels are used at every step of the way, from fertilizers and pesticides to food processing and transportation. In fact, it takes ten calories of fossil fuel to produce a single calorie of modern supermarket food.[3]

Four of the top ten killers in the US today are chronic diseases linked to diet: heart disease, stroke, Type 2 diabetes and cancer. The modern American diet is a public health catastrophe of fast food and empty calories. This is particularly true for inner city populations which often live in food deserts, which have plenty of liquor stores and fast food chains, but not a supermarket in sight, thanks to redlining of minority neighborhoods.

However, all these problems also offer tremendous opportunities: if we can create healthy, diverse, regional food systems that run largely on sunshine rather than fossil fuels, it will lead to millions of green jobs, better health for our population, greatly diminish our greenhouse gas emissions and dramatically cut our need for imported oil. Already there are some very positive signs. For the first time in a century, the number of farms in the US has increased. The new farms are mostly small, many of them operated by women, and many of them cater to local markets.[4] There is a tremendous surge of interest in eating local foods, reflected in the rise in urban gardening, school gardens and farmers' markets. Even the big supermarket chains are finding it profitable to contract with local farmers for some of their produce.

Why the Ithaca Farmer's Market Works

Several key elements make the Ithaca's Farmer's Market special. For one thing, it is a very local, producers-only market. Only farmers, producers and craftspeople living within a 30 mile radius of Ithaca can sell at the market. This rule is strictly enforced. According to Monika Roth, the Agriculture and Environmental Program Leader at Cornell Cooperative Extension of Tompkins County, "Too many markets break the rules on local. People should stick to being a local market, set boundary rules and police it."[5] The result of the local orientation is that people build a strong sense of community over time, and the market supports a growing diversity of local farmers and craftspeople. Consumers also develop an appreciation for what is seasonally available and develop relationships with individual farmers.

Because the market is now open for eleven months a year (five more months than the upstate New York growing season), some farmers have developed season extension crops that can be profitably sold at the market. One example is the bright bunches of gold, orange or red tulips sold by Jen and John Bokaer-Smith, farmers at West Haven Farm. The tulips are grown in a winterized greenhouse at EcoVillage at Ithaca and are ready to enliven customer's homes in early spring. After a long, grey winter, people are eager and willing to buy fresh-picked bouquets. Another season extension is the crisp, green hydroponic lettuce grown by Challenge Industries, a local nonprofit that offers jobs for people with disabilities (see Chapter 5). Yet another approach is Blue Heron Farms, which has perfected winter storage for root vegetables, which are then available in the middle of winter. Monika Roth thinks that the market has the potential to become year-round. "If they can do it in Alberta, Canada, which is much colder than Ithaca, they could do it here."[6]

Another reason for the success of the Ithaca Farmer's Market is the variety it offers. It maintains a ratio of 20% crafts, 20% prepared food and 60% agriculture. The market maintains very strict guidelines, and prepared food and craft producers go through a peer juried process in which members vote on who gets to sell their product. "It can feel uncomfortable," said Jen Bokaer-Smith about judging your peers, "But it produces high quality stuff."[7] Farmers, in turn, are visited by board members to ensure that they have a working farm.

Growing the Farmer's Market from its humble origins to its current, robust state has not been easy. There have been plenty of bumps along the way. In any organization there are different personalities and different visions. There were times when there was a lot of emotional conflict between people on the board. Jan mentioned, "Sometimes there are still issues that get people riled up." But for the most part, the Farmer's Market can be considered the biggest success of the local foods movement in Ithaca. "It changed the way people eat. Now they eat fresher foods, more diverse foods…none of the farmers are getting rich, but people see that they can make a living and save arable land as farmland. There is more diversity. In fact the bigger supermarkets pick up on the trends that we start. Now people want mesclun greens and kohlrabi."[8]

Can the Ithaca Farmer's Market be replicated elsewhere? It would take quite a while to get to the scale and quality that Ithaca offers, and it definitely helps to live in a college town with tourist traffic. However, there are lots of ways that smaller markets can be started. Cornell Cooperative Extension of Tompkins County has created rural satellite farmer's markets. Starting in 1999, they worked with 4-H youth to develop markets in small towns. Cooperative Extension secures produce on consignment from local farms and sets up a farmstand that is managed by youth in a rural community. According to Monika Roth, the combination of having a team of four to eight kids involved, with a staff supervisor who may be a work-study college student, leads to multiple positive outcomes: fresh, local produce is available to townspeople, the young people (which may include some at-risk youth) get important job skills (including how to identify, cook and enjoy fresh produce) and they develop teamwork. The whole program costs very little to run, and there are now 30 vendors that serve three rural towns. The town of Trumansburg now has over 30 vendors, as does Lansing.

In order to develop a local farmer's market, there have to be local farmers. In the Ithaca area, small-scale farmers in the 1800s took very little to the marketplace. "Everyone grew their own chickens and cabbages," explained Monika. In the 1920s, there was a move to dairy farms. In the 1970s the back-to-the-land movement became popular. Some Cornell students started farming cooperatives, or private farms such as Littletree Orchards, which continues to this day as a favorite local pick-your-own orchard. Moosewood, the now-famous cooperative vegetarian restaurant, started in 1973 and provided another outlet for locally grown produce. About this time Greenstar Cooperative, a highly successful member-owned grocery store, also started.[9]

Buying Local: Greenstar Cooperative Market

As wonderful as the Ithaca Farmer's Market is, it is primarily a three-season affair that despite its popularity is only reaching a small percentage of Ithaca residents. Since people eat all year round and eat a variety of foods, it's important that other parts of the food system also make a commitment to local purchasing. It has been estimated that if everyone were to buy even 10% of their food locally, that would mean an additional $26 million dollars would stay in Tompkins County. As Greenstar's Marketing Manager, Joe Romano told me, "That is an amazing number, but what is more amazing is that it is an additional amount that would be added to our local abundance every year. If you think about the additional revenue that money would generate by being invested back into the community it just grows and grows exponentially."[10]

I met with Joe on an eerily warm January day — 64°F — and we crossed the street from Greenstar's colorful, bustling natural foods store to a small, stuffy office building. We passed a big outdoor sign that declared, "We sell more local products than anyone else." Greenstar, like the Ithaca Farmer's Market, is a very popular local institution. Started around the same time as the Market, it celebrated its 39th birthday in 2010. Now boasting two local natural foods stores, including a deli and a bakery, it is a $13 million business with 150 employees and 6,300 member-owners. This represents about one fifth of the population of Ithaca!

It is always a delightful experience to walk into Greenstar to do my shopping — there is a sense of ownership and pride in the values that are demonstrated everywhere. Joe told me, "The biggest signs in the store are not about a sale on milk for 39 cents, they are about our mission and values." A recent survey clarified who the members are and what they hold important, he told me. The core shoppers answered a question about who are we? as "funky, fun, knowledgeable, passionate, mature co-opers." They are 71% female (while I thought this was a surprise, Joe pointed out that usually far more women than men do the shopping, so this is low for women.) They seek what Greenstar has to offer: locally produced, fair trade, healthy, natural, fresh, organic and ethically produced food.[11]

Greenstar is one of the few places in the US that sells fair trade, organic bananas produced by a cooperative venture in Ecuador. Bold blue signs proclaim "local" on many items in the produce department and even state what farm they came from. Items that are not local are clearly labeled so that you can choose whether it is worth the extra carbon footprint to buy something from California or even further away from Chile. A deli provides nourishing soups, salads, entrees and desserts, with nine kinds of organic and fair trade coffee. Regular cutlery is provided for in-store eating, and to-go containers and cutlery are made out of compostable corn products.

But the best thing about Greenstar is not just the delicious, fresh food or the ethical values behind the store. Perhaps the most compelling reason to shop at Greenstar is the strong sense of community. It is a kind of village green where people socialize over the produce aisle, while waiting in line at the cash register, or having a cup of coffee and a muffin while discussing politics.

Like many other examples in this book, Greenstar creates value on multiple levels: it builds community, builds the local economy, promotes environmental practices and operates by ethical standards. Like the Farmer's Market, it is also a cooperative that teaches people to work together and that seeks to build an alternative economic structure that values human needs rather than individual profit. Joanna Green, a long-time local food advocate, noted another aspect of Greenstar's success. "As a stable institution, it's a training ground in real democracy. It helps people to learn how to work effectively together in a group. It's a local institution that was built from the grassroots up, and it doesn't depend on just one or two people."[12]

The Cluster Effect

Ithaca provides an excellent example of a maturing regional food system that is working well on many levels. To the newcomer, it is astonishing that so many things are in place: the myriad number of local, often organic family farms, the excellent Farmer's Market, the support of local institutions such as Cornell and Ithaca College for local foods, the dedication to composting that is evident everywhere from the zero-waste festivals to the local schools which compost even their lunch trays, the restaurants which offer gourmet local fare and tantalizing wine tours. As Edible Finger Lakes magazine publisher Michael Welch and his wife and magazine editor Zoe Becker told the New York Times, central New York is having a golden culinary moment, with lots of home cooks and restaurant chefs who know how to coax the best from the local cheese, produce and fish. "It's just a really great place to eat right now."[13]

What is less obvious is that these carefully integrated systems did not happen overnight. Instead, they built slowly over the last thirty years. "These were institutions which came about synergistically," said Joanna Green, who for decades worked at Cornell's Small Farms Program. "It was a chicken and egg development that happened incrementally over time. The Farmer's Market and Greenstar have anchored the development of the local food system here, lending stability and providing steady markets."[14]

It is a well-known phenomenon that when businesses that produce a common product cluster together, the result is lively competition which ultimately brings more business for everyone. Think of restaurants in a city—the Chinese restaurants are all in one neighborhood, the Italian in another. People know where to go to get the food they want. Similarly, the Finger Lakes region, and Ithaca in particular, display all the hallmarks and synergies of a local food and farming cluster: geographic proximity, strong economic ties and social networks among producers, multiple products and distributors, engaged support institutions and both competition and collaboration. The result is a very healthy local food and farming system, one that bestows numerous benefits on both producers and consumers.

A key part of Greenstar's mission is local production. How does Greenstar promote local products, besides the colorful "local" signs? Liz Karabanakis, Greenstar's former Member and Community Services Manager, explained some of the many ways. There is a smaller markup for locally produced goods, so they can compete more effectively with mass-produced global products. The location in the store is important, including having certain items at eye level. There are often free tasting samples of local products. Greenstar consciously forms partnerships with local farmers, and there are often profiles of farmers in *Greenleaf*, the store's monthly newsletter. "We're part of building a vibrant agricultural community." Liz told me. "Although local has become trendy, this is what we've been doing for 38 years."[15]

But retailing local foods is not necessarily easy, Monika Roth shared. There are a number of obstacles, including a short growing season in upstate New York, farmers lacking the capital investment to grow their farms, the distribution network for local farmers needing to be strengthened and lack of a centralized storage facility.[16] Greenstar does work with local distributors Regional Access, Fall Creek Produce and Finger Lakes Organics as its first priority for produce. However when it comes to other products, finding local sources of goods is harder. Liz Karabanakis explained, "Either we buy goods from United Natural Foods which is a national conglomerate, or our buyers have a lot of extra work to work with local producers on a one by one basis."

When I asked Liz about her vision for the future, her eyes lit up. "We need consumer education to help build demand for local foods. There are issues across class, race, equity and accessibility. We're working with Sustainable Tompkins and the Greater Ithaca Activities Center (GIAC), a nonprofit which serves low income families, not just upper middle-class white people. We're building a vibrant agricultural community and providing support for farmers. The feasibility of a viable local foods system rests on a distribution network on an institutional level — we need to get all the local institutions on board, whether their motivation is food security, public relations or better nutrition. I'm confident that Greenstar has an important role to play." She finished with, "We are reconnecting consumers with food, and information is key."

Liz was invited to be a keynote speaker at Greenmarkets in New York City, to speak about Trends in Food Retail. She shared some of her talk with me. "I found that consumers are now splitting their food dollars differently. They spend most of their money at 'super-centers' that sell everything, not just food. They have sacrificed freshness, taste and nutrients for affordable prices. All the environmental costs are externalized. But consumers save a small portion — maybe 10% of their food dollars — for gourmet, fresh food from farmers' markets and cooperatives." She continued, "When I talk to students, they often want to save for a hybrid car or take navy showers to help the environment. I tell them, 'Don't skip doing those things, they're great, but let me give you an easy tip — we all eat three times a day. You can make an enormous difference in your choice of foods.'" Liz left me with one last thought, "Food is hope."[17]

Sara Pines sorts food for
Friendship Donations Network.

Feeding the Hungry

For over two decades, Sara Pines, the founder of Friendship Donations Network, has been gathering food donations from local supermarkets, farms and bakeries. The leftover food, which amounts to about 2,000 pounds (one ton) a day, is saved from being thrown into the landfill and gets redistributed to 22 food pantries, soup kitchens and work sites employing low income workers around the region. Sara, one of the founding residents of EcoVillage, calls herself "a little old lady," but her volunteers call her the Tornado. The win-

ner of numerous awards for her work, Sara has enormous tenacity. She and her volunteer-run operation feed about 2,500 people a week.

Her passion to feed the hungry comes from personal experience. When she was still a child growing up in Palestine, her father was killed, and for a while she and her mother were homeless. The experience left her with a deep-rooted desire to make sure that no one goes hungry and that no food is wasted. Her program is a smart way to tap into an unused resource — day-old food — and it makes an enormous difference for many peoples' lives. This program could be replicated in almost any city.

Community Supported Agriculture

Twenty years after the Farmer's Market and Greenstar got their start, a new phenomenon emerged: the Community Supported Agriculture (CSA) farm. CSAs provide a partnership between farmers and consumers. Farmers sell *shares* in the harvest of the farm long before the first seeds are even planted, thus getting much needed capital at the beginning of the growing season and securing a guaranteed market for their produce. In exchange, consumers get weekly distributions of their share of the harvest. They develop a relationship with the farmer and enjoy some of the freshest produce around. It is truly a win-win model for everyone.

The first CSA in the US started in Massachusetts in 1990. Ithaca is a town that loves innovation, so it was no surprise that just two years later there were already three CSAs in the Ithaca area. Now, 18 years later, there are 20 CSAs that serve the Ithaca area, according to Debbie Teeter, who puts out a local food guide for Tompkins County. Like Monika Roth, she also works for Cornell Cooperative Extension of Tompkins County (CCE). Debbie told me that 2,000 local families get food from CSAs — this represents about 6% of the county's population, a very large number given that CSAs were only introduced a couple of decades ago. The CSAs provide not only vegetables, but there are also ones that specialize in meat, eggs, bread or fruit.[18]

Full Plate CSA

I met Chaw Chang at a Sustainable Tompkins Local Foods Gathering in 2006. After the potluck of local food dishes was cleared away, and after prizes were given out for the "most scrumptious" and the "most local" (won by a man who used venison from a deer he killed in his own backyard), the 60 people present listened to Chang talk about his farming experience. I was struck by his energy and enthusiasm. Chaw, together with his wife Lucy Garrison-Clauson, run Stick and Stone Farm which grows produce such as squash, heirloom tomatoes and leafy greens. They wholesale produce to Greenstar, Ithaca College and several restaurants. But perhaps the biggest innovation is their collaboration with Remembrance Farm and Three Swallows Farm to offer the innovative Full Plate CSA. By harnessing the power of three farms, it allows each farm to concentrate on growing fewer crops, yet still provides great diversity in the shares provided. There are now over 400 shareholders in this CSA.

Healthy Food for All

Everyone should be able to have access to fresh fruits and vegetables, but it is not always easy for low income people. This brings up the question of how to create food equity — that is, the ability and the right for people of all incomes to enjoy healthy, nutritious food. Luckily the federal Farmer's Market Nutrition Program provides special vouchers to low income families to purchase fresh produce at farmer's markets.

However, until recently, it was very difficult for low income people to join a CSA, mostly because membership requires an upfront payment of several hundred dollars — cash that can be hard to come by. In Ithaca, the options have been expanded by an innovative low income CSA program, Healthy Food for All. The growth of the program has been phenomenal, increasing from 18 families to 120 in just four years. It is now a partnership between Cornell Cooperative Extension and six local farms, United Way, Ithaca Health Alliance, Greenstar Cooperative Market and a local foundation. Not only do the families enjoy weekly supplies of freshly picked produce, they also gather in the Extension offices once a week for popular cooking classes so they know what to do with unfamiliar items in their shares, such as Jerusalem artichokes or kale. Free, on-site child care during the classes makes a big difference for the participants, who also learn the importance of eating a variety of produce, tips on making fresh food more attractive for children and how to cook with the seasons.

Neisha Butler prepares fresh produce in cooking class with Healthy Food for All.

"I wasn't a vegetable person before. Now I know there are lots of different things you can do to make them good," said one participant. Another woman beamed, "This was a really, really positive experience for my family. I feel a lot of gratitude that I was able to have such good quality food that I normally wouldn't be able to afford and that my family was able to eat really healthy."[19]

Finger Lakes Culinary Bounty, another brainchild of CCE's local foods champion Monika Roth, links together Finger Lakes farmers with restaurant chefs who use local ingredients to produce gourmet, mouth-watering dishes. For dedicated locavores, seeking out these restaurants is a real treat, helped out by a website showing their locations. In an exciting recent development, Finger Lakes Culinary Bounty wineries and restaurants teamed up with local farmers to produce four *Harvest Dinners* as fundraisers for Healthy Food for All. The gourmet dinners are each held at a local farm, enhancing the dining experience. One of the dinners is held annually at EcoVillage at Ithaca. The first year West Haven Farm paired with the chef from one of my favorite local restaurants, Just a Taste, and also featured local wines. It was very satisfying knowing that the money raised from a $75 a plate gourmet meal allowed local people who have limited resources to join a CSA farm the next summer.

In this system everyone wins—farmers and local chefs get the appreciation they deserve for growing and serving excellent local foods, community members who support the program get an incredible meal while learning about local farms and low income community members get access to a program that not only provides healthy, nutritious foods but that also builds a sense of community.

Cornell Dining Triples Local Food Purchases

It's important to have major players on board. Cornell University, which spends $9 million a year on food for its 31 dining locations, made a commitment in 2006 to triple its purchase of foods from local and regional farmers. Their produce contract required its fruit and vegetable supplier to buy one fifth of its food locally. In 2007 that grew to 25%, and that was increased to 33% by 2009. This remarkable step has many ripple effects: it supports the local economy, it cuts back on fossil fuels and it reduces global warming. It also gives the students a chance to make a choice—they may pay slightly more for locally produced food from small farms, but they can also take a stand for the environment and for fresh, more sustainable foods.

There are some hurdles to overcome. With the short Northeast growing season, local produce is hard to find in the winter. To offset a limited winter selection, Cornell Dining purchases lots of root vegetables and apples in the fall—ones that can be stored for use during the deep freeze of winter. It also buys locally grown hydroponic lettuce year-round.

Finding enough farms to supply the increased demand for local foods by Cornell, Ithaca College and other institutions is a real challenge. Farms in the northeast tend to be small. As Cornell Dining senior executive chef Steven Miller said, "When you are feeding four people, it is easy to buy locally. When you're feeding 24,000 people a day, it becomes very different." For example, Cornell sometimes has to purchase from four or five farmers just to get enough beans for a meal.[20]

For Cornell's president, Dr. David Skorton and his wife Dr. Robin Davisson, local food is nothing new. "One of the first things we did in moving to Ithaca was to join a CSA," Davisson confided in a speech at a fundraising dinner for EcoVillage at Ithaca's new Groundswell Center for

Local Food and Farming. "It made us feel at home." [21] *Luckily for EVI, they joined West Haven Farm. Davisson has helped to lead the charge for Cornell to rapidly increase the percentage of locally purchased food. Having the president of Cornell and his wife in full support of buying locally is a big plus. As Cornell throws even more of its economic clout into local farms it may provide just the stimulus needed for more people to try their hand at farming. Imagine small, local farms as a growth industry!*

An Integrated Local Food System at EcoVillage

While the local foods movement is about growing and marketing farm fresh food, it is also about creating a sense of community. And when that community lives in close proximity, all kinds of wonderful synergies can happen. At EcoVillage we hold community meals four times a week during most of the year. Typically there are between 40 and 80 people who gather for an evening meal cooked by a volunteer team. Cooks plan their meals around what is seasonably available from the EcoVillage farms or other local farms, creating fresh, tasty dinners. In the winter we have figured out dozens of recipes to make from all the stored root vegetables. In the summer it is a relief to get away from using parsnips and potatoes! Whatever time of year, it's a pleasure to sit with friends and neighbors and catch up from our busy lives over a delicious meal.

At EcoVillage we are very fortunate to have two organic farms which operate as CSAs. West Haven Farm, started by farmers and EcoVillage residents Jen and John Bokaer-Smith, provides 250 kinds of fresh produce, herbs and fruits to over 1,000 people a week in the greater Ithaca area during the growing season from just ten acres of land leased from EVI. The farm, which started in 1993, sells 60% of its produce to shareholders and the other 40% at the Ithaca Farmers Market.

In contrast, Kestrel's Perch Berry Farm was started just recently by another EcoVillage resident, Katie Creeger. Katie, who otherwise makes a living as a landscaper and a translator, had always dreamed of having her own farm. She now runs a successful business that is an organic, pick-your-own CSA berry farm. As far as we know, it's the first of its kind in the US. People come from all over the area to pick juicy quarts of fresh strawberries, raspberries, black raspberries, red and black currants, gooseberries and thornless blackberries. Tuesdays at EVI are busy days, with shareholders arriving to pick up their shares at West Haven, then ambling over to Kestrel's Perch to pick the week's share of berries. It is a lovely time for children to play together and adults to chat while they are picking in adjacent rows. Kestrel's Perch even has a special kids' picking section featuring hardy alpine strawberries, which are just the right size for a child's snack.

But the farms are just part of the local foods story at this EcoVillage of 160 residents. Many people also have their own community garden plots, and during the summer months, gardens are overflowing with leafy greens, peas, beans, squashes, garlic and tomatoes. Many people freeze or can their extra produce, and one neighborhood of 30 homes keeps two chest freezers for individual's use. Several EcoVillagers have teamed up to make a solar dehydrator (which works fine except in rainy summers!). Others have crafted movable solar cookers...large mylar-covered reflector plates direct sunlight onto a simple, glass enclosed box. My friend Jeff Schwartz recently invited me over for a solar pizza lunch, which he had handily cooked in his homemade solar oven. It was delicious, and wonderful to know that no fossil fuels were used at all. Gradually we are learning from each other more and more about eating seasonally, growing our own and putting food by for the winter.

One fascinating project was building an underground root cellar to store all those wonderful fall harvest root vegetables — potatoes, beets, carrots, onions, turnips and parsnips — through the winter. My friend and next-door neighbor Tina Nilsen-Hodges worked with a team of Ithaca College students over the course of a school year to plan it. The students, after researching root cellars extensively, came up with a preliminary design to be built out of wood. The price tag, at a whopping $26,000, made the residents blanch whiter than a stored potato. So the next group of students looked at more affordable designs. They came up with an intriguing although labor-intensive idea: why not make a root cellar out of earth bags?

Working with a local green builder, the residents spent most of one summer constructing it. First the hillside next to the Common House was excavated, and we put in a foundation of rammed earth tires. Although I only put in a few hours on the foundation, my muscles still remember the rhythmic thump, thump, thump of tamping the earth into a tire with a sledgehammer at a rate of 40 pounds of earth per tire. Once the foundation was set, we held dozens of day-long work parties to put up the walls. Earthbags are made from feedbags stuffed with a combination of earth, clay and sand. One person holds the bag open over a wooden frame, while the other person pours the mixture in and tamps it down. The finished earthbag looks and feels like a giant brick. It is then stacked on other bags and held in place with a few strands of barbed wire that catch the mesh of the bag above.

One day a group of us worked in the pouring rain. Although we were cold and wet, we were laughing most of the time. When it came time for lunch, someone literally hosed off our clay-covered overalls so that we could go inside without tracking in a roomful of clay. The circular earthbag walls were covered with an earth-based plaster both inside and out, and a wooden frame held a sod roof in place. Although it was half the price of the first design, this earthbag root cellar was at least twice the labor. But it was fun to work together with all ages chipping in to help. The finished root cellar has now been in use for several years, and it provides space for 2,000 pounds of roots to be stored each winter.

In the Ithaca area we have an excellent start on creating a local food culture, but it's not just happening here. All over the US people are waking up to the joys of eating more seasonally and locally. I hope you will consider how you, too, might take part. Whether it is starting an urban garden or shopping at a local farmer's market, a delicious adventure awaits!

3

Green Building/ Green Energy

It is one of the coldest days I remember in my 18 years of living in Ithaca. Outside the fields are sparkling with a new layer of creamy snow which fell overnight, adding to the foot of snow already on the ground. I see tracks that tell the story of a large rabbit bouncing over to my snow-covered flower garden, nibbling and hopping off in a hurry. There are deer tracks further out, graceful hoofprints in a line. My neighbor skis past my backyard and waves. He is bundled up so much I can barely tell who it is. No wonder he wants to cover up—it is a bracing 8°F outside! The amaz-ing thing is that I am perfectly toasty even with no heat on in my house. The thermostat says 70°F; the heat has been off since Jared left for work at 8 AM, and it is now mid-morning. But the sun is pouring in through the 14 foot high, triple-glazed windows in our passive solar home, and I close my eyes to let the embracing warmth sink in. As I take off my sweater, I can't believe that it's so cold outside. I feel grateful to live here, with a wide expanse of open field, lines of forest and the blue hills to the south, and my EcoVillage community of 60 houses clustered closely around my home like a warm blanket on the north, east and west. Now that energy prices are soaring, I also feel grateful to live in a home that makes such good use of the sun's heat. Last year Jared and I spent just $500 for heat and hot water for the entire year! Some of our friends who live in less well-insulated homes are spending that much or more every month in the winter (January 16, 2009).

Solar Capital

Over the last ten years, green building and renewable energy use has exploded in Tompkins County, with Ithaca as a hub. In fact, according to an article in the *Syracuse Post Standard*, not only is Ithaca considered the solar capital of New York State, but if you look at a map showing the location of solar installations by US zip code, "Ithaca stands out like a supernova."[1] How can this be? For those of us who live here, it is a well-known adage that Ithaca is considered the second cloudiest city in the country, after Seattle. How then, did this small city in upstate NY become a solar capital? It was not by accident.

To find out more, I gathered together a group of green builders and renewable energy advocates. Those who had been around for a while told me that in the 1960s and 70s, the same back-to-the-land young idealists that were described in the last chapter as being the pioneers of the small organic farm movement in this area were also building their homes from scratch. Mike Carpenter, a long-time Ithaca builder who also owns a solar business, shook his head as he told me that many of those structures have now fallen into disrepair. "People didn't really know what they were doing back then."

Another and more sophisticated wave of green building came a couple decades later. Steve Nicholson, a resident of the small town of Caroline, built his own off-grid solar home in 1990. He recalls that at that time there were only two electricians who were state licensed solar installers in the whole state. New York state offered a 50% rebate for off-grid homes for one year, and the installer close to Ithaca installed solar electric panels (also called photovoltaics) for 35 out of the 50 homes that qualified for the rebate. "The installer made an advocate out of me," Steve recalled. "He told me it wasn't enough to have solar panels on my roof, I should tell other people about it." Steve has been a vocal supporter ever since.[2]

The High Cost of Construction As Usual

In the US, buildings account for a whopping 40% of total primary energy use.[3] Part of this is driven by size of homes: even as average family size has shrunk, the size of new homes in the US has increased from 1,000 square feet in the 1950s to 2,400 square feet in recent years. To provide heat and air conditioning and lighting to these homes and even larger McMansions is terribly costly, not only in dollars but also to the environment. Increased construction of suburban homes and shopping malls has also steadily taken over prime farmland and wildlife habitat and increased the need for more highways, more infrastructure and more commuter miles driven. Our drive to build also results in massive amounts of garbage. Construction waste accounts for 24% of landfill debris.[4] It doesn't have to be this way.

In 1996, EcoVillage at Ithaca (EVI) built its first neighborhood of 30 passive solar, superinsulated homes — the first neighborhood-sized green development project in the county — but we didn't install photovoltaic (PV) panels because there was no rebate or tax incentive in place at that time, and PVs are expensive. In 2002, however, when we built the second neighborhood, there was a new statewide program which offered a package of rebates and tax incentives that cut the cost in half. Almost half of the new homeowners chose to pay for solar panels, and some also installed solar hot water as well. If one stands to the south of the two neighborhoods and looks back it is striking to see 14 sets of shining silicon panels on the roofs of second neighborhood homes, and none on the first neighborhood — all due to the power of New York's solar incentive programs!

In 2010, Ithaca has about one third of the solar installations in the whole state, according to Steve. There are eight qualified installers just in Tompkins County. I asked him why solar was so popular in such a cloudy place. "When people congregate in one place they learn from each other," he mused. "Perhaps it's also because we're centrally isolated. Concepts can spread virally in a small community."[5]

Just as we saw in the Chapter 2, having a cluster of like-minded businesses — or in this case individual homeowners, organizations or builders with similar values — makes an enormous difference. But passive solar homes and solar PV panels are only part of the story. Green building design encompasses far more than that. I decided to check out the popular Green Buildings Open House (GBOH) to see the range of creative ideas that are demonstrated in the nearby area.

What Is a Green Building?

While there is no one standard definition, the GBOH brochure describes it well. "Green building involves optimizing the way a building uses resources (air, water, energy, light, materials) in order to create a health-promoting, well-functioning space for the inhabitants while minimizing the negative impact on the environment."[6] *This definition is broad enough to include retrofitting conventional buildings with energy efficiency measures and/or renewable energy, renovation projects using recycled materials and new construction designed to be as sustainable as possible. But it also may address the location of the building and its surroundings: Is it near public transit? Does it promote community? Can one reach essential services by biking or walking?*

Green Buildings Open House

On a blustery, cold weekend in early October, over 600 people eagerly traveled to multiple sites around Ithaca and surrounding towns by bus, by car and by van. One hearty group even went by bike. It was the 2008 Ithaca Green Buildings Open House, organized locally by Cornell Cooperative Extension (CCE) of Tompkins County and the Ithaca Green Building Alliance (IGBA), and also part of larger regional and national events sponsored by the Northeast Sustainable Energy Association and the American Solar Energy Society. "The tour has gotten to be so popular we added a second day," one event organizer told me. "We were amazed at how many people showed up."[7]

Twenty five private homes and two non-residential sites were included in the Open House. Sites were open from 10 AM to 4 PM on either Saturday or Sunday, and homeowners were on hand to show off their site's green features and to answer questions. In addition to self-guided tours, people could opt to take shuttle vans guided by green building professionals for a small fee. There was a fascinating mix of people: in addition to architects and builders there were families with kids in strollers and retirees.

The goal of the Green Buildings Open House is to educate and inspire people to make their own choices about green building, and to "inform you in enhancing the comfort, health, and sustainability of your own home or workplace."[8] Because any building project involves multiple trade-offs, it is very helpful to be able to talk to the homeowners and building managers to find out what techniques were used and how well they work.

One site was especially interesting to me. Mike and Carrie Koplinka-Loehr live with their four children in a completely solar house that uses no fossil fuels. The passive solar design provides most of their space heating, with backup from 48 evacuated tube solar collectors which also provide their hot water. Their 72 photovoltaic panels provide all the electricity needed for a large family. They have an air to air heat exchanger (which captures heat from air that is vented from the house and warms cool, fresh incoming air).

But the most interesting feature is that this house represents state-of-the-art design by Cornell students and faculty. The house was built as part of the national Solar Decathlon — a biennial competition among colleges and universities to build the greenest home. Finished homes need to be small enough to transport to Washington, DC where they are placed on the Washington Mall for viewing. The Koplinka-Loehrs purchased the 2007 Solar Decathlon house and built an addition for their family. Over 300 Cornell students had been involved in the conceptualization, design and construction of the original house, along with faculty advisors. This is an excellent example of putting the brain power of an Ivy League university to work on a practical issue!

Another special site on the tour was the Dorothy D. and Roy H. Park Center for Business and Sustainable Enterprise at Ithaca College. This $18 million dollar building was built to LEED Platinum standards, the highest certification level of the US Green Building

The Park Center for Business and Sustainable Enterprise at Ithaca
College is LEED Platinum.

Council. It is the first facility for an undergraduate business program
in the world to achieve this standard, and when it opened it was one
of only nine LEED platinum buildings on a US college or university
campus. The building is not only built to the highest green standards, it also has a spacious, sunny interior with lots of natural light.

Almost 90% of the building materials were manufactured locally, one third of the total were recycled and three quarters of the
new wood materials were from sustainably-managed woodlots. Almost all of the construction waste was diverted from landfills by recycling or salvaging. The building is designed to use 37% less energy
than a code compliant building. It employs light-colored or shaded
paving, native plant landscaping, a vegetated roof, superinsulated
exterior walls, extensive daylighting and occupancy sensors in the
classrooms that turn lights on or off. Centralized controls monitor
and automatically adjust heat, ventilation and air conditioning. Low
flow faucets and dual flush toilets connect to a stormwater reclama-
tion system. The College purchases half of the building's electricity from renewable sources. There is even a Sustainable Café which
features organic items and locally grown food in season. Even the
cutlery, cups and plates are compostable!

Like the Solar Decathlon house, there is also a story behind this
impressive building. In 2003 Ithaca College hired a new provost,
Peter Bardaglio, who had a passion for sustainability. I remember

giving him a tour of EcoVillage at Ithaca in the early days of his tenure. As we walked through the densely clustered neighborhoods of
passive solar homes with kids playing on bikes and neighbors tending front yard tomatoes, his eyes lit up. As I spoke about the on-site
organic farms and hands-on educational programs with students I
could tell that Peter really got it. He understood the importance of
creating a whole systems approach to sustainability. Later he told
me that the visit influenced him profoundly. "It was a seminal moment for me," he confided. "I realized this is what learning is, this is
what real knowledge is."[9]

Bardaglio went on to become a very strong advocate for sustainability at Ithaca College. He threw his weight behind the budding
Partnership for Sustainability Education (PSE — further described
in Chapter 6) between EVI and the IC Environmental Studies Program, and when the initial National Science Foundation grant that
supported the partnership ran out, he secured permanent funding for it through the college. He was a strong spokesperson for
teaching sustainability across the curriculum and for encouraging
then-president Peggy Williams to sign the American College and
University Presidents' Climate Commitment.

Before he left the college five years later, Bardaglio had created
a legacy at Ithaca College in two ways: he seized the opportunity
to envision, promote and raise funding for a state-of-the-art LEED
platinum business school, one that promoted a curriculum based
on sustainable business theory and practices; he also consistently
brought college-wide attention to the sustainability issue and lec-
tured nationally about the innovations that IC was taking. In 2008,
Ithaca College won the Campus Sustainability Leadership Award
for a college of its size from the national group, Advancement of
Sustainability in Higher Education (AASHE). While many people
at Ithaca College (especially PSE coordinators) can take credit for
that designation, it was Bardaglio's tenacious leadership in the administration that provided the space and support for sustainability
initiatives to grow.

After leaving the Ithaca College campus on south hill and its
panoramic view of Cayuga Lake, the Green Buildings Open House

continued downtown. Of course not all the buildings on the tour used dramatic, state-of-the-art building techniques. Many were modest retrofits of older housing stock. One such example was a house in the downtown area worked on by Ithaca Neighborhood Housing Services (INHS), a 30 year old, nonprofit housing organization that is best known for recycling houses in the Ithaca area. While this renovated house is a typical single family home that doesn't look different in any way than neighboring buildings, it was able to achieve a LEED Gold certification for affordable single family houses — the second in New York state (INHS also built the first). In the Green Buildings Open House brochure, it was modestly described as "nothing fancy — just a really well detailed, carefully constructed house."[10] INHS was also involved in the LEED for HOMES pilot project to help develop a national standard for green building. Scott Reynolds, who works for the agency, told me, "We want to show that housing can be affordable, attractive and resource efficient."[11] In the future, INHS plans to build all of its single family new construction projects to these standards.

Permanently Affordable Green Housing

Ithaca Neighborhood Housing Services has built over 125 affordable homes over the last three decades. The low income owners who buy these homes are getting a great deal, due to state and federal subsidies. The only problem is that when these first-time homebuyers sell their homes, the price is often no longer affordable. Now a new program, known as the Community Housing Trust, will help to solve that issue. Owners who buy a home under this program will be able to recoup their costs and take a modest 2% a year increase in the home's value. "However, if the value of the house rises faster than that the extra value stays within the house," explained INHS executive director Paul Mazzarella. "We wanted to make sure that our valuable subsidies have long-term benefits."

But INHS goes a step further, by building homes that qualify for the highest level of green building — LEED platinum. This means that residents' fuel bills will remain low for the life of the home. "We're very proud to be using green construction," Mazzarella said. "There are few homes built that achieve that rating, and barely any affordable homes build to such standards." [12]

Nearby, another home has been constructed by owner-builders Todd Saddler and Laurie Konwinski. Their two-story home, built over three years in the heart of a residential neighborhood, has been inspiring to many people, as it has gone up, step by step. It uses a lot of common-sense principles — facing due south, it picks up heat and daylight from its passive solar orientation. Like EVI homes it has double wall construction filled with R35 dense packed cellulose insulation. It has grid-tied photovoltaic panels to produce electricity, a lovely masonry stove that provides both heat and hot water, radiant floors, and it uses local lumber. It is located within walking distance of most activities — something that I miss in my EcoVillage home. Fiercely idealistic, Todd and Laurie have found a way to put their ideals to practical and inspiring use. Describing their style of architecture as "Ithaca Peasant," Todd told visitors, "Our home brings us into contact with the natural beauty of sun, soil, wood, fire, air, water and our fellow human beings." He added with a twinkle, "Tomorrow is our permanent address." Laurie pointed out, "If humanity spoils this beautiful planet we are given we won't have a new one to go to. We've made our best effort to build a home which supports a sustainable lifestyle on as many levels as possible." [13]

Whether new construction, retrofit or state-of-the-art use of renewable energy, clearly there is a lot going on with green building in the Ithaca area. EcoVillage at Ithaca has taken it to a neighborhood level.

Origins of EcoVillage at Ithaca

In 1991, my friend and colleague Joan Bokaer started drumming up support to build an ecovillage in the Ithaca area. I was living with my family in San Francisco at the time, newly divorced with two young children. The previous year I had spent as organizational manager on

another of Joan's projects, an environmental walk across the United
States. The Global Walk for a Livable World included 150 people from
six different countries. We walked an average of 20 miles a day, six days
a week, and stopped in 200 cities and towns across the US to do environmental education. We gave lectures at college campuses, taught classes
in elementary schools and did non-stop media interviews. Working with
local church groups, college faculty and students and environmental
groups along the way, we helped to start recycling programs (very new
at the time), planted trees, encouraged people to eat less meat and
live a simpler lifestyle. We even talked with people about the concept of
global warming, which in 1990 was barely on the radar screen of scientists, let alone the general public. We started on Martin Luther King Day
in Los Angeles and ended at the United Nations in late October, with a
rousing speech from the head of the UN environment program.

At the close of the Walk, one young woman summed it up for all of
us, "The Walk changed my life. Now I know I can do anything I set my
mind to do." With that spirit still in mind, when Joan called me up six
months after the walk was over to invite me to move to Ithaca and help
her create an ecovillage, I felt immediately that it was the right thing
to do. But first I needed to make sure the time was right and that there
was enough seed money to pay me a small salary. After the experience
of facilitating an initial five day envisioning retreat that brought together
over 100 people, I decided to pull up my deep roots from the Bay Area
and move to Ithaca, which had a reputation as a fun, cosmopolitan and
progressive college town, to co-found the EcoVillage.

While Joan left her work with EVI in 1996 to found other projects, I
am still here, working as executive director of the EcoVillage at Ithaca
nonprofit. Over the years we've been able to build a kind of living laboratory for sustainability that has won national and international awards
and is considered a key example of sustainable community development.
What makes EVI special? In addition to conserving land by densely
clustering our housing, having two organic farms and creating engaging
hands-on educational programs, we have created a small village of 160
people who care for each other like a large, extended family.

EcoVillage at Ithaca—Cooperative Solar Housing

EVI has 60 homes, with gardens, a pond, two Common Houses and parking all densely clustered on just 10 acres of land, with another neighborhood of 30 homes planned for construction. All buildings are designed as passive solar, with large windows on the south side and big roof overhangs to block the summer sun. Homes are constructed as superinsulated duplexes, which is very energy efficient. Although the primary heat source is solar energy, in the First Resident Group (FROG) there is a mini-district heating system, which supplies backup space heating and hot water to each cluster of eight homes. Currently this system runs on natural gas boilers. When we have the money and the plans in place, we will be able to retrofit the whole neighborhood of 30 homes by simply converting the four energy centers to a renewable fuel source.

As we design our third neighborhood of 30 homes, called TREE (third residential ecovillage experience), we are exploring the use of Passiv Haus design, a pioneering approach to superinsulated homes that originated in Germany. In these homes, walls are so well insulated that whole homes can be heated with the equivalent amount of heat provided by one burner on a stove. The body heat of the residents and waste heat from appliances, in addition to passive solar gain, keep these homes very toasty. Because they are so airtight it is

Jim Bosjolie

Almost half of homes in EcoVillage at Ithaca's SONG neighborhood generate their electricity with rooftop solar panels.

also important to ventilate them well with heat recovery ventilators. Currently there are only a handful of these homes built in the US, but they are increasingly popular in Europe, with over 21,000 built. EVI would like to help popularize the design as a terrific way to save energy.

Plants for Green Roofing

Motherplants is a certified women-owned nursery in upstate New York, dedicated to growing plants for green roofs. Their business has become quite successful in just a few years, and specializes in the drought-tolerant, shallow rooted species adapted to vegetated roofs. People choose green roofs for a variety of important reasons. They reduce stormwater runoff; moderate building temperatures, reduce heating and cooling costs; reduce heat radiation from buildings which causes the urban heat island effect; add to a building's aesthetic value, and increase green space for human enjoyment and wildlife value. For these reasons, green roofs count toward the environmental building certification known as LEED.

Big Red Goes Green

Cornell University, nicknamed Big Red, is the economic engine of Tompkins County. It employs a full 10,000 (10%) of the county residents as professors, researchers, administrators, chefs, clerical and maintenance staff. Together with Ithaca College and the local community college, it brings 25,000 students to Ithaca every year, essentially doubling the population of the city during the school year. For a while, it seemed that Cornell lagged behind some other colleges and universities around the country on sustainability issues. Ithaca College was already starting to teach sustainability-oriented courses, composting all of its dining hall food scraps and forging a formal partnership with EcoVillage at Ithaca to teach courses on the science of sustainability.

Meanwhile Cornell was making big strides, albeit some controversial ones, in changing its physical plant. In 2000 it launched a Lake Source Cooling system, conserving 80% of the electricity Cornell uses to cool its buildings by passing the cold water of Cayuga Lake through heat exchangers. The system drew criticism from local environmentalists who were concerned that the system, which discharges water that has been warmed to 48–56°F at the surface of the lake, could create algae blooms and other unhealthy conditions. After eight years of operation, however, the Lake Source Cooling system seems to be creating minimal disruption in the lake's ecosystem, by some accounts, although it is still opposed by some environmentalists.

Ten years later Cornell took another major stride towards becoming more energy self-sufficient. At the end of 2009, the university finished a major upgrade of its central heating plant, allowing it to generate almost three quarters of its own electricity. After years of researching options, Cornell chose to build an addition to its aging, coal-fired facility by adding two natural gas turbines that produce steam for a generator. Known as Combined Heat and Power (CHP) or cogeneration, the facility captures exhaust steam from electrical production and funnels it into the campus-wide heating system, thus producing both heat and power at the same time. "We will be running a lot more efficiently than standard plants," said plant manager Ed Wilson.[14]

As the Cornell CHP plant came online in January 2010, a dramatic drop in total greenhouse gas emissions was expected. Kyu Whang, vice president of Facilities Services, told a group assembled for a tour of the plant, "We've only completed our Climate Action Plan exactly four months ago and we can stand here and say we're cutting our emissions by 28 percent. That is a major accomplishment."[15] The largest source of Cornell's greenhouse gases is through on-site combustion, and the CHP plant will make this far more efficient. By switching fuel sources from coal to natural gas and producing heat and electricity together, the CHP plant will provide 70% of the electricity needed for campus while also supplying heat to the buildings. It also may be able to use either liquid or gas biofuels in the future, as they become available.

According to the US Environmental Protection Agency (EPA), combined heat and power plants achieve between 60 and 80% efficiency. Traditional coal-fired plants, such as AES Cayuga (Ithaca's main electricity provider), achieve only about 33% efficiency because most of their heat is discharged through cooling towers.

Peter Bardaglio described the impact of coal this way, "Thanks to mountaintop removal, more than 470 mountains in four Appalachian states have been destroyed to date.... Given the inefficiency of coal, this means only about 156 of those mountains went into providing electricity. The other 314 mountains were not only destroyed, they were a complete waste."[16]

In February of 2007, Cornell president David Skorton signed the American College and University Presidents' Climate Commitment. By pledging to become carbon-neutral, signatories agree to develop a comprehensive plan for eliminating emissions of greenhouse gases associated with global warming. The Combined Heat and Power project is expected to reduce annual emissions of carbon dioxide by 50,000 tons, nitrogen oxide by 250 tons and sulfur dioxide by 800 tons.[17] As the largest player in Tompkins County's economy, Cornell's commitment to providing cleaner, less polluting sources of heating and cooling energy provides an excellent example (more details in Chapter 12).

A Rural Example: Energy Independent Caroline

In 2005, the town of Caroline in Tompkins County became the second municipality in New York state to purchase 100% windpower for municipal use. Now, several years later, it is developing a business model to produce sufficient wind energy to power the entire town of Caroline's 1,400 households, roughly 1.5 megawatts of electricity. As part of a grassroots education and outreach campaign, the Energy Independent Caroline committee received $1,500 from Cornell's community partnership program to distribute one compact fluorescent light bulb (CFL) to every household in the town. A joint Cornell University/Ithaca College planning team decided to

Dominic Frongillo

It takes all ages to organize energy independence in the town of Caroline.

organize the massive distribution. Wendy Skinner, coordinator of SewGreen, a local nonprofit organization that teaches people about reusing fabrics, sponsored a Sew-In which created 1,200 colorful cloth bags for the distribution.

"The idea exploded," recalled Dominic Frongillo, a key young organizer for the initiative, "She would drop off these bag-making kits at Brooktondale Community Store and people would take them home and each week, she'd come back and another stack of bags would be made. People were so excited to be part of this larger community effort…it was really fun!" Dominic learned some sewing skills himself in the process. And then there was the distribution. "We had a group of Cornell students who planned this like a campaign. We stayed up until 4 AM plotting out the routes for distribution. And on April 21 during a three hour period we had 75 people who fanned out across the Town of Caroline and distributed the bags by car, by foot, by bike and even by horseback!" In addition to a CFL, the reusable bags had information about how to save energy in the homes, a survey of what people were already doing and what barriers existed for them to take more measures and questions and information about the wind energy project. "So all of a sudden we're a household name…people were actually waiting to get the bags."[18] The students got to learn hands-on skills and information about planning a campaign.

The Evolution of a
Young Sustainability Leader

Dominic Frongillo is one of Tompkins County's most active young lead-ers, and he is passionate about community sustainability. Until recently he lived in the same house he grew up in, in the small town of Caroline, NY. Curiously, his parents are the ones who moved out and left town to teach in South Carolina. During his senior year in high school, Dominic had the good fortune to be part of WISE, a community service program. His mentor was Tim Logue, a community planner. Dominic loved work-ing with middle schoolers to ask them to plan what they wanted their community to be like in 10 years. "I found that incredibly empowering—that a community could articulate a vision for itself. What an amaz-ing democratic process for a community to set goals for itself and then achieve them."

This early interest asserted itself again in college at Cornell, when Dominic chose an independent major in Community and Sustainability. He was influenced by professor Rob Young, in City and Regional Plan-ning. "He told us, 'The only way that we will survive is to create the world of our dreams'," recalled Dominic. "That was an incredible moti-vating factor." After graduating in 2005, Dominic first thought he would go into the Peace Corps to experience community and make a difference in the world. "I'm really interested in how we solve problems at the local level," he told me. "You can make a really big impact at the personal level, you can turn a life around and you can also work at the policy level...but on the community level you can see both of those things." Then it dawned on him that he could do those things while working in his own home town.

Even before graduating from Cornell, Dominic had been involved in town politics in Caroline, helping to put together the Town Comprehen-sive Plan. "We had old-timers sitting down with newcomers and talking about agriculture, open space and infrastructure, and what the county would look like...No one used the word sustainability," recalled Dominic, "but that's what it was all about." He ran for Town Supervisor and won.

"My goal is to get 100 other young people to run for office. That's my measure of success." Dominic recounted organizing 160 young people *from local high schools and colleges to go to Washington, DC in March 2009 to take part in PowerShift, a national mobilization of young people to lobby for clean energy and green jobs. He was especially impressed by Van Jones, a powerful black leader who did a stint working for the Obama administration, who told them, "'You are part of the biggest revolutionary change in history of how we relate to ourselves, the economy and the planet, and we can raise millions of people out of poverty in the process.'"* [19]

Black Oak Wind Farm

On the other side of the county, plans are underway to build a wind farm on Connecticut Hill, in Enfield, which has a similar sized rural population to the town of Caroline. The Black Oak Wind Farm is being developed by Enfield Energy, a business that expects to be able to generate 35–50 megawatts — enough to power all the households in Tompkins County! While the project has generated a lot of controversy, with some local landowners who are very upset about the prospect of seeing twenty 2.5 megawatt turbines out their windows, Black Oak Wind Farm finally got the green light from the town.

In January 2009, the Town of Enfield passed a local Wind Ordinance, governing the development of any wind resources in the town. The law provides Enfield Energy the framework within which it can design the wind farm. The local law covers everything from property setbacks to noise levels, insurance and safety. Enfield Energy is working to secure financing for the project, choosing turbines and siting them; the company plans to begin construction sometime in 2010 or 2011. "It's been an unfathomable amount of work," John Rancich, the owner of the company told me. Despite reluctant support from the town, there have been many, many hurdles.

Rancich, who is from Enfield, is dedicated to his local roots. "We will employ local contractors, train local people to operate the wind farm and will return a portion of the profits from the Black Oak Wind Farm to the Town of Enfield, helping improve local services and reduce the tax burden on residents. We will not be selling the energy out of the area, but will sell it locally for use here in our own county."[20] The site for the Black Oak Wind Farm was chosen because it is the windiest place in the county and because it already has a high-voltage transmission line crossing the site, making a grid tie-in feasible.

In a guest column in the *Ithaca Journal*, Steve Nicholson, also an early advocate of wind energy and a member of Tompkins Renewable Energy Education Alliance (TREEA), explained why this group of educators and activists supported the Enfield wind farm. "Data from the EPA shows that this amount of electricity, if supplied by NYSEG [the local utility that uses coal-fired plants] will produce emissions of approximately 98,000 pounds of nitrogen oxide, 350,000 pounds of sulfur dioxide and 60 million pounds of CO_2. It takes about 12,000 acres of trees to absorb this amount of pollution, or 6,250 cars would have to be taken off the road to accrue these same environmental benefits." Nicholson continued, "While we recognize the value of an unchanging skyline, we can also see smog in every direction. According to the EPA, air pollutants have reduced visibility from 90 to 20 miles in the eastern US. We believe resident wildlife and humans face a much greater danger from coal-burning pollution than from sharing the landscape with wind turbines."[21]

Not only are wind farms not polluting, they have a very small footprint on the land, using just 3% of the land in the case of Black Oak. The remaining land will continue to be used for farming, ranching and forestry, as well as an Alternative Energy Education Center, set up to work with area schools and to offer hands-on exhibits to the public.

One very interesting tie-in for the Black Oak Wind Farm is that its profits are planned to be used to build a zero net energy development, Carrowmoor, across the street from EcoVillage at Ithaca. Carrowmoor, when finished, is designed to include 400 residences, most of them designed as luxury homes, although some permanently affordable housing will be part of the mix. Some of the green features will be densely clustered housing (leaving 113 acres of open space), 100% use of windpower, a walkable community, underground parking, commercial space which will include storefronts with basic goods for residents' use, rainwater harvesting and re-gionally sourced materials and labor. Right now Carrowmoor is on hold until the Wind Farm is up and running. "Otherwise I'm totally stretched financially," Rancich confided.

John Rancich, developer of both Black Oak Wind Farm and Car-rowmoor, epitomizes a new kind of green developer — one who sees the potential of making a good profit from green buildings and use of renewable energy. He also has a community spirit. On his website, Rancich said that the intent is for Enfield Energy Wind Farm to be "turned over to, owned and managed by Town residents themselves, rather than having an outside corporation develop the site and dis-appear with the profits." Moreover, the profits from the wind farm "will help pave our roads, repair our school and fight our fires."[22]

Bringing It Together:
The Ithaca Green Building Alliance

In an effort to communicate between the many businesses that are involved in green building and renewable energy, Brent and Diana Katzmann founded the nonprofit Ithaca Green Building Alliance (IGBA) in 2005. This group of about 50 entrepreneurs meets regu-larly to network and share new information. Brent, who runs a nat-ural building business with his wife, shared some of his thoughts with me.

"There is a spirit of collaboration in the green building commu-nity here that is deeply woven into our business practices," he said. Many green builders seek to rethink not only the built environment, but also their own way of working. "While many of us ultimately compete for the same customers, it is quite common that we end up bringing each other on board as subcontractors or consultants for these projects." Brent sees the green building industry maturing at a rapid rate, leading to more specialization among the members of IGBA, who may choose to focus on straw bale, zero-energy, Passiv Haus, affordable green or other approaches. "As a result, our collab-orative approach is already evolving to address broader issues that affect all of these approaches: encouraging local production and dis-tribution of frequently used green building materials; gathering and sharing actual performance metrics for the many buildings we've created in order to better evaluate the real life effectiveness of our varying choices in materials and methods."[23]

One collaborative effort is the Green Building Seminar Series, co-sponsored with CCE-TC, which often features local experts who share detailed information on everything from Green Heating Options to Wastewater Treatment Systems. Mike Carpenter is working on an interactive database which will include information on the cost of construction, performance metrics and contact information for many green buildings in the area. This cooperative spirit among green building professionals in Tompkins County is a great example of the whole being greater than its parts.

Tompkins County has a very healthy and growing network of green building and renewable energy projects, from rural towns to urban institutions, from CFL distribution to Combined Heat and Power plants, from passive and active solar homes to large-scale wind farms. Despite its cold and cloudy weather, this county has become the solar capital of New York state. Not only does it have a network of collaborative green building professionals, but it also offers a tremendous variety of educational programs for the public. This chapter has not even touched on some of the many other initiatives here, including Performance Systems Development, an energy consulting firm (first started by a resident of EVI) which now works with local governments around the country; Taitem Engineering, an innovative energy engineering firm which among other things has pioneered an air conditioner run on geothermal energy; the Danby Land Bank, which leases farmland to grow biomass fuel crops and many, many more. Just as the local food and farming movement has taken off in recent years, green building and renewable energy is a close second, with innovative ideas popping up everywhere and a remarkable openness to sharing ideas and information.

Building a Livable City

Smart Land Use and Transportation Alternatives

*The average American household spends $8,000
a year to own, maintain, insure and gas the family cars
(which are parked 95% of the time).*

ITHACA CARSHARE BROCHURE, CITING AAA STUDIES

*On average, Americans spend 19 cents out of every dollar earned
on transportation expenses. The nation's poorest families spend
more than 40% of their take-home pay on transportation.*

THE ENVIRONMENTAL JUSTICE RESOURCE CENTER

*The quality of life depends on how we build our cities.
The higher the density and diversity of a city, the less
dependent on motorized transport and the fewer resources
it requires, the less impact it has on nature.*

RICHARD REGISTER, ECOCITYBUILDERS

Car-Free at Last!

We were on our way out of town for a special getaway in mid-December. The B&B was booked, the car was packed and I felt that special glow of "we're on vacation" spread like a wide grin across my face. We were worried about the approaching snowstorm, but snow tires and winter driving savvy made us confident we could easily make the 200 mile round trip. Then, leaving the outskirts of Ithaca,

Jared accelerated. There was a terrible grinding noise, and I looked over to see the gear shift pop back into third. He tried again to shift into fourth gear, and again that grinding noise assaulted our ears. Oh no! We had worked hard to schedule this three-day weekend, and now it seemed doomed. After a quick assessment, we decided to take a risk and continue, skipping fourth gear for the rest of the trip, and shifting directly from third to fifth. Luckily it worked!

After a great getaway, we consulted with our mechanic, a hard-working guy we were getting to know all too well, as our 12 year old car needed increasing numbers of repairs. "You'll need a new transmission," he told us. "I can get you a good used one and install it for $1,500." This was a critical moment. We had three choices: a) continue to put large amounts of cash into *Tango*, our dear old car with 180,000 miles on it, b) buy a new used car, for even larger amounts of cash or c) give up owning a car entirely. While the last option seemed radical, we giddily agreed that now was the ideal time to try it out. It became our New Year's resolution, and as of January 1, 2009, we parked our car for the last time.[1]

While this was a huge step, we had been preparing for it for years. We had made a fairly smooth transition, as a family of four, to letting go of a second car eight years before. We were inspired by other EcoVillage families who figured out how to manage with just one car. "Communication is key," one couple told us. So, on Sunday evenings we would coordinate the car schedule for the week, including shopping, after-school activities, errands and work. I frequently was the chauffeur, dropping Jared at work, Jason at the high school, then driving myself to Cornell and shopping on the way home. It seemed like a lot of driving, so Jared and I started biking to work frequently in spite of Ithaca's steep hills, and our high-school-aged sons became excellent bikers as well. We all used the bus, and I gradually transitioned to working at home part-time. Living at EcoVillage made things easier, too, since we could always ask a neighbor to pick up last-minute groceries or borrow a car in a pinch.

Now our sons are grown, I work at home full-time, and Jared bike-commutes to work year-round. On cold winter mornings he suits up in neoprene bike tights, neoprene boots, double layers of gloves and a neoprene face mask. I have to make sure to kiss him goodbye before that Darth Vader mask appears!

Biking Is the Most Efficient Transport!

The bicycle has many attractions. It alleviates congestion, lowers air pollution, reduces obesity, does not emit climate-disrupting carbon dioxide, reduces the area of pavement needed, and is priced within reach for the billions of people who cannot afford a car....

Few methods of reducing carbon emissions are as effective as substituting a bicycle for a car on short trips. A bicycle is a marvel of engineering efficiency, one where an investment in 22 pounds of metal and rubber boosts the efficiency of individual mobility by a factor of three. On my bike I estimate I get easily 7 miles per potato. An automobile, which requires at least a ton of material to transport one person is extraordinarily inefficient by comparison.[2]

Baby, You Can Drive My Car

One huge help has been Ithaca Carshare. This innovative car sharing program rents cars by the hour to members, on a 24 hour, seven-days-a-week schedule. It is one of over 50 successful car share programs in North America, which jointly serve over 320,000 members sharing nearly 7,500 cars. Ithaca, with about 30,000 residents, is the smallest city to date with a car share program.

Car sharing may be the start of a new paradigm in how we view transportation. In the car-oriented United States, the type of car one owns is often considered an important part of one's identity. Car sharing takes away the ego attachment to one particular car, allowing people to think more freely about the real goal of getting from one place to another. One journalist from Los Angeles reflected that the car sharing trend shows that "the actual car is not all that important. It is really just a means to an end. It's a transportation appliance, a node in a system made possible by the Internet."[3] It's also easy to use. After joining as a member, you can sign out a car online, parked in various locations around town, then use an electronic key to gain access. You can drive the new, well-maintained car anywhere you like, as long as you get it back on time to its original location.

As much as I loved old *Tango*, I have to admit that it is a joy to drive a new, reliable car that is always clean and has a full tank of gas. While it is easy to take it for granted, Ithaca Carshare had a long, difficult gestation. Yet it is one of Ithaca's biggest success stories to date for transportation alternatives.

Ithaca Carshare initially grew out of research funded by a minigrant from a partnership between Ithaca College and EVI. Dan Roth, the project coordinator, pulled together a Car Share Summit in January 2006. The mayor showed up, as well as key transportation planners for the county, the city, Cornell and Ithaca College. Speakers from two successful independent car share programs, one in Boulder and one in San Francisco, gave the audience of over a hundred transportation advocates a big boost. We had a collective sense of excitement: if they can do it, we can, too!

From the beginning, Ithacans, true to form, wanted to start a nonprofit, locally-controlled car share service. Most cities with car share programs used FlexCar or ZipCar, the two big car share companies at that time. But Ithaca has a fiercely independent spirit, and the planning group applied for and received funding for a $177,220 state grant to jump-start its own program—all within the same year as the Car Share Summit. A soft launch was planned: to place two cars at EVI in February 2007 to work out any initial kinks in the program. So far, so good. Unfortunately, despite the promising start, getting insurance proved to be a headache. Insurance companies just didn't know what to do when faced with multiple drivers, and the few companies that were willing to offer a quote charged as much per car as they would charge an aggressive taxi driver in traffic-clogged New York City. It was simply not affordable.

Despite these issues that threatened to stop the project, the staff and board of the new nonprofit hunkered down and kept researching options. Finally, on Earth Day 2008, Ithaca Carshare announced that it was ready for membership sign-ups. In a triumphant press release, coordinator Jennifer Dotson shared that their insurance

Jim Bosjolie

Sharing a car can be fun. Author is in the back of car with other EcoVillagers.

agent had come through with a Valentine's Day present on February 14, in the form of an auto insurance policy that was not only affordable, but allowed us to accept members as young as 18. Just a year and a half after the initial Summit, Ithaca Carshare was officially on the road!

Now that the program is running, it has become very popular. In its first two years, it has expanded from placing six high-mileage Nissan Versa hatchbacks on the streets of Ithaca to nine Nissan Versas, two Honda Fits, a Scion xB and a Toyota Tacoma pickup truck. With a tag line of "good for you, good for the planet," Ithaca Carshare's website explains why it is a green option:

- Studies show that for each carshare vehicle, up to 15 privately owned vehicles come off the road.
- Carshare members walk, bike, and bus more.
- By helping people "kick the car-owning habit," carsharing reduces vehicle usage, fossil fuel use, and greenhouse gas emissions.
- Carsharing helps reduce traffic congestion, improving local air quality[4]

But there is another important plus to car sharing. Jared and I are finding that not only do we plan our trips more carefully to accomplish multiple errands, we also have found that by not owning our own car, our social life has increased! One example is a recent trip to the Dance Flurry, an annual three-day event in Saratoga Springs which draws 5,000 people to a fun-filled music and dance festival. Rather than our usual solo trip, we carpooled with two friends we rarely get to see. We had so much fun, chatting during the four hour trip each way and sharing delicious meals before and after the Flurry, that we are already planning ahead to carpool next year!

Land Use Patterns Drive Environmental Problems

Despite its advantages, giving up a primary or even a second car is not possible for many North Americans. The majority of our population lives in suburbs, with homes separated from workplaces, schools, healthcare facilities and with few public gathering places. Most couples work two jobs to make ends meet, and it can be hard to juggle all the needs of a family while managing infrequent public transit. It wasn't always this way.

"Simply put, the suburbs — where houses on average doubled in size and miles driven annually has tripled since the 1950s — are the best possible invention for mindless consumption," wrote authors Dave Wann and Dan Chiras. "They may well be the single largest environmental impact the world has ever known."[5] While suburbia has gobbled up rich farmland close to cities and driven car-oriented development, cities have had their own woes.

I experienced this firsthand in Lima, Peru, where my family lived for two years when I was a child. The *barriadas*, those vast shanty-town slums on the outskirts of Lima, were home to tens of thousands of poverty-stricken people who had migrated from the Andes to the glittering city in search of jobs. I'll never forget seeing lines of women and children, waiting for hours in the hot sun, for a chance to access one village water tap for all their drinking, washing and bathing needs. Open sewers carried human waste and garbage past every house, and one in every five children died before the age of five, often of malnutrition. Unfortunately, these slums are growing. Of the three billion urban dwellers today, it is estimated that one billion are slum-dwellers.[6] American moviegoers got a small taste of this urban poverty by watching "Slumdog Millionaire," the Oscar winner of best movie in 2008. One young man from Nepal, who grew up on the streets of Kathmandu and was adopted at age ten by an EcoVillage resident, commented of the movie, "That was my life, minus the millionaire part."[7]

...And Solutions—Ecological City Design

But cities don't have to be the problem. They can in fact be solutions. The EcoCity World Summit, held in San Francisco in October of 2008, brought together 150 presenters and thousands of participants from around the world to a remarkable four-day conference, all focused on a positive vision of what the city can become. As Kirsten Miller, the conference director said in a welcoming statement, "We need to rethink and rebuild our human civilization to exist in balance with living systems." She continued, "[there] are enough of us to help launch a design revolution: the city, town and village built for people and nature instead of for cars and cheap energy. We are seeking no less than to transform the way we inhabit planet Earth, and we are here to discuss, refine, and energize the vision." Richard Register, conference co-convenor added, "It is remarkable that more of us don't connect the largest creation of our species — [cities] — to the largest of our environmental, resource consumption and biodiversity problems — and to their solutions.... We may well find out that the far happier, healthier way of building cities is also the most culturally enriching and equitable way, the way most beneficial for all life on the planet, the way that also rescues us from the destructive forces we have unleashed, and is at the same time the way that can actually work."[8]

This was the Seventh International EcoCity Conference, and Joan Bokaer and I each had the privilege of presenting our work; Joan spoke about Connect Ithaca, a new organization that seeks to reconfigure Ithaca as a pedestrian and bike friendly city with excellent rapid transit, and I spoke about EcoVillage at Ithaca, an experiment in densely clustered cohousing neighborhoods, organic farms, land preservation and hands-on education.

But the conference evoked an earlier time — in 1996, EcoVillage at Ithaca had co-convened the Third International EcoCity Conference with our sister village of Yoff, Senegal, and we therefore knew many of the players. In fact, one of the first people I saw on entering the conference center in San Francisco was Serigne Mbaye Diene, a Senegalese man who years before lived in Ithaca as a Cornell graduate student. It was Serigne who had had the vision of linking our nascent EcoVillage at Ithaca efforts as a sister village to his 500-year-old traditional fishing village near Dakar. The conference that Joan and Serigne co-convened in 1996, with the guidance of Richard Register, drew hundreds of people from around the world and presented a lot of similar themes. It also produced tangible results over time. It helped set the stage for a national network of ecovillages in Senegal. In addition, it provided a basis for excellent university programs linking US college students with traditional villagers. Together they learn hands-on applications of alternative technologies that improve the environmental conditions of the villagers and offer options for ongoing jobs in areas where unemployment can be 50% or greater.

A Walkable City with Transit Options

While cars have driven modern North American development patterns, Ithaca has tried, with some success, to keep its core city intact. Ithaca has some suburbs, but the city itself is quite compact and walkable. In fact, Ithaca was named #1 for Green Commuters by AARP. More people in Ithaca walk to work — 40% — than in any other city in the state, including Manhattan, which has 22% walk to work commuters.[9] That is quite remarkable, given the cold climate and the steep hills!

This has been a long-lasting trend. As Carol Kammen, a local historian noted, "At one time Ithaca was a walking city. Some people kept carriages or hired a cart and driver from a livery stable. In 1877, for example, there were three livery stables in the center of the city. To leave the county there were steamboats that transported people up the lake, there were a few stage lines, and after the 1830's there was travel by train."[10] When Cornell was established in the 1870s, a horse-drawn wagon carried people up the steep hill to the campus. In the 1880s trolleys were popular, but they were replaced in the 1930s by buses.

In 1988, the city, Cornell and the county consolidated bus service into Tompkins Consolidated Area Transit (TCAT), which now has more than three million riders a year. With the severe economic downturn at the end of 2008, TCAT experimented with giving riders a 50 cent fare (a dollar less than usual) for off-peak riding hours from July through October. The promotion yielded a 23% increase in ridership in its first month alone.[11] Unfortunately TCAT was unable to sustain the lower fares due to big deficits from the rising cost of gasoline. But there have been other experiments as well. TCAT offers VanPool, in which groups of 4 to 14 commuters receive a van, insurance and maintenance to offer easy, affordable commuting options from areas not served by TCAT. Cornell has encouraged this option and provides free membership in Ithaca Carshare for VanPool members.

Cornell is in the midst of revisioning its transportation options. Already a national leader with several award-winning programs in place, Cornell has successfully moved one third of its commuters out of single-occupancy vehicles into alternative modes. In a proactive transportation study conducted from 2006 to 2008, Cornell looked at transportation-related impacts of potential Cornell population growth over the next decade. "The desired outcome will be strategies that promote a best-in-class transportation system with greater participation in walking, bicycling, transit use, park-and-rides, and other alternatives to single-occupant vehicle commuting."[12]

Some of the proposed innovations are already underway. The community-wide VanPool and Ithaca Carshare programs described above were both aided by seed money from Cornell. No-fee evening and weekend bus passes for students create easy mobility and support bus service at times that it is traditionally underused. And Cornell provides a one-year, no-fee bus pass to all new Cornell students to "foster a transit culture at the university." One striking long-term innovation is that Cornell plans to invest $20 million over ten years in support of housing initiatives, transportation demand management programs and related transportation infrastructure improvements that will benefit the local community as well as Cornell.[13] This is particularly significant, given the lack of adequate affordable housing near the city and how many workers live outside the county in order to spend less on housing. So by building less expensive housing, Cornell will help to solve a social problem as well as significantly cut transit miles and therefore greenhouse gas emissions. It is a great example of leveraging funds for a sustainable solution that positively affects social, economic and environmental goals at the same time.

The Ithaca Commons

The City of Ithaca has long been an innovator in land use. One example is the Ithaca Commons, a downtown pedestrian mall in the heart of the city. Stretching over two city blocks of streets closed to cars and filled with trees, the Ithaca Commons has a variety of shops, banks, restaurants, outdoor cafes and one large and two small pavilions that serve as performance venues. It provides a wonderful, casual way to socialize and brings together locals and tourists alike. On summer evenings there are free concerts, and even in the depths of winter there are festivals, such as Light in Winter, a unique science and art festival. There is also an ice sculpture contest and a chili cook-off. We can thank former Ithaca mayor Ed Conley for his vision and leadership in creating the Commons. Conley, who served four two-year terms as mayor, worked hard to prevail over many downtown merchants who thought the Commons was a bad idea. Conley, an Ithaca native, was elected mayor in 1971 by a nine vote margin. As a working class man he took office at a time when city politics was dominated by professors who could afford the $12,000 salary. In order to make ends meet, Conley supplemented the job with other part-time jobs, including working at a service station.[14] But despite this financial and time handicap, his vision of a vibrant city center, for people not cars, became a key legacy that continues to create social capital today.

Some of the most popular cities in the world are known for their city centers which are closed to cars. I have been fortunate to visit a few: Copenhagen, Denmark; Quebec, Canada; Boulder, Colorado; Charlottesville, Virginia; and Burlington, Vermont. In each of these cases, the vibrancy of people on foot, interacting with merchants or strolling along tree-filled streets, is a real joy. As our industrialized, globalized world moves at an ever-increasing pace, having a human-scale city center that moves at walking speed is relaxing and rejuvenating. Mix in some live music, delicious local food, public sculpture and the beauty of flowers, trees, and water features, and it can be a tremendous draw. I certainly hope that the Ithaca Commons will continue to thrive into the future, with the addition of thoughtful improvements.

Ithaca Biodiesel

A nonprofit organization started in 2007, Ithaca Biodiesel recycles used veggie oil from restaurants and makes it into a fuel suitable for cars. Veggie oil burns more cleanly than diesel fuel and recycles a product that would otherwise be wasted. It is not considered a net contributor to global warming because soybean or other crops first absorb carbon dioxide from the atmosphere and release it when burned, all in the same year, as opposed to fossil fuels which release carbon that has been buried for millions of years. Ithaca Biodiesel also outfits diesel cars to run on veggie oil. As the bumper sticker on one car at EcoVillage proclaims, "Drive vegetarian." This fledgling organization boasts a handful of dedicated volunteer workers. One of the group's successful fundraising methods was to hold a Grease Wrestling Tournament in which competitors wrestle, fully-clothed, in used veggie oil, coming out smelling like French fries.

In an educational endeavor with many ripple effects, Mark Wienand, an Ithaca Biodiesel technical advisor, helped four Lehman Alternative Community School Students (LACS) to convert a 17 passenger diesel-powered school bus to veggie oil. The conversion cost $1,000 which the school paid for with a grant. The conversion will save the school money in the long run, because rather than filling up at a gas station LACS students will be able to use discarded vegetable oil from restaurants. But more importantly, the conversion provided the students with a very empowering hands-on learning experience. Ian Gray, a junior at LACS, said, "One of the main reasons I'm doing this is because you always hear people in the progressive community talking about reducing our dependence on foreign oil and pursuing alternative energy sources. But that's all talk and we are trying to put that philosophy of sustainability into action." [15]

Recycle Ithaca's Bikes (RIBS)

When my son Daniel lived at home one summer after college, he got around almost exclusively by bike. In fact, he had three of them, including one he built himself. It was through him I learned about RIBS, an innovative program of the Southside Community Center, whose mission is "to support sustainable communities by promoting the reuse and maintenance of bicycles." In exchange for a little volunteer labor, you can even earn a secondhand bike. The program, which started in 1990, is open Tuesday, Thursday and Saturday afternoons. There is a women's class on Wednesday evenings.

Along with the funky artistic fence of painted bike parts outside, RIBS exudes a wonderful do-it-yourself attitude. When it is open, people of all ages and diverse backgrounds spill out onto the sidewalk to work on repairs. There are Cornell professors mingling with low income high school students, and it is often the teens who teach the adults. The program serves 250 kids and 200 adults each year. It's a great example of teaching sustainability on multiple levels: from recycling used bikes, to empowering people to learn new skills and creating a safe place for a diverse group of people to enjoy getting to know each other.[16]

RIBS is a program of the Southside Community Center.

Some people take the message of self-sufficiency to the max. One day my son coasted down West Hill to RIBS with his bike that needed repairs. The next day he fixed the bike and managed to tow it back home, up the steep hill, while riding his other bike. Now that's alternative transportation!

EcoCity Ithaca: Three Visions of the Future

In an interesting confluence of events, the City of Ithaca, the Town of Ithaca, Tompkins County, Cornell University and Ithaca College have been in the process of revising their long-term, comprehensive plans. This provides an unprecedented opportunity to shift gears to become a more sustainable city. While Ithaca already features many excellent examples of green design, planners also want to improve its livability over time through smart growth, transit-oriented development and green transportation. These can all lead to a better quality of life, reduce use of fossil fuels and lessen risks of climate change.

However, the inertia of a car-dominated culture can be hard to change. Ithaca experiences traffic jams and clogged roads, especially exacerbated by the commuter traffic from outlying areas. The initiatives which follow are ways that address high density, people-oriented, urban environments — ways that Ithaca can become more of an eco-city.

PodCar City

Are private cars on their way out? Some people in Sweden and Ithaca think so. On September 14–16, 2008, Ithaca hosted the second international PodCar City Conference. Several hundred people attended, traveling from as far away as Sweden, Brazil and China. The conference was initiated by The Institute for Sustainable Transportation (IST) from Sweden and Connect Ithaca, LLC, a group which "aims to evolve Ithaca, NY into a pioneering Eco-City that would become a template for urban development in the US."[17]

If podcars sound like a futuristic, space-age transportation concept, it's not surprising. While there are yet no working prototypes, podcars are planned to be computer-guided, electric vehicles that travel on their own networked system — usually elevated monorails, which people could access from stations spaced regularly along high density corridors. Podcars would typically seat two to eight passengers, giving travelers the freedom and privacy of their own cars while reducing traffic and parking woes. A party of one or more passengers would punch in their destination, somewhat like a horizontal elevator, and go directly there with no interim stops. Because podcars are very lightweight, they would not take much energy to run, making it feasible to power them by using solar or wind-generated electricity. Personal rapid transit (PRT) is not a new concept. A limited version of this kind of system was built in 1975 in Morgantown, West Virginia, and it still transports university students downtown and back. I had the chance to travel in it in 1990, and it seemed similar to an automated airport shuttle to me — a convenient way to get around the steep green hills and valleys of Morgantown.

Podcars have both strong advocates and strong detractors. In Ithaca, key transportation planners such as Fernando de Aragon, director of the Ithaca-Tompkins County Transportation Council, are in favor of giving it a try. "As we look 20 years ahead we had to take into account climate change," he said. "How are we going to move our goods and people into the future? A new mode of transportation doesn't come along very often. We had the rail, then the car...the technology still needs to prove itself. It has great potential. It's getting us to start planning now. We need to." His thinking was echoed by Gary Ferguson, executive director of the Downtown Ithaca Alliance. "[This] links communities together in a way that people can get from one place to another seamlessly...the Pod Car concept deserves special attention."

On the other hand, skeptics like Vukan Vuchic, a professor of transportation and engineering at the University of Pennsylvania, think that a PRT system "is operationally and economically unfeasible." Vuchic continued, "In the city, if you have that much demand, you could build these guideways and afford the millions it would take, but you wouldn't have capacity. In the suburbs, you would have capacity, but the demand would be so thin you couldn't possibly pay for those guideways, elevated stations, control systems and everything else."[18] Michael Smith, a history professor at Ithaca College, quoted Vuchic in a recent lively sustainability listserv exchange about PRT, and added his own thoughts. "I have to say that I think investing in PRT in this city would be a terrible waste of resources. The bus system is already very good for a city this size and if we put the kind of money they're talking about for PRT into that system it would be great." Smith went on to say, "As this project has been discussed a trophy mentality about it seems to be short-circuiting common sense."[19]

Meanwhile, a number of cities in Sweden, Poland, the UK and Masdar City (a zero-carbon city planned for construction in Abu Dhabi) are actively planning PRT systems. Santa Cruz, California, where students currently ride a bus which can take 40 minutes to go two miles up the hill to campus, is also considering one. Leaving aside for a moment the question of whether PRT actually works or not, the prospect of changing transportation patterns in a big way has got Ithaca hopping.

Downtown Ithaca 2020 Strategy's Big Ideas

1. *Mixed Uses: Downtown must have mixed-use projects and mixed-use streets.*
2. *A Dense Urban Core: Downtown density and downtown success are inextricably connected.*
3. *Reducing Automotive Usage in Downtown: We will pro-actively seek to reduce downtown dependence on the automobile whenever possible.*
4. *Transition Zones at Downtown's Edges: The heights and densities of downtown should begin to scale down toward the neighborhoods.*
5. *A Preference for Pedestrians: The community wants a downtown that has a walkable scale and is considered pedestrian friendly.*
6. *Maintaining the Retail Street: We must act to protect, preserve and enhance the downtown retail core.*
7. *The Commons as a Transit Hub: The Commons should be considered a key part of the community's public transit system.*
8. *In-Fill Development: In-fill development is an environmentally conscious way to maximize limited downtown real estate.*
9. *Clustered Destinations: There is a need for the community to seek to cluster pedestrian foot-traffic generating uses into downtown.*
10. *Downtown as a Community Center: Downtown should remain the community's focal center for major events, celebrations, and community gatherings.*

11. *A Leader in Green Practices and Sustainability: Downtown should*
    serve as a showcase for the community's broader interest in green
    and sustainable practices.[20]

Southwest Park

Along the inlet channel that feeds Cayuga Lake, there is a 62 acre
site of undeveloped land owned by the City of Ithaca. On the east
it is bordered by an ugly strip of the backs of big box stores, but on
the west the channel flows, with Cornell and Ithaca College crew
boats gliding by, and ducks and Canada geese swimming in the cold
water. As the last large piece of developable land on the flatlands in
the City, it is the site for a proposed housing development, dubbed
Southwest Park, that would include at least 600 units of affordable,
mixed income housing as well as businesses that would provide
local services, such as child care facilities, small stores and doctor's
offices. The dense development could support a high quality urban
transit service that would minimize car usage. Twenty acres of open
space, one third of the site, would be set aside for wildlife and recreation.

The Southwest Park project is moving along, albeit slowly. A vision statement was created by a committee in 2005. The vision includes Smart Growth principles:

- It locates new housing in proximity to jobs, services and shopping, thus reducing sprawl.
- It adds residential to the mix of uses in the southwest corner of
  the City, which is now a commercial district.
- It has the potential to reduce vehicular trips because of its location and enhances public transit, bike and pedestrian options.[21]

But the vision plans to not only meet Smart Growth goals, but exceed them, "by the vigor with which they embrace the goals, but also
by the extent to which they incorporate diversity, permanent affordability, environmental and sustainable features."[22] I was pleased to
see that the statement also includes reference to a variety of housing

styles and ownership, including cooperatives and cohousing. It was good to also see some of the same principles that EVI demonstrates, of densely clustered housing with large amounts of open space, put into play in an urban environment. The City engaged a consortium of nationally known new urbanist designer/developer firms to start the design process, but they waited for the City to complete wetland delineation and other due diligence tasks.

David Kay, a City Planning Board member, told me he thinks Southwest Park will be a tipping point that will push Ithaca to define its economic, ecological and social future as part of a strategic plan. "There will be resistance, just as there is to other innovations, but I think there's enough history and momentum in that direction that this will tip it over." He explained that the development is on public rather than on private land, so it will force a kind of dialogue in the public arena as to how the city spends its money.[23] Assuming that the plan goes forward, it will be a major step towards creating a dense, walkable, urban village, one that is affordable to many people who currently have to commute into the city.

The Aurora Street Dwelling Circle: Green Infill Development

A microcommunity with similar principles to EcoVillage and Southwest Park is planned for downtown Ithaca. Architectural designer Rob Morache has teamed up with builder Sue Cosentini to create what they are calling a 5-2-One community. Their website explained the term, "The 5-2-One initiative asserts that through our combined efforts, intention and creativity we can reduce the ecological footprint of 5 people or 5 households down to that of one person or one household." This is because "if everyone on Earth lived as Americans do, we would need 5 Earths to sustain us." Since we only have one Earth, we must make an effort to live within those limits.[24]

The Aurora Street Dwelling Circle plans to build four more housing units on a vacant lot between two existing houses (one of which contains two units). The vision is that the seven member households will share a commitment to sustainable living and mutual support. They will share open space in a community courtyard with food and herb gardens, access to a social gathering area, a compost bin, a

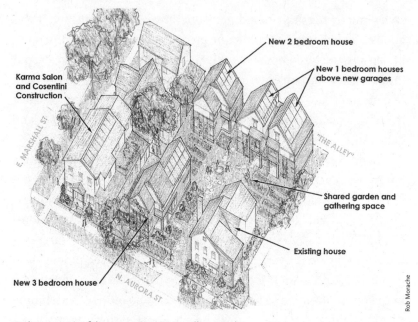

New 2 bedroom house

Karma Salon
and Cosentini
Construction

New 1 bedroom houses
above new garages

"THE ALLEY"

E. MARSHALL ST

Shared garden and
gathering space

Existing house

New 3 bedroom house

N. AURORA ST

Rob Morache

Bird's-eye view of the Aurora Street Dwelling Circle.

bicycle garage and the basement of one of the homes will be used for storage, a workshop and a root cellar.

The community will encourage reducing car use by 80% through car sharing, biking and using transit. The community will obtain food from local CSA farms, as well as growing, preserving and storing their own garden produce. The houses themselves will be built to the German Passiv Haus standards, in which the building is so well insulated that it needs little or no outside heat source, resulting in a dramatic reduction in energy use and cost of living.

Because living in close quarters with other people is not necessarily easy, residents will take some training in listening skills to build trust, respect and better communication. As Rob told me, "These skills will be essential as we progress towards a future which will face energy and resource depletion, climate change, and economic instability. We will have to rely more on each other, learn from each other and find comfort in the basics: food, friends and family."[25]

If it works out as envisioned, it could be that microcommunities like this Dwelling Circle will be a smaller and easier alternative to build than a cohousing project, particularly in an urban environment. This kind of urban infill development in ordinary, middle-class neighborhoods could potentially be easily replicated in other cities. I hope it catches on!

Taken together, these three visions of the future provide visionary ideas for both micro and macro scale neighborhoods that are part of the larger City of Ithaca, linked together with mass transit that also encourages pedestrian and bike-friendly streets. It will be fascinating to see how Ithaca does develop over the next 10 to 20 years. Ithacans, and their surrounding county, are determined to shape a positive future.

5

Local,
Living Economy

*Economics is not abstract, inanimate or impersonal. It is
not a construct of law or calculation of finance. Rather,
economics is highly personal — a web of relationships, of
individuals to one another, to our communities and to the
natural world on which we depend. Economics is the material
reflection of the spirit and character of those relationships.*

CHUCK MATTHEI, FOUNDER OF EQUITY TRUST, INC.

Sustainable Enterprise and Entrepreneur Network

It was a Monday evening in March 2009 and about 75 people filled
an upstairs meeting room at Island Health and Fitness club. We
were small business owners, nonprofit leaders, sustainability coordinators from Cornell and Ithaca College and a few people from
local government. We had gathered for a special event put on by the
Green Resource Hub — the first gathering of a regional Sustainable
Enterprise and Entrepreneur Network (SEEN), meant "to support
our local green businesses and help create a resilient and sustainable
local economy." The online flyer advertising the event had a bright
yellow sunflower, peeking like a sun over a honeycomb with bees
buzzing around. The byline said, "Mother Nature knows the value
of creating healthy and cooperative relationships in her networks.
Shouldn't we do the same?"[1]

In time-honored fashion, the Green Resource Hub had invited a
guest speaker who was many steps ahead of our local efforts. Holly

Harlan is founder and president of Entrepreneurs for Sustainability (E4S), one of the most successful green business networks in the US. She is a colleague and friend of Jon Jensen, head of the local Park Foundation, who used to live in Cleveland.

I had the privilege of meeting Holly earlier that day, when she came up to EcoVillage for a tour. We compared notes on how people change. She is convinced that the key to deep cultural change is to build networks of like-minded people. When people see another small business saving money from adopting green features, they want to try it themselves. "They learn from their buddies," she told me. Likewise, I described how living at EcoVillage can also generate rapid behavioral change. One person tries bike commuting, and others see that it is not only possible but fun. We inspire each other to take on new challenges and risks — and to green our behavior.

Green Drinks Ithaca kickoff gathering.

Her talk was "Connect-Learn-Do: How Cleveland Businesses are Redesigning for a Sustainable Economy." Holly introduced her methods to the audience. "When someone has a way to save money, design new products, find new markets, energize employees, improve personal and planetary health and leave a legacy for your grandchildren, would you be interested?" she asked. Everyone raised a hand. She went on to talk about emerging industry opportunities: energy efficiency, solar thermal, entrepreneurial farming, food waste composting, wind power, deconstruction of old homes and more. While these are all things that would be useful in Cleveland, they are certainly applicable in Ithaca, too. This inspiring educational evening was a good start for Ithaca's green business network.

From this first meeting, SEEN has evolved into a happening network with increasing numbers of green member businesses and organizations who "work together to achieve ecological, social, and financial success," according to its mission. Monthly networking events are beginning to knit together a community of like-minded entrepreneurs. Some of these events include inspiring speakers who address green business concerns, while others, like the Green Drinks Ithaca, are informal times to gather for fun.

Transitioning to a Local Economy

Ithaca seems ripe for a transition to more of a local economy. There is already a very strong local foods movement as noted in Chapter 2. As mentioned earlier, buying locally makes enormous differences. The web of relationships that is formed through residents buying from their neighbors provides a rich tapestry of social capital. The more people invest in their own community, the more ties they develop to other people and the more local jobs are created. Local buying stimulates a win-win cycle.

Compared to much of the rest of the US, Tompkins County is in reasonably good economic shape, but it also faces complexities. On the one hand, the county has a highly educated populace; it is often said, "even the mail carriers have PhDs"; 47% of the population has a bachelor's degree or higher.[2] Roughly one half of the county's economic base comes from educational services. Cornell, nicknamed Big Red, has a very big red footprint, not just in the county but also in New York State. As the third largest non-governmental employer in the state, it wields $3.3 billion in annual economic influence and provides 23,000 jobs to Central New York and 36,000 jobs statewide.[3] Although both Cornell and Ithaca College have had to retract their spending during the recession, cutbacks have been in the 5% range, and the local unemployment rate has been consistently lower than surrounding counties and the national average.

On the other hand, upstate New York is an economically depressed region. Lucrative manufacturing jobs are disappearing, and many people suffer from either unemployment or underemployment. According to the Tompkins County Living Wage Coalition, over one third of New York State residents do not have sufficient income to meet their basic needs! New York also has the worst income inequality and largest gap between its minimum wage and average wage in the US.[4] The official poverty rate for Tompkins County households is 7%, less than the national average but still unacceptable. There is an imbalance between wages for many jobs and the relatively high cost of living. As just one example, housing costs are 40 to 60% higher than in surrounding counties, yet wages are not proportionately higher.[5] This is a tough, ongoing problem which needs to be addressed through a combination of higher wages with more affordable housing in the city and county.

Building Economic Justice— Alternatives Federal Credit Union

When I first moved to Ithaca in 1991, I asked various people what bank they used. Most people I knew chose the Alternatives Federal Credit Union (AFCU) because of its remarkably progressive mission, "to build wealth and create economic opportunity for underserved people and communities." I decided to become a member and have been very happy with the results. Deciding to use my money to support social justice and the local economy feels great, plus the staff is diverse and friendly, the lobby is filled with interesting artwork by local artists and I almost always run into friends. It feels more like a local market than a bank—a place that builds social capital as much as financial assets.

We are very fortunate to have this award-winning community development credit union in Ithaca. First established in 1979, AFCU has 9,000 members, of which two thirds have low to moderate incomes. Bill Myers, the visionary founder and long-time CEO of AFCU, retired in 2007, but his legacy lives on. Bill has dedicated his life to helping people from all walks of life to become financially self-sufficient and helped to launch very innovative programs and services, some of which have served as models on a regional or even national basis.

The Living Wage Standard
This initiative was started in 1994 to address internal staff concerns about compensation standards. AFCU now updates it every few years to determine the minimum income a single person working

full-time needs to live in Tompkins County. The updated study looks at housing, transportation, healthcare and other necessities, as well as recreation and savings to come up with an annual figure. In 2010 the Living Wage Standard was \$11.11 per hour or \$23,104 per year,[6] an increase of 13% since the last study was done in 2006. Alternatives is one of 62 employers in Tompkins County that provides this Living Wage. Leni Hochman, Chief Operations Officer of AFCU, says the reason is simple: "Because it's the right thing to do." She continued, "Alternatives' mission is to promote economic justice. We have programs and services designed to help people in this community move out of poverty, to become financially self-sufficient. It follows that we provide our own staff with a fair and just wage."[7]

Tompkins County Workers' Center, a project of the nonprofit Center for Transformative Action at Cornell, uses the updated figures to advocate for workers and organize campaigns to help workers get a Living Wage. The Worker's Center recently started certifying Living Wage Employers and publishing the list on their Web page, thus providing a moral yardstick for other businesses to follow.

The Free Tax Preparation Program

This program matches trained community volunteers with low income households to prepare taxes. It helps ensure that eligible families receive the Earned Income Tax Credit, a refundable federal income tax credit. AFCU will even make a short-term, low interest loan to individuals, based on the credit they will receive. One of my friends, who volunteers for the program, enjoys meeting new people and being of service. "Plus it's a great way to bring federal money back into the community, for people who really need it," she told me. Interestingly, even the US government agrees. The Internal Revenue Service gave AFCU an award for their work on this program.

A Great Deal for Low Income Savers

AFCU was one of the first places in the country to offer Individual Development Accounts (IDAs), a program to help low income people invest in their future. This amazing program seems almost too good to be

true. Initially funded by $20,000 from AFCU and later augmented with
private donations and foundation funding, it offers matching funds for
low income people to save substantial funds for buying a house, start-
ing a business or going to school. In some cases, such as the First Home
Club IDA, participants' savings of up to $1,875 are matched at a 4:1 ratio
with $7,500 for a total of $9,375 for a down payment on a home! Other
programs offer a somewhat more modest match of 2:1 for basic savings
accounts or microenterprise development. As one participant said, "I
started the IDA because of the match. It's hard to believe that anyone
who had the opportunity would turn it down." In the last year alone,
110 community members started IDA accounts.[8]

The Credit Path

All of these member services and outreach tools are part of what
is known as the Credit Path model of financial empowerment.
Originally conceived by Bill Myers as a way to understand members' financial situations and to incorporate the needs of low income
members into AFCU's business plan, the Credit Path describes
where people are situated at various points along a continuum between poverty and self-sufficiency. According to the AFCU website, "Our job, as a community development financial institution,
is to help our members move along that continuum by empowering them to make decisions, and offering opportunities, that will
move them towards financial self-sufficiency." The site continues,
"We've found that financial education — developing spending and
savings plans, acquiring business skills, planning for home ownership — is often the key to helping members move more swiftly, but
securely, through the process of building financial strength without
unnecessary risk. Financial education combined with access to capital creates a powerful combination."[9] Now AFCU is developing the
Credit Path as a replicable model that other organizations can use.
It recently completed its fifth Credit Path Seminar for community
development practioners. The annual two-day seminar includes a

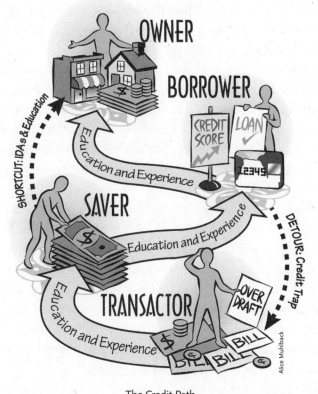

The Credit Path

tour of the community that gives participants the chance to meet Alternatives' members and to see the practical results of their work.

Tristram Coffin, Alternative's new CEO, gave this overview perspective, "Our main niche is the social equity side of sustainability — the notion that the community can't have a permanent underclass of people without access to resources and opportunity if we are to create a truly sustainable community."[10]

Garden Gate: Fresh Food to Your Doorstep

One innovative business that connects local, organic farmers with locavore customers is Marlo Capoccia's Garden Gate Delivery service. After her first child was born, Marlo felt the need to get the freshest, most nutritious foods available by going directly to local farms. And while she was at it, why not bring home food for the neighbors? Now a mother of three, Marlo and her husband Fred run a food delivery service that brings back the concept of the "milk man," except they have expanded it to a farmer's market on wheels. Using a 14-foot van named Stella which they retrofitted to run on veggie oil, they deliver breads, cereals, dairy, eggs, fruits and vegetables, meats, pasta, wine and beer, most of it sourced from within 25 miles of Ithaca. They also team up with Full Plate Farm to deliver their winter CSA shares directly to customers. Garden Gate is an excellent example of combining many sustainability goals in one green business.[11]

Getting help from AFCU with a Getting Down to Business class, individual counseling and loans was critical to Marlo's start-up. She confessed that "even though I knew a fair amount about what foods I wanted to sell and what a delivery model might look like, I had NO idea how to run a business." This kind of assistance for small businesses and microlending is part of AFCU's mission; the credit union notes on their website that "Small businesses, especially start-ups, are engines of local economic development. Small businesses play a major role in job creation in New York, creating 80% of all new jobs."[12]

Marlo's advice to others is: "Start small, it really is OK to just start tiny... People really like variety and that's a hard thing to manage. It's not profitable for quite a while, but the relationships you build almost make it worth it by itself. Last year the thing I kept being surprised about was how important those connections were."[13]

Local Currency: Ithaca Hours

We sometimes joke here in Ithaca that we print our own money, but it is actually true. As the oldest and largest local currency system in the US, Ithaca Hours prints money that can only be used locally. It is counted as real, legal tender and is taxed by the IRS. Over 900 local businesses and entrepreneurs accept Ithaca Hours as cash, and about $100,000 is currently in circulation.

Ithaca Hours, the brainchild of Paul Glover, a wildly creative and somewhat controversial former Ithacan, was started in 1991. At that time the average hourly wage in Ithaca was $10 an hour, so it was decided that the Ithaca Hour would be worth $10, roughly equivalent to an hour of work. The original purpose of the nonprofit fund was to combat Ithaca's underemployment and low wages. People who were unemployed could be paid for their services in Ithaca Hours, then go to the local grocery and buy food. At the same time, the currency was intended to help promote local businesses and keep money in local hands.

"One great example is that if you shop at Walmart with regular money, as soon as you use that money, it leaves the community and goes to the corporate headquarters, which is in Arkansas," said Amanda Block, a member of Ithaca Hours outreach staff. "If you use Ithaca Hours in local businesses, [money] will stay in the area. That supports the local economy and keeps it healthy."[14]

An A–Z online and print directory lists businesses that accept Ithaca Hours, from "Accountants and Bookkeepers" to "Yoga Instructors," with other participants as diverse as Bang's ambulance, painting contractors and real estate rentals sandwiched in between. Some businesses, like Ithaca Bakery, accept payment for small amounts, such as ½ Hour (worth five dollars), in Ithaca Hours. Others, like the Finger Lakes Permaculture Institute, accept 100% payment in Hours for classes.

Despite being looked at as a model by many other local currency efforts around the US and even the world, Ithaca Hours has languished in its home town in the last decade. Even Greenstar, a very loyal supporter, had a hard time deciding to continue accepting Hours since relatively few suppliers accepted them, and their stockpile grew beyond their capacity to spend it. While Greenstar made a values-based decision to continue using Hours, it shouldn't have to be that hard a choice. A local currency doesn't work well unless a critical mass of consumers and businesses are using it regularly.

Steve Burke, president of the board of directors for Ithaca Hours and owner of Small World Music, noticed an enormous increase of interest in Ithaca Hours in 2009. "It's quadrupled," he told me. "We have gotten interviewed for articles in *USA Today*, *Time* magazine, *Newsweek* and *Der Spiegel*. A Korean film crew is coming, too."[15]

Steve decided to leverage all the interest that has picked up with tough times. When he received word that the *New York Times Magazine* planned a trip to Ithaca to cover Ithaca Hours, he approached Mayor Carolyn Peterson. "I asked her, wouldn't you like to be able to tell them that the City supports using its own famous local currency?" Since then, the City of Ithaca has decided to consider paying some wages and benefits in Ithaca Hours and accepting Hours for payment of some fees (such as trash tags). Steve also approached Agway, a local farm supply store. For the first time, they showed interest, especially when reminded that shoppers and other local businesses that already use Ithaca Hours will become loyal customers.

Certainly, if times get even tougher in the future, local currencies such as Ithaca Hours are bound to fill an important niche, just as they did during the Great Depression. In the meantime, there are many other ways that Ithacans are encouraging support of local businesses, no matter what currency is used.

Local First Initiative

I met with Jan Norman, a friend and a member of the EcoVillage Board of Directors, to find out more about her vision for supporting the local economy. Jan is a real spark plug. Since she first moved to Ithaca in 1971 she has personally launched or operated seven different small businesses, most of them centered around kid's toys (such as Cat's Pajamas) or hand-crafted clothes (like her current business, Silk Oak). She has also served on the Greenstar Council and convened the Farmer's Market Board, all while raising six children.

I met with Jan at Gimme Coffee, a popular local coffee shop that roasts its own beans. She brought her own mug for chai and launched into an animated talk about her excitement in visiting a branch of Business Alliance for a Local Living Economy (BALLE) on a recent trip to Massachusetts. I resonated with Jan's enthusiasm, since I was already familiar with this innovative network of 20,000 entrepreneurs across the US and Canada, united by a vision of fostering vibrant communities, a healthy natural environment and prosperity for all. To me, growing an Ithaca BALLE network made total sense.

Jan told me, "There are some pieces missing from the puzzle in Ithaca. Some of the different elements don't realize what's in it for them. They think of sustainability as only relating to the environment. But by supporting a local living economy you can have it all. I'm really excited!" She went on to tell me, "I'm really getting more than ever that this [local business network] is a huge missing piece of this conversation. If you bring it along, you're going to have a radical shift. The business aspect is so important with big box stores and the internet; so much money is being pulled away from our local economy. BALLE Networks provide an alternative."[16]

Less than a year after this conversation, Jan and a colleague, Leslie Ackerman who is the Director of the Business Cents program at AFCU, had launched Local First. This initiative encourages Ithacans to Think Local First when purchasing goods and services. The founders collaborated with Autumn Newell of Tuff Soul (a recycled clothing shop) and Kelly Moreland of Mama Goose (which sells secondhand baby and children's clothes and toys), building on a previous local passport campaign that Autumn had started the year before. During the 2008 holiday season, they issued a Local Lovers Challenge. Even the name was a draw — who wouldn't want to be a local lover? Participants got a little card, listing the names of about 50 local businesses. The card was stamped each time you bought an item from a participating business. If you accumulated five stamps, you were eligible for a lottery offering great prizes. Two of the local business owners who participated in Local First told me it was their best holiday season ever, despite the recession! It's clear that there is a strong desire to support local businesses if consumers are encouraged to do so.

The Downtown Ithaca Alliance (DIA) is another important player in this movement. In addition to helping to revive the Ithaca Commons (Chapter 4), they promote over 100 locally owned downtown businesses through methods like hosting special events, promoting free downtown parking and providing business consultations. According to DIA executive director Gary Ferguson, tourists love the Commons and the small original shops which are so different than their big box stores at home.

Ten Thousand Villages—A Fair Trade Store

While buying local products is very important, it is nice to occasionally buy special gifts from other countries. My son Daniel volunteered after school one semester at Ten Thousand Villages, a delightful store on the Commons, one of seven such stores around the US which specialize in handcrafted items from around the world. Fair trade provides under- and unemployed artisans opportunities to earn vital income and improve their quality of life by establishing a sustainable market for their hand-crafted products. Ten Thousand Villages is a nonprofit program of the Mennonite Central Committee and is a founding member of the World Fair Trade Organization, a global network of more than 350 fair trade organizations in 70 countries. By building long-term, collaborative rela-tionships with suppliers, stores that carry fair trade products are creat-ing a new way of doing business—supporting local economies around the world.

Green Jobs for All

Of course, supporting local businesses is only one side of the equa-tion. On the other side, there needs to be jobs to employ our young people and retraining for people in the manufacturing sector who are getting laid off. Local activist Gay Nicholson, president of Sus-tainable Tompkins, likes to talk about a systems approach to devel-oping a green economy. "When you take a systems view you really need to be working on all parts of that spectrum to try and stimulate all along that pipeline."[17] To Gay, who has been studying this issue for years, it is all about the interrelationship of market demand and both consumer and business education. Gay has been an impor-tant champion of promoting local economic development through systematically connecting key players to provide just these kinds of functions.

Gay Nicholson, Sustainability Pioneer

Gay Nicholson is an articulate powerhouse, someone who knows how to get things done and who has put her considerable talent and energy into the Ithaca sustainability movement. She serves as board president and CEO of Sustainable Tompkins, a title which suits her intense involvement in creating cutting-edge conferences, new programs and networking with city leaders, business owners and grassroots activists alike.

Gay migrated to Ithaca in 1979 to get her Master's in crop science and later her doctorate at Cornell. She spent ten years in the sustainable agriculture field and learned integrated pest management just as the principles were being discovered. As a graduate student, Gay and others were assigned to figure out inspection standards for organic farms. She laughed and said, "if you saw bugs crawling around, that was a good thing, because it meant they weren't spraying pesticides." A group of students formed EARC, the Ecological Agriculture Research Collective. "We got a lot of grief from professors for our gender, our generation, what we were doing. After getting my doctorate, I sensed that sustainable agriculture was getting on its feet. But hardly anyone was interested in promoting environmental stewardship to the general public. I knew I didn't want to become a tenured professor, and I had put a lot of roots down in Ithaca." So rather than becoming an academic, Gay became a community organizer.

Peter Nicholson

Gay Nicholson, president of Sustainable Tompkins.

Gay was hand-picked to help jump-start Sustainable Tompkins (ST) in 2004 and conducted a feasibility study on how to create a sustainable county. Early on she concluded that a combination of a top-down, bottom-up approach was best. Gay works tirelessly with elected officials, business leaders and grassroots activists. Some of her projects have been holding a Finger Lakes Bioneers conference (linked by satellite to a

national conference in California), starting the Marcellus Shale chal-
lenge (see.Chapter 10) and creating a regional carbon offset program
whose proceeds fund energy efficiency retrofits for low income housing.
"Sustainable Tompkins serves as a catalyst to start other groups," Gay
said earnestly. "We're a small group but we leverage larger, systems level
redesign work." [18]

ST regularly offers public education programs. In 2008, my friend
and EcoVillage colleague Elan Shapiro created a series of programs
called Equity and Sustainability, organized by ST and its community partners. On May 6, a lively program on "Green Jobs for the
Finger Lakes: Employing Local People in a Sustainable Economy,"
brought together presenters from local green businesses engaged in
renewable energy, real estate and green building on the one hand,
with Susan Christopherson, a Cornell professor and her graduate students in a green economic development class on the other
hand. The class had spent the semester researching the job creation
potential in the energy efficiency and renewable energy sectors
and analyzing how state and local policies can drive the creation
of green jobs. Among other findings they concluded that Ithaca
needs more business support services, job training and a skilled
workforce.

One of the presenters was Pat Govang from e2e Materials, a
local green business success story. Started by Anil Netravali, professor of fiber science and apparel design at Cornell, and Patrick
Govang, president of e2e and former industrial partnerships director for the Cornell Center for Materials Research, this start-up
company takes advantage of the area's advanced technology expertise. e2e makes biodegradable composite alternatives to a number
of petroleum-based products. One example is a resin made from
soy protein which creates an alternative to particleboard that is as
strong as soft steel. Not only does it use a renewable resource, but it
has the added advantage of not off-gassing formaldehyde. In addition, wood chips used in particleboard are often imported from the

Pacific Northwest and resin from Saudi Arabia. In contrast, the soy protein is locally grown.

"We're taking manufacturing and turning it upside down." Govang declared. "We can empower people to make products from local materials that at the end of their lives will biodegrade."[19] Comet, a San Francisco–based skateboard company, actually moved to Ithaca to take advantage of this new product and is providing regional manufacturing jobs. Soy is grown locally, and increased demand means more regional agricultural jobs. So the net effect of e2e is to increase regional green-collar jobs, use local materials and create a new, environmentally friendly product which replaces an old product that causes pollution.

Finger Lakes Fresh:
Employing Workers with Disabilities
in Sustainable Agriculture

An exciting new and growing business, Finger Lakes Fresh, is a hydroponic greenhouse that employs 18 workers with disabilities. In the middle of winter, I can get a fresh bouquet of salad greens or baby pac choi from Greenstar and know that it is locally grown without pesticides. Better yet, I know that this produce provides green jobs to people who might otherwise have a hard time finding work. Finger Lakes Fresh is a business that is owned and operated by Challenge Industries, Inc., a nonprofit agency that provides training, job placement and support services to individuals with disabilities and other employment barriers. Challenge, which won an award for best nonprofit of the year for Tompkins County in 2008, was founded in 1968, and in one year alone assisted over 800 individuals to work in local community businesses. Challenge also partnered with 300 area employers to help find jobs. Rather than a sheltered workshop, Challenge places most of the people it supports in businesses outside of its own purview.

Finger Lakes Fresh uses cutting edge technology developed by Cornell University researchers to grow greens year-round in New York State. By growing lettuce in a controlled environment, with an even temperature, under lights, while floating on supports in a nutrient solution, "the plants think they're in Hawaii every day," quipped Patrick J. McKee, president of Challenge. This enables Finger Lakes Fresh to harvest 3,000 heads of lettuce every day, "about 20 times the amount that is grown per square foot in fields in California," according to McKee.[20] One thing I appreciate about buying this lettuce is that the roots are left on, keeping it very fresh even a week after it is harvested. Soon Finger Lakes Fresh plans to start using renewable energy, utilizing waste biogas captured from the Ithaca Waste Water Treatment Facility and two local dairy farms.

In addition to its social and environmental mission, Finger Lakes Fresh is also good business. The customer base has expanded to seven Northeast states, with revenues of over $600,000 a year. In fact, Finger Lakes Fresh has provided an ongoing income source for Challenge, while other funding sources have been cut back with the recession. This is a green business that could be replicated in other states.

Sustainable Workforce

The National Apollo Alliance defines green-collar jobs as "those associated with building, managing, constructing, assembling and servicing the clean energy sector of the economy all over the country," according to Keith Schneider, national communications director. The Apollo Alliance is comprised of a coalition of business, community and environmental leaders with the common goal of establishing energy independence and efficiency across America. "It's a new economic development strategy emerging as a response to rising energy costs and global warming," he added. These new jobs provide wages and benefits to support a family, as part of a triple-bottom-line approach. "We envision a profound shift in the underpinnings of the economy," Schneider said. "It is happening and at a much faster pace than anticipated."[21]

While Tompkins County is greening its workforce over time through training programs at TC3 (Tompkins, Cortland Community College — the local community college) as well as area business and consumer education courses, a lot remains to be done in both job training and attracting a skilled workforce. To give students a sense of the opportunities they could find in working for local green businesses, Sustainable Tompkins teamed up with TC3, with funding support from the Park Foundation and New York State Energy Research Development Authority (NYSERDA) to offer the first Green Collar Career Fair on November 5, 2008.

The Fair included 40 regional exhibitors who promoted careers in various sectors of sustainability, including energy efficiency, renewable energy, alternative transportation, green buildings and local farms and food. The response was tremendous! Over 450 high school and college students preregistered and arrived in biodiesel buses for morning workshops, followed by the general public in the afternoon. Interactive displays included a car run on vegetable oil, a stationary bike to generate electricity and the opportunity to take a compostable Comet skateboard out for a spin in the parking lot. Given the recession, most of the 40 exhibitors did not have jobs to offer at the moment, but there was a strong sense of potential expressed by Jan Quarles of Sustainable Tompkins, one of the hosts of the event. "A lot of young people start looking for work in cyberspace and assume they will have to move out of the area to get a job," she said. "We want to show them there is this emerging, burgeoning sustainable movement all around them. I feel that green jobs are the one solution to our two biggest problems: the environment and the economy."[22]

While there are many factors that lead to growing a local green economy, they are all interwoven. Ithaca is fortunate to have excellent examples of a credit union that is based on economic justice, its own local currency, various efforts to Buy Local, the beginnings of a Sustainable Enterprise Entrepreneur Network and a BALLE chapter, as well as local job creation and a great potential for developing a green collar economy. Other people around the country have noticed these efforts. "Ithaca has been a leader in penetrating the status quo, breaking some of those boundaries and establishing new rules of the game," said Schneider of the National Apollo Alliance in an interview with the *Ithaca Times*. "For a long time [Ithaca] has been considered a place to look for models to apply locally and nationally."[23]

6

Educating for a Sustainable Future

"Commit to Reduce Your Carbon Footprint," proclaimed the poster as I entered the campus center for the Ithaca College Climate Change Teach-in. A nearby table informed me that we must lower CO_2 emissions to a maximum of 350 parts per million (ppm)...that is the highest level they can reach before tipping into catastrophic climate change. But now, in 2009, we were already at 385 ppm. Rather than feeling numb and powerless, students were encouraged to make an immediate commitment to changing their lifestyles. The large poster was filled with colorful Post-it Notes with these declarations by different students:

I will reuse more. Stop buying products that create waste!

Glass jars are your friends for life.

Eat vegetarian.

Refuse to drive.

I will ride my bike more to make the earth happy.

I will install a clothesline in May.

I commit to spending less, earning less and driving less and buying less.

Spend more time outdoors.

I will plant a vegetable and herb garden over the summer.

And a humorous one:

I'm going to continue to turn off the heat in my roommate's room.

I was struck at how effective these post-it notes were in bringing the overwhelming reality of climate change down to a manageable scale, with very personal commitments to a simpler, less resource-intensive lifestyle. The lecture hall was packed when I arrived. There must have been a hundred students listening to a panel on the business case for sustainability. Many of them had been assigned by professors who offered extra credit for coming to this teach-in.

Poznan, Poland, the site of the UN Forum Convention on Climate Change, sprang to life through the eyes of Astrid Jirka, the Ithaca College (IC) professor who taught a three-credit course, International Environmental Policy, which included a week long field trip by the 20 students to this global conference. Andrew Grossman, a junior, told me that just a couple of weeks before traveling to Poznan, he had attended a model UN program at the University of Pennsylvania. Each student played the role of a diplomat. "I was Saudi Arabia," he told me. Then, at the Climate Change conference he got to sit behind the actual delegates from Saudi Arabia. Everything he had been learning in class suddenly sprang to life. "The most important thing I took away from it was the importance of business incentives," Andrew said. When you change the way the world does business, it has a profound effect.

Senior Rachel Roscoe shared her perspective. "I got to meet people who are right now feeling the effect of climate change. These are no longer questions on a test…hearing straight from indigenous people who are already affected by climate change was eye-opening." Both Andrew and Rachel agreed on how sobering the conference was, and that there are no good answers to the energy puzzle. Every solution poses severe consequences. Even hydroelectric dams can create dead zones. Manufacturing biodiesel in developing countries can be an ecological and social disaster. "You can't have an eco-solution without a social solution," Rachel concluded.

How did Ithaca College get involved in this global event? In 1999, Environmental Studies student Sean Vormwald went to a climate change conference in the Netherlands. The experience was so compelling that later, as a graduate student, he worked with the Provost's office to file an application for Ithaca College to have "official non-governmental observer" status at subsequent conferences. A group of IC students and faculty went to Montreal in 2004, Nairobi in 2006, Bali in 2007 and now Poznan in 2008. It took just one motivated student to open the door for Ithaca College to delve into the international debate about key issues.

A distinguished diplomat from Barbados, Selwin Hart, was next at the podium, the invited guest of honor. As a representative of the Alliance of Small Island States (AOSIS), a group he called the "conscience of the conventions," Hart agonized over the choices. "How can we effectively negotiate when for us the stakes are extraordinarily high? We only have two or three representatives per country, while developed nations may have 150." AOSIS has consistently pushed for the most radical reductions in emissions (capping temperature rise at 1.5°C above pre-industrial times or more than 85% emissions reductions by 2050 from 1990 levels) while OPEC has consistently opposed them. He left us with a question, "How will we achieve these numbers?"[1]

Ithaca College Is a (Collaborative) Winner

In November 2008, the Association for the Advancement of Sustainability in Higher Education (AASHE) announced the winners of its annual Campus Sustainability Leadership Awards. Ithaca College won in the category of four-year colleges of its size. The awards recognize institutions "that have demonstrated outstanding overall commitment to sustainability in their governance and administration, curriculum and research, operations, campus culture, and community outreach."

Not only did IC win this prestigious award, but one of its students did as well. Senior Sarah Brylinsky claimed the Student Leadership Award for the year, for "demonstrating outstanding leadership in promoting campus sustainability."[2]

Garnering these two national awards in one year was a remarkable feat. How did Ithaca College (and one of its top students) achieve such recognition? I knew an important piece of the story. While IC had long promoted civic engagement and had a nationally known recycling program, the word *sustainability* was barely known in 2001. It was that year that IC biologist Susan Allen-Gil first brought her environmental studies students on a field trip to EcoVillage. She liked the practical demonstration of an environmentally oriented lifestyle, and after some discussion, proposed that we jointly apply for a National Science Foundation grant to develop curricula to teach four courses on the Science of Sustainability.

Susan's move was brilliant. It brought together two unlikely partners: EcoVillage at Ithaca — a grassroots, educational nonprofit and intentional community — and IC — a four-year, established liberal arts college. In ecology, it is a well-known principle that the edge where two ecosystems meet, such as the ocean and the shore or the woods and the meadow, is by far the most biologically productive area. The same holds true, it seems, for organizational ecosystems. By having to navigate between these two different worlds, we've all had to stretch and grow, and at the same time exciting new collaborations have emerged. The interface between us has been boldly creative and intensely productive, with far-reaching ripple effects that none of us would have imagined at the outset.

The three-year matching grant was funded, and much to my surprise, suddenly there was money to pay EcoVillage residents to teach semester long courses on topics such as Sustainable Communities, Sustainable Land Use and Energy Conservation and Renewable Energy. These courses not only exposed students to interdisciplinary concepts but always included application of theory, through hands-on projects, either at IC, EVI or in downtown Ithaca. And EcoVillage instructors such as Elan Shapiro and Karryn Ramanujan were given the chance to demonstrate a new pedagogical approach, based on team-based learning, self-reflection and community service projects that balanced ecological, social and economic concerns.

We held bi-monthly meetings between EcoVillage coordinators and IC faculty to discuss next steps. Early on, our Partnership for Sustainability Education (PSE) decided to fund mini-grant projects. We invited IC faculty to apply for $1,000 summer grants that would enable them to develop curricula for courses based on sustainability principles. For many faculty, including Jason Hamilton who became a well-known speaker on the topic and later the president of the Board of New Roots, a sustainability-oriented charter high school, getting a mini-grant was a first exposure to sustainability.

The mini-grant program soon expanded to include EcoVillage educators, some of whom had never worked with college students, to lead students in practical projects that applied sustainability principles. One good example was two mobile solar trailers, which EcoVillager Greg Pitts designed and built with IC students. They each consist of two photovoltaic panels, a battery and an inverter installed on a small metal trailer, which can be hauled around to provide electricity to power outdoor events, as a demonstration at environmental fairs or to provide the juice for power tools at a remote site. One is parked at IC and one at EVI.

But the partnership did not rest on its laurels. Susan Allen-Gil pushed us steadily to think about how to best achieve our goals of "infusing sustainability across the curriculum" at IC and developing EVI's educational capacity. Several other highly successful methods were used. Using money from the grant, we established an ongoing Sustainability Cafe series, with monthly presentations on the latest sustainability ideas by faculty, students or community experts. Seven years later, long after the grant ended, this forum continues. The Cafes use "teachable edibles," a tradition which started when Elan advocated for bringing healthy, local foods snacks to the forums, as a visceral way to educate people about an alternative to packaged cookies and coffee.

Sarah Brylinksy, Student Leadership Award

Sarah is a remarkably articulate young woman. At age 21, having just graduated from Ithaca College, she was hired as Program Coordinator for the new Center for Environmental and Sustainability Education at Dickinson College, a small liberal arts college in Carlisle, Pennsylvania. I ask her about what influenced her choice of career. "My education at Ithaca College was definitely the thing that influenced me the most in my life. The provisions for sustainability education shaped me in ways

I did not expect, I did not plan for." Originally going to Ithaca College to learn about jazz or psychology, Sarah confided that "it's because of peoples' constant message of sustainability and opportunities available and lovely mentors that I am where I am now."

As a freshman, Sarah did not get into her first five choices for Freshman Seminar, so instead she took a team-taught course, "People, Planet, Prosperity." Halfway through the semester, she related, she finally understood what sustainability meant. She recalled, "I sat there in class thinking: This is it! I found it! This is everything I feel strongly about, confirmed and articulated." One of her professors, David Saiia, (a recipient of a PSE mini-grant) offered the chance to spend the summer in Ecuador, working on microenterprise with Fundacion Maquipucuna, a group which he had supported for several years. Although she was neither a business major nor an environmental studies major, Sarah wanted desperately to go. She told David, "I'm trying to find my soul, my way." She was not disappointed. She and the other students helped a group of women to further develop a sustainable jewelry and textile arts cooperative, among other activities. "It was a transfer of a lot of the theory that I had learned about sustainability…immediately put into a more tangible practice," she recalls. "That was it. They had me hooked." This all happened in Sarah's first year at IC.

Sarah also learned how to apply the broad theories of sustainability to her concerns about ecofeminism. "Gender development concerns and environmental development concerns overlap in such an international but also very local and technical ways for me." She feels an obligation to pass on her knowledge to students at Dickinson. "I try to make small subsets of these larger values really accessible to people…. It's important when you can apply the theories to what's dear to your heart."

Her new role at Dickinson is varied and engaging. "We are trying to make sustainability a part of every discipline, a part of every student's curriculum by the time they graduate," she told me with a big smile. "So much of sustainability is about common sense. It's about being a good neighbor."[3]

Another role that Partnership for Sustainability Education plays is providing faculty development seminars, with a focus on sustainability. One year, our PSE group arranged for two IC faculty, funded by the Provost's office, to go to a training Sustainability Across the Curriculum Leadership Workshop hosted by the Piedmont Project at Emory University in Atlanta. The Piedmont Project, based on an earlier experiment, the Ponderosa Project at Arizona State University, brings together cohorts of faculty members to learn about sustainability and their regional environment. "Many of society's most significant and complex problems can best be addressed and resolved through multi-disciplinary inquiry," the Piedmont Project website explained. "Universities are ideally equipped to address these problems, but rarely do so effectively. As part of a broader, university-wide awakening to environmental and sustainability concerns, the Piedmont Project focuses on curricular change, to support faculty intellectual development to address these urgent societal issues."[4]

Susan Swensen and Jason Hamilton, both IC biology professors, came back with a lot of excitement for sharing their experience. They began offering the Finger Lakes Project, an innovative faculty development seminar, now in its fifth year. The Finger Lakes Project typically attracts about 50 faculty from Ithaca College, Cornell, Wells College and Rochester Institute of Technology, as well as EVI educators. The goal is to empower faculty to learn how to teach sustainability topics in a way that is exciting, place-based and participatory.

Finger Lakes Project Workshop
Learning Outcomes

Provide a fertile environment to explore how systems thinking can be used to understand, integrate, and teach the relationships between social, economic and ecological health.

Explore ways in which each participant's particular discipline relates to sustainability issues.

Demonstrate how content and approaches from a variety of disciplines can be integrated into an experiential learning experience to understand a particular place and time.

Engage in reflective dialogue about what the core of Education for Sustainability really is.

Develop a supportive community of co-learners that can serve and an inspiration and resource for further development.[5]

Each of these tools — mini-grants, cafes, faculty development seminars and project-based learning — have been individually and collectively powerful. Overall, they have helped Ithaca College to transform into a remarkable institution, one which has inspired students to become inspiring leaders, faculty to "walk their talk," operations staff to push the sustainability edge and administrators to change policy. Ithaca College has earned its award for national leadership. The partnership has also given legitimacy to EcoVillage educators to share their lived knowledge and the confidence to begin planning for their dreams — including an eventual EcoVillage Center for Sustainability Education.

But that is really just the beginning. The accumulated impact of that first three-year NSF grant is still going on. IC Provost Peter Bardaglio was so enthused about the PSE that in 2005 he lobbied and obtained funding for the partnership as a permanent budget line for the college. Just as important as helping to change the culture of a college, the partnership also helped to launch a new organization that has had tremendous impact on the whole county — Sustainable Tompkins.

Marian Brown — Ithaca College Sustainability Coordinator

Marian is a quiet but exceptionally effective organizer. Her curly gray hair and ready smile suggest a grandmotherly presence, but far from being retired she puts in a grueling 60–80 hour work week. Her job encompasses not only helping to start and support sustainability initiatives on campus—a never-ending task—but also representing Ithaca College at the numerous meetings of eleven different community sustainability partnerships around town (see the sidebar on page 112). "The sustainability framework provides linkages between the college and the community that are more robust than anything before," she told me. And Marian is often the personification of that link.

Marian, who has worked at IC for 28 years, shared that "This is the most fun I've ever had, because it's tapping into so many pieces of myself. It's both deeply fulfilling and at times deeply exhausting." The job not only allows her to work with staff, students and faculty but also to help change the institution at a higher level. For instance, in working on the Climate Action Plan for IC, she saw the college's chief financial officer change from stressing the dollar

Marian Brown, de facto sustainability coordinator at Ithaca College.

side of the triple bottom line equation, to advocating for building two three-million-dollar wind turbines down the line. "It's so rewarding to see people grabbing onto something larger than themselves. I'm amazed to see institutional leaders take risks. The vision [of a sustainable future] is really powerful."

One of Marian's deep-seated interests is to provide community-based, hands-on learning opportunities for students, both on and off campus. She stresses how important it is to do this carefully. "You have to vet and work with the community partners, provide them with a reasonable idea of what a student learner can offer them, assess student skills and pair students with the right group. Then you have to train the students and support them, and work with the faculty to teach them more about community based learning, including setting learning objectives and monitoring performance," she told me.[6]

Ithaca College
and Sustainability Partnerships
in the Local Community

Partnerships in Sustainability Education—*collaboration between IC faculty and EcoVillage educators*

Finger Lakes Buy Green—*multi-sector advisory team collaborated to create a web resource on regional sources of green products*

Finger Lakes Environmentally Preferred Procurement Consortium—*multi-sector collaboration of organizations to pool purchasing volume to secure good pricing on environmentally-preferred products*

Mayors Climate Agreement Community Outreach Council—*Mayor Carolyn Peterson reached out to local stakeholders to advise her on strategies to reduce greenhouse gases.*

Ithaca Carshare—*a regional car share program*

Tompkins County Climate Protection Initiative—*multi-sector collaboration, bringing together representatives of institutions and organizations working on county-wide strategies to combat the challenges of climate change*

Cayuga Sustainability Council—*a quarterly meeting of representatives of about 50 local sustainability-oriented organizations who meet to share information and resources*

Sustainable Tompkins—*an organization dedicated to supporting regional sustainable development*

Tompkins Renewable Energy Education Alliance—*a regional organization dedicated to advancing knowledge about and integration of renewable energy technologies and strategies in the region*

Sustainable Tompkins: A Little History

It started like this. In 2003, our PSE team hired sustainability education consultant Ed Quevedo, a high-powered speaker from the Bay Area, to give a presentation as part of our faculty development series. The lure of an outside speaker can be tantalizing, and a lot of faculty showed up—some were introduced to sustainability for the first time.

One thing that Ed mentioned in passing was his involvement with helping to create Sustainable Sonoma [County] in California. This was intriguing, as we all sought ways to bring the sustainability message to the whole community. So after a lot of discussion, we decided to invite him back for a half day meeting. Our PSE team, including IC professors Garry Thomas and Susan Allen-Gil, and Elan Shapiro and I from EVI brainstormed people to invite to this special event. We wanted a good mix of influential people — from local government, to businesses, to nonprofits, to academia and activists. Thys VanCort, then head of City Planning and Development got involved and offered us a room at City Hall. I was concerned that we had no plan for follow-up and suggested that we help to seed a part-time staff position, as organizing on this scale was too big for volunteers to tackle.

The Sustainable Tompkins County event snowballed into a powerful gathering of key local leaders. After sharing about how Sustainable Sonoma got organized, Ed Quevedo asked participants to brainstorm their own visions for the future. People were electrified by the possibilities. Similar to the Car Share Summit (see Chapter 4), just knowing that other people across the country were taking action was enough to mobilize dormant energies in the participants. This event heralded the birth of a new organization, Sustainable Tompkins, which has had a major role in shaping the sustainability discussion in this county.

But it wouldn't have happened without a key individual, Gay Nicholson (see Chapter 5). Gay was just back from taking six months off to travel the US. Elan identified her as someone with the skills to do the organizing work required, and money was raised from a variety of local partners.

As part of the initial feasibility assessment, Gay organized a series of five study circles designed to engage local leaders in thinking about the following topics:
- Renewable energy and responsible construction
- Sustainable regional economies
- Infrastructure design for sustainable communities
- Systems for community well-being
- Moving toward a sustainable culture

Each study circle met three times over six weeks in the spring of 2004, with a total of 80 people. The groups were asked to develop three proposals to further achieve sustainability in Tompkins County. The study circles were a hit.

Simultaneously a series of Sustainability Salons were organized by Gay and Elan. Held in coffeehouses around the county, they offered hosted conversation groups where residents talked and exchanged ideas about sustainability. Students from an Ithaca College class Elan was teaching provided some of the facilitation and note-taking. A six-week op-ed series on sustainability and feature articles in the local papers brought wider public attention to the issues.

This was followed by the Sustainable Tompkins Summit, a major event which drew about 200 community leaders for a catered dinner and acknowledgment of their roles in helping to shape the discussion. Each study group then presented its top ideas for further development. People had a chance to circulate and vote for different projects, which ranged from building an integrated, mixed-use affordable green neighborhood in downtown Ithaca to creating a project to help children to eat well and get exercise. The excitement over the various ideas was palpable. By the end of the evening, there were scores of volunteers signing up to take the next steps on each of the selected projects. Sustainable Tompkins was launched!

The whole effect was striking — county leaders in many sectors, students and ordinary citizens were all being exposed to the interconnections between the environment, the economy and the society — the triple bottom line of people, planet, prosperity — resulting in an enthusiasm that surpassed the organizers' expectations and led to the beginning of an emerging social movement.

Sustainable Tompkins: Educating for Action

Since then, Sustainable Tompkins (ST) has exploded in growth and activities, and many of the original projects are well underway. Originally a coalition of diverse groups, ST has recently become a nonprofit educational organization. Its mission is "to promote the long-term well-being of our communities and region by integrating social equity, economic vitality, ecological stewardship, and personal and civic responsibility." It serves as "Connector, Convener and Catalyst," with a four-way strategy of "top-down, bottom-up, build awareness and build infrastructure."[7] It has been astonishingly successful, especially since most of the people involved are volunteers. Some of the myriad activities have included:

- Monthly educational gatherings on different themes such as Sustainable Transportation, which brought together public transportation and bicycle advocates with low income residents
- A searchable online sustainability map of Tompkins County, which lists over 100 groups engaged in diverse aspects of sustainability[8]
- A Just Sustainability Initiative to bring together the work and vision of both economic justice and sustainability movements; this has included resident-based study circles in Ithaca's Northside and Southside neighborhoods, teaching home-energy improvement workshops and offering mini-grants for model neighborhood practices
- The donor-supported mini-grant program has distributed $10,270 to 25 projects since 2008, to encourage local self-reliance, strengthen neighborhood connections and promote long-term community well-being; for example grants have included $500 to the Whole Community Project to purchase gardening tools for loan to downtown community gardeners and $500 to GIAC to purchase seeds for its Northside Community Garden
- Organizing major conferences with partner organizations — for example Health and Sustainability Conference, Green Collar Career Fair and Sustainable Technology Showcase

Sustainable Tompkins continues to be on the cutting edge of educating and organizing around sustainability topics in our community.

EcoVillage at Ithaca Center for Sustainability Education

Meanwhile EcoVillage at Ithaca continues to expand its educational potential, not only through the partnership with Ithaca College and more informally with Cornell University, but also through hosting more than a thousand visitors a year, holding workshops and events and most recently through envisioning plans for an ambitious educational center that can more fully utilize its resources as a living laboratory of sustainability practices.

In 2007–2008, we conducted a Feasibility Study. We envisioned a tree with six branches: a sustainable secondary school, sustainable agriculture programs, expanded training and consultancy, a sustainable business incubator, a cultural events center and a small conference center. Of these branches, two have already materialized: New Roots spun off to become a public charter high school, based downtown, but it maintains ties to EcoVillage partly through its farm-to-school lunch program. In addition, Groundswell Center for Local Food and Farming has started to offer workshops and courses to beginning farmers.

Growing New Roots

New Roots Charter School, a public high school committed to sustainability education and social justice, has a student body that includes 40% students who are low income, 18% students of color and 25% students who have learning disabilities (twice that of the other public schools in Ithaca). It draws students from an amazingly wide

New Roots students study local streams.

radius: 15 school districts in the surrounding region send students to New Roots.

The school's vision is a big one:

> New Roots Charter School will empower young people as citizens and entrepreneurs that create just, democratic communities, and thriving green economies that restore the natural world that sustains us. Excelling in both traditional and innovative curriculum areas, our students will learn actively, think critically, and solve problems creatively and collaboratively, developing the knowledge and skills to redesign our communities for social, economic, and ecological sustainability. We will support all students in defining and realizing their goals and aspirations, and in recognizing their ability to take leadership in improving the lives of their families and community. We will put the best available tools — and the power of informed optimism — in the hands of tomorrow's leaders.[9]

Founder and principal Tina Nilsen-Hodges' biggest motivation for starting New Roots was recognizing the relationship between outdated educational systems based in the industrial and corporate orientation of the 20th century and how they contribute to the unsustainable practices that threaten our communities. Instead she said, "I wanted to create a school community that could model that education could be joyful and engaging and also allow young people to build a sense of self that would allow them to step into this brave new future that we face, with climate change and other attendant problems, and still feel confident and grounded and with the kind of skills they need as entrepreneurs and leaders and community builders and people who feel invested and part of their region."

It hasn't been easy. When I talked to Tina during the first year of the school's operation she told me that, like any new start-up venture, it has been an "intense crucible." Teachers and students alike come from traditional public school backgrounds but are trying to create a new culture from scratch. Tina laughed at the analogy that came to mind, "It's like putting the wings on an airplane as you're bumping down the runway. Everything is new. There is nothing to fall back on."[10] Despite the hurdles, it is clear that New Roots is already making a transformative impact on the lives of many students.

A vital dimension of New Roots Charter School is its connection with the surrounding community. There is a strong emphasis on learning through doing. Students spend every Wednesday afternoon engaged in service learning projects, a method of teaching, learning and reflecting that combines academic work with meaningful service. Often students are able to walk to the organizations where they help out. Just a few examples are: providing reading and homework buddies to kids at local schools; teaching seniors technology skills such as how to use a cellphone; sewing fuel- and money-saving draft dodgers (to wedge under doors to keep out cold drafts) for low income residents using reused fabric at SewGreen; refurbishing used computers through the Ithaca Youth Bureau's Computer All Stars Program. Tuesday and Thursday afternoons are often used as time for internships, where students can learn skills of their choosing, alongside a caring mentor, including working at preschools, a glass studio, a bakery, the History Center, an auto shop or a hairdressing salon.

New Roots is one of the cutting edge schools around the country that uses the Expeditionary Learning model, which includes five core practices "learning expeditions, active pedagogy, school culture and character, leadership and school improvement, and structures" which "work in concert to promote high student achievement through active learning, character growth, and teamwork."[11] Learning expeditions offer students an active way to work on solving real-world problems with the help of a local expert. One exciting example was a project which New Roots tenth graders explored during their first semester. As a team, they conducted a multidisciplinary investigation of the proposed and highly controversial Marcellus Shale natural gas drilling issue (see Chapter 10), exploring its social, economic and environmental dimensions. They were able to connect to this important issue through work in their global studies, geometry and biology classes, then give a final presentation to the whole school.

Groundswell Center for Local Food and Farming

Another exciting development that has emerged from the initial visioning work done for the EcoVillage Center for Sustainability Education is a new sustainable agriculture education program. Groundswell's mission is "to help youth and adult learners develop the skills, knowledge, and inspiration for building sustainable local food systems." [12]

At a fundraising dinner for an earlier version of Groundswell, my friend and former EcoVillage neighbor, Joanna Green (introduced in Chapter 2) came up to me. "Liz, I know what I want to do with my life now," she told me, her face glowing with conviction. "I want to be the person who makes Groundswell happen." True to her word, Joanna took early retirement from her job at Cornell, where she had worked for over two decades in sustainable agriculture education and research. Drawing on her extensive network of contacts in local food and farming, she put together a terrific advisory board, including representatives from Cornell Cooperative Extension, Ithaca College, graduate students, farmers and more. Although we only had a tiny amount of funding to offer, Joanna spent months working pro bono to pull together her team, identify needed programs and get them started.

As this book went to press, Groundswell was teaching its first eight-week Summer Practicum in Sustainable Farming and Local Food Systems. Students earned six credits through Tompkins Cortland Community College (TC3), with both academic learning and plenty of hands-on training on three farm campuses — West Haven Farm (an organic vegetable farm at EcoVillage), Kingbird Farm (a horse powered farm 30 miles from Ithaca that specializes in grass-fed beef, pork, poultry and eggs) and Northland Sheep Dairy (also 30 miles away, a farm that provides training in production and marketing of gourmet sheep's milk cheeses). West Haven Farm manager Todd McLane joined Joanna in teaching the course. "As a farmer, I love having the opportunity to provide good wholesome fruits and vegetables to my community," he shared. "But I also have a passion to teach, whether it's exposing someone to their first farm experience or showing the proper way to hand hoe a bed of broccoli." [13]

Groundswell also initiated an innovative program that was first developed by farmers in the Hudson Valley. The new Finger Lakes CRAFT (Collaborative Regional Alliance for Farmer Training) offers advanced training to aspiring farmers in the Ithaca area. The CRAFT approach builds on the training provided by individual farmers to their interns and employees during the course of the growing season and includes nine day-long training sessions at one of the three farms mentioned above. The CRAFT approach has been highly successful in increasing the quality, depth and breadth of new farmer training in several other regions in the US and Canada. And communities with a CRAFT program tend to attract the most serious and committed trainees, which is a great benefit to participating farms. We're excited to be developing this program right here in the Ithaca area.

I asked Joanna how she felt about Groundswell's progress. "In a way Groundswell is a culmination of decades of work—a weaving together of many of the existing strands in the local food system with some new ones notably: EcoVillage, Cornell Cooperative Extension, the farms, TC3, IC, Cornell and local public schools," she told me. "It's also a very replicable model I think."[14]

And There's More

In this chapter we've looked at a broad spectrum of sustainability education initiatives, from the awards that Ithaca College has garnered, to an inside look at a partnership between IC and EVI, to the founding and some of the programs of Sustainable Tompkins and the growth of New Roots Charter School and Groundswell Center for Local Food and Farming from their EcoVillage roots. While this covers some of the ground between high school, college and adult learners, we have touched just a small portion of the sustainability education endeavors in Ithaca.

In addition to the ones mentioned above, Cornell has an Office of Sustainability and the Center for a Sustainable Future, both of which "leverage the strengths of an Ivy League University dedicated to a Land Grant mission."[15] The Johnson School Center for Sustainable Global Enterprise helps research solutions to environmental and economic problems through an entrepreneurial business approach. The county has some amazing Green Teams happening at the elementary school level (see Chapter 11), a wonderful Finger Lakes Permaculture Institute, lots of informal workshops (many put on by CCE-TC, Greenstar, ST and others) and a strong commitment by several key local museums to focus on educating about climate change and other topics. For instance, the Museum of the Earth has a Global Change portal which leads teachers and students to useful resources in order to study "the most pressing environmental issue of the 21st century." Museum of the Earth defines *global change* as not only climate change, but also biodiversity loss, ozone depletion and other environmental changes with global impact. Global change, they note, "while relevant to every scientific field and human endeavor, is most centrally studied through Earth system science."[16] They provide outreach through exhibits, curriculum, presentations, professional development and website resources.

Likewise the Sciencenter, a very innovative local science museum for kids, has dedicated itself to sustainability in both its message and its operations. The executive director of the Sciencenter, Charlie Trautmann, visited 34 European museums in 2007 to see how they address issues in sustainability and global warming, then came back to write a report and implement many of the lessons learned. His report includes a new tool, called the Museum Sustainability Index, which museums can use to self-assess their own progress in becoming more sustainable organizations and communicating the science of sustainability to the public.[17]

So, from educating new farmers, to working with students from elementary through graduate school to workshops for people of all ages, the sustainability message has permeated this county deeply. One key thing to remember is the importance of supplementing theory with hands-on, experiential learning that is applied to helping to solve real-world problems — this applies to students of all ages. For we often learn best when we are engaged learners. With so much at stake, the world needs all of us to be engaged — to both learn and to take action.

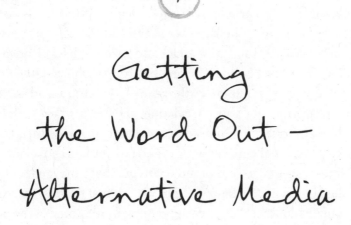

Getting the Word Out — Alternative Media

Finger Lakes Environmental Film Festival

It was the first week in April 2009, the week of the Finger Lakes Environmental Film Festival (FLEFF), and there was so much going on, it was hard to choose among the many events. There were unusual film screenings, presentations, workshops, performances, digital media and art installations. They took place all over Ithaca, from the Ithaca College campus, to downtown, to the independent movie theaters, Cinemapolis and Fall Creek Pictures.

I decided to see a film called "The Garden," shown at a local alternative movie theater. It was a surprisingly powerful documentary about the largest urban garden in the US — 14 acres of land wrested from development in South Central Los Angeles by a dedicated group of Latin American immigrants.[1] The garden had plots used by dozens of families for growing their own food. But it had so much more — over time it had become a community of people who loved the land and who felt empowered by their ability to be more self-sufficient in the midst of the stark background of inner city poverty. In many cases the immigrants brought deep knowledge of farming from their home countries, so this little chunk of land had great personal significance. It was an oasis of beauty in the midst of freeways, with full grown fruit trees shading verdant vegetable patches.

There were politics involved at every level — the community garden was originally started as a form of healing after the devastating LA riots in 1992. The landowner allowed the people to use it
for many years, then abruptly decided to snatch it back. Under the
direction of a strong Latina woman, the group mobilized to fight to
keep the garden. As bulldozers threatened, the group worked with
pro bono attorneys for a stay of eviction, and they worked with City
Council members who promised to come to their aid. As their cause
got better known, the mayor and several movie stars spoke out and
helped to raise a huge sum of money to purchase the land, only to
have the landowner back down from his original promise to sell to
the group. In another deeply disappointing move, some of the poli-
ticians were shown to support the farmers with their rhetoric, but
behind the scenes they used their actions to undercut the group. In
a heart-breaking scene, the carefully tended plots are plowed under,
and the land reverts to a vacant lot. Watching the weather-beaten
faces of the farmers as their garden gets bulldozed brought me to
tears. This arbitrary and willful destruction of a community asset
that provided both physical and spiritual sustenance seemed pure
evil. We were left to ponder what brings strength and vitality to a
community — and what destroys it.

And this was just one of 67 films screened over the course of
the week! The yearly Festival seizes the opportunity to expose thousands of students and area residents to a wide variety of ideas. As its
mission statement says:

> FLEFF at Ithaca College embraces and interrogates sustainabil-
> ity across all of its forms: economic, social, ecological, political,
> cultural, technological and aesthetic. The festival is in the spirit
> of UNESCO's initiative on sustainable development. This initia-
> tive has redefined and expanded environmental issues to explore
> the international interconnection between war, disease, health,
> genocide, the land, water, air, food, education, technology, cul-
> tural heritage, and diversity...the Festival engages interdisci-
> plinary dialogue and vigorous debate. It links the local with the
> global. And it showcases Ithaca College as a regional and na-

tional center for thinking differently — in new ways, interfaces and forms — about the environment and sustainability.[2]

In addition to its many goals, the Festival engages 100 competitively selected festival interns. These students, chosen across disciplines and from freshmen to seniors, take three one-credit courses, offered through the Division of Interdisciplinary and International Studies at Ithaca College, the Festival's main sponsor. Besides acting as staff of the Festival, the students use their experiential learning as the background for developing a professional understanding of the subject matter. They work in teams, from operations to blogging. As one alumna said, "the interns are the festival."

Some Good News for a Change

As I strolled out of the movie theater, I picked up a copy of the latest *Positive News US*, Ithaca's own quarterly newspaper which concentrates on finding the most empowering, interesting news around the globe. On the front page the paper proclaimed: "We envision a world in which people treat each other with respect and kindness, where we consider the Earth to be our home to care for and to enjoy... And we know that this world is in the process of emerging... *Positive News* is a reflection of this widespread emerging movement and tells its stories."[3]

I quickly scanned the headlines. "Ecuador's Historic Vote: Nature Gets Legal Rights" was the lead story on the front page. The article applauded Ecuador's new constitution, voted for by a record two thirds of the population, which set a ground-breaking precedent — the first in the world to grant Nature the same inalienable rights as human beings. It was inspired by the indigenous Quichua concept, *sumak kawsay*, which translates as "balanced living." According to Maria Fernanda Espinosa, Ecuador's ambassador to the UN, "It aims to supersede the assumption that having more will enable better living."[4] The article informed me that Ecuador has an abundance of unique habitats, from the Amazon rainforest to the Andes and the Galapagos Islands and is very culturally diverse, with a full quarter of its population made up of indigenous peoples. The new constitution reflects the traditions of the native people who see Nature as a sacred mother and call her by the name *Pachamama*. It sets an amazing legal precedent — one which may bring Ecuador into direct conflict with some of the multinational corporations that extract timber, oil and minerals and have been a mainstay of Ecuador's economy.

While the first article made me cheer, the second front-page article made me laugh. The headline read "Exposing Poverty," above a photo showing a group of men and women on the London tube — in their underpants! Apparently more than 100 people took part in setting a new world record for the largest gathering of people wearing underpants. The event was organized by Pants to Poverty, a fair trade organization, to mark Guinness World Records Day. This group has the aim of selling ethical underwear that is fair trade certified, sweatshop free and made from organic cotton. Staged right before Christmas, the event was meant to teach people about the devastating effects of manufacturing "bad pants" from carcinogenic dyes to exploitation, but educating in such a humorous way that founder Ben Ramsden said, "I'm sure we will make a few stressed-out morning commuters smile."[5]

As an antidote to the mainstream media, which focuses on the most dramatic, often violent and negative news, *Positive News US* tells the story of ordinary people who are doing extraordinary things. Ithaca Hours founder Paul Glover explained, "There's a lot of negative news in the world, and if that's all that people can think about, if that's where our imaginations are locked, then things will spiral in that direction. That's why we need a new medium for news about a better future that we all deserve and are capable of creating."[6]

Positive News US is part of a larger network of papers, started in the United Kingdom, with editions in Hong Kong, Spain, Argentina and Germany. It was brought to the US by Ilonka Wloch, a Polish émigré, who first picked up a paper in Ireland and decided to distribute it when she moved to Ithaca in 2001. "When I started distributing it, people were so excited," she told me, "They said you should do something like that here." Although she had no prior experience in writing articles, media, fundraising or business and had only rudimentary computer skills, Ilonka was inspired. "I'm a very optimistic person," she said. She gathered supporters, including Paul Glover, who helped her go around and get local businesses to advertise in the premier US edition.

When I asked Ilonka what inspired her, she thoughtfully replied, "I have such a deep passion for change in the world, and I'm holding inside myself a picture of what is possible... By presenting people with what works, not stressful information, although we do include information about the issues at hand, but writing about solutions, it opens us up to be more receptive ourselves to creating change."[7]

In a very short period of time, *Positive News US* has grown to a circulation of 20,000. Most of these copies are distributed within Tompkins County, but 20% go to cafes, stores, libraries and schools around the East Coast, and an additional 15% get circulated nationally. Ilonka recently moved to the West Coast, so a *Positive News California Edition* is planned.

One example of youth empowerment that has stayed with me is a story about a six-year-old Swedish boy, Marcus Marcus, who was outraged to find that sharks are caught for their fins, which are cut out and made into soup. He decided to start his own international campaign to Save the Sharks. His father, Fredrik Marcus, said, "My goal was to show my son that one person, even small people, can make a difference." The campaign website that father and son created has garnered 20,000 signatures from 58 countries and is now available in four languages. "You must do something," young Marcus explained. "That's what it's all about. You must do something."[8] Reading *Positive News US* is a habit I don't want to break.

Community Supported Books

Just as farmers have developed Community Supported Agriculture as a way of gaining support from loyal customers who purchase a share in the harvest of the farm, Community Supported Books (CSB) is a new program developed by one of our local bookstores, Buffalo Street Books. Locally owned, independent bookstores around the US have been very hard hit by internet retailers such as Amazon and big chain bookstores such as Barnes and Noble and Borders. And the state of the economy has not helped, either.

CSB will help Buffalo Street Books survive throughout the cycles of crests and troughs of running a small retail business. Whereas a farm generates income primarily during harvest season, a bookstore generates its highest income at the beginning of each of the school terms and during the winter holidays, explained owner Gary Weisbrott. With CSB, a customer puts money into an account at the bookstore, then draws purchases against that balance. At any time, the customer may withdraw remaining funds. For deposits of $500 or more, customers get special discounts. It is yet another way that customers can support a local business, and cushion it against a lack of sales in between holiday and school rushes.

Tompkins Weekly

While *Positive News US* includes news from around the world as well as local news, another free local paper concentrates on activities and events right here at home. *Tompkins Weekly*'s editor and founder Jim Graney explained his motivation, "Without a comprehensive venue for examining local issues, we as Tompkins County residents lack the opportunity to come together and learn what is happening across our whole community."[9] The paper provides a look at local issues, a comprehensive calendar of community events and profiles of community residents making news. Among other things, it has a well-read Signs of Sustainability article series, organized by Sustainable Tompkins and sponsored by Alternatives Federal Credit Union. This series includes an article on some local aspect of sustainability each week. A group of a couple dozen people (including myself) take turns writing these short introductions to some interesting aspect of our work.

For example, Signs of Sustainability has included an article about solar cookers by Shawn Reeves, founder of EnergyTeachers.org; an article about the Zero Waste Festival Alliance, a new group that recently formed to minimize garbage at Tompkins County's numerous summer festivals by Kat McCarthy from Tompkins County Solid Waste; and an article about energy conservation by Sharon Anderson, Environmental Program Leader at Cornell Cooperative Extension of Tompkins County. Together, these and other authors represent a Who's Who in the local environmental movement.

Of course, Ithaca being the community it is, there are a number of other free newspapers as well. The *Ithaca Times*, another weekly, is bigger and splashier than *Tompkins Weekly*. There is also *Ithaca Child*, which caters to families. It's great to have many free sources of local news!

Green Guerrillas

One enterprising group is the Green Guerrillas, part of Southern Tier Advocacy and Mitigation Project (STAMP) which was founded in 2005 in response to the frequency with which young people are referred to juvenile and adult court systems. STAMP challenges criminalization and incarceration by encouraging self-respect, em-powerment, leadership and self-determination among young people and families. The Green Guerrillas byline is "sustainable storytellers who challenge the status quo." They are a group of talented young

Green Guerrillas youth media tech collective at Taughannock Falls.

people who are committed to sustainability and social change. They make documentaries about inspiring people and events. They also present the Community Cinema, a monthly series of films by other independent filmmakers that aims to educate and create "accessible opportunities for civic engagement."[10]

I enjoyed attending one of these film showings recently, "Taking Root," a documentary about Kenyan Nobel Peace Prize laureate Wangari Maathai.[11] My friends and I arrived ten minutes early at the Henry St. John's building, one of two community centers serving Ithaca's Southside neighborhood, and the screening room was already packed. We staked out seats on the floor in the front, but some of the later arrivals had to stand for the whole program. About 125 people of all ages and races attended, including at least 16 of my EcoVillage neighbors.

The evening started out with a quick introduction of some of the Green Guerillas and a short excerpt of a current film they were working on. Then "Taking Root" was introduced. It was deeply engaging to me to see footage of Maathai herself in action, and of the Green Belt movement she inspired. When the lights went on after the show, I was amazed to find out that several Kenyans who had worked with Maathai were present. Although at first reluctant, they did speak to the rapt audience and told more of the inside story, including some disillusionment they felt with Maathai's election to parliament and her consequently more conservative role. Then the audience was treated to a short discussion with Samite, an amazing Ugandan musician who has, fortunately for us, settled in Ithaca. In addition, we feasted on a huge array of fruits, salads, drinks and desserts that Liz Karabanakis had arranged, a donation from Greenstar Cooperative Market. Overall, quite a satisfying evening!

The Izzy Award

The same busy week as the Fingerlakes Environmental Film Festival was taking place, Ithaca College's Park Center for Independent Media hosted a big ceremony to inaugurate the first annual Izzy Award for special achievement in independent media. On March 31, 2009, the beautiful old State Theater filled with 800 people who eagerly came to honor two pillars of independent journalism: Amy Goodman, host and producer of the popular radio show "Democracy Now!" and Glenn Greenwald, whose blog appears on Salon .com. The Izzy Award was named after the legendary dissident journalist Isidor Feinstein "Izzy" Stone, who courageously challenged the US government during the height of the McCarthy era through his groundbreaking newsletter, *I. F. Stone's Weekly*. Greenwald and Goodman were chosen to share this first Izzy Award for "their pathbreaking journalistic courage and persistence in confronting conventional wisdom, official deception and controversial issues."[12]

The evening began with Jeremy Stone, I. F. Stone's son, reflecting on his father's life and legacy. "When I first heard about an award for people who most 'resembled' Izzy, I had high hopes that I might finally win a prize," he quipped. "Unfortunately, the selection committee appears to have been concerned with behavior [rather than looks]." Even though his father loved his work, he was often lonely, Stone said. "His capacity for thinking independently, and acting on principle, isolated him from just about everyone. In the McCarthy era, because he spoke in defense of Jeffersonian principles, people were afraid to be seen with him. When he supported the rights of Palestinians, Jewish institutions would not invite him to speak. And when the National Press Club refused to serve his black guest lunch, he quit the club," Stone told the audience.

Stone went on to praise the two award recipients, and to draw parallels between them and his father. Glenn Greenwald, a former constitutional lawyer, started blogging in 2005, acting as his own editor and publisher in the I.F. Stone tradition. In 2007 he moved his popular blog to Salon.com, where he posts meticulously researched weekly pieces that skewer government and big media alike for hypocrisy and deception. Stone said, "Glenn Greenwald is a close reader of official documents and a principled critic of the tendency of the Executive Branch to exceed its rightful powers. He has been a fearless critic of government officials and complacent reporters."

Amy Goodman, in turn, "speaks up for the disenfranchised and gives her audience facts they don't hear from the traditional media," Stone reflected. And like *I. F. Stone's Weekly*, "Democracy Now!"

takes no advertising or money from corporations or government. Amy Goodman has built "Democracy Now!" into the largest public media collaboration in the US, and it offers a daily cutting edge broadcast on television, radio and the internet which features issues, experts and debates that are rarely heard in corporate media. "She confronts authority no matter how high. And she has repeatedly shown physical courage." He concluded with "I. F. Stone once said: 'If the government makes a mistake, the newspapers will find out and the problem may then be fixed. But if freedom of the press were lost, the country would soon go to pieces.'"[13]

The Park Center for Independent Media (PCIM), which just started in 2008, is part of the larger Roy H. Park School of Communications at Ithaca College. The Park School aims to help students "explore the myriad ways people and organizations 'talk' to one another: not only through words, but also through image, sound and design." PCIM carries this mission further by sponsoring a competitive summer internship program which gives students a chance to hone their skills at some of the best independent and progressive media institutions in the US, including Bill Moyers/Public Affairs Television, Center for Media and Democracy, Common Dreams, "Democracy Now!" and Alternet.[14]

Your Impact

As yet another outgrowth of Ithaca College's interest in sustainability and independent media, recent IC environmental science graduate Andrew Bernier premiered a monthly show entitled "Your Impact" on the college's student-run radio station WICB in the fall of 2007. WICB, which broadcasts to a wide area "with a potential 250,000 listeners," won the 2008 Best College Radio Station from the MtvU Woodie Awards. It allows students to have a hands-on experience in producing shows. "Your Impact," "is designed for members of Tompkins County (and the world) to both educate and learn. We discuss just about any topic and how it is sustainable or how it could be more sustainable. From healthcare practices and building techniques to personal finance and education, the list is truly endless," Andrew wrote in an introductory e-mail. "Everyone from individuals to commercial companies are encouraged to use the show to share their knowledge… We'll even sprinkle in simple daily tips that you can do to make your life more sustainable… And remember, no matter what your choices are, be it social, environmental or economic, they all add up to be your impact."[15]

Whether it is an exploration of sustainability through the lens of film, independent broadcast or print media, internet blogs or academic inquiry, there is a lot going on in the Ithaca area. All of it celebrates the importance of an independent spirit — getting away from corporate-controlled mass media. A healthy culture requires active questioning and analysis and many sources of information. I see Ithaca as fostering an explosion of independent media. It is as if we are building new, community-scale neural pathways that transmit information that is locally based and cutting edge. At the same time, these pathways integrate with the larger national and international scene to bring a very rich brew of information and analysis and application of sustainability and social justice principles to our community. While it can be overwhelming at times, it certainly keeps us all connected.

8

Health and Wellness for All

We think that access to health care is a basic right, and not a privilege. We have shown that it is a right that we can give to each other, simply and cooperatively.

ITHACA HEALTH ALLIANCE BROCHURE

It's time for my annual dental checkup. I am so thankful that I have healthy teeth. Several friends of mine have had to undergo root canals, gum surgery and other expensive and invasive treatments, costing many thousands of dollars. No one I know has dental insurance, so having the bad luck to have bad teeth becomes a terrible financial burden. I'm pleased to get a clean bill of health this time. Before paying at the front desk I whip out my Ithaca Health Alliance card which gives me a 10% discount. Overall a painless visit to the dentist.

In a country which faces a growing healthcare crisis and in which one in six citizens are uninsured, Ithaca faces the same issues in microcosm. In Tompkins County, the number of uninsured rose by more than 100% from the year 2000 to 2005, according to the US Census Bureau.[1] Currently more than a quarter of the county's population is not insured! Despite this shocking statistic or perhaps because of it, Ithaca is pioneering some innovative approaches to the healthcare dilemma, from looking at sustainable healthcare as a system-wide approach to providing a free clinic, from developing healthy school lunches to gathering grassroots fundraising support for innovative programs. These creative measures are in addition to a baseline wealth of more traditional medical and holistic wellness services in Tompkins County: an excellent local hospital — Cayuga Medical Center, the Finger Lakes School of Massage (every other person in Ithaca is a massage therapist it seems), a Convenient Care center, an active Planned Parenthood chapter and more alternative healthcare practitioners per square foot than almost any place in the world.

As with every other topic covered in this book, the approaches to health and wellness overlap extensively with other sustainability efforts. Long-term wellness is promoted by programs such as those ensuring access to healthy food or through emphasis on city planning and transportation alternatives that promote walking and biking instead of driving. As we promote solutions in one area, they tend to create positive effects in another — a real win-win approach.

Providing Our Own Care: Ithaca Health Alliance

When Paul Glover lived in Ithaca, he was a one-man whirlwind of visionary ideas, some of which grew into amazingly successful projects. One of them was Ithaca Hours (discussed in Chapter 5). Another was the Ithaca Health Alliance (IHA). Started in 1997, its mission is "to facilitate access to health care for all, with a focus on the needs of the uninsured."[2] IHA uses community memberships and volunteer hours from medical practitioners to create a community healthcare system that does not rely on insurance companies. Like Ithaca Hours, IHA's wide network of caring people provide a safety net for low income people. In the process they both create remarkable social capital. Rather than relying on government fixes or corporate accountability, both organizations emphasize creative ways that local people can support each other through providing services in an organized and dignified manner.

At the beginning, most of us who joined IHA for the low membership fee of $100 per adult per year did so just to support a good idea. Over time we benefited from a growing number of practitioners (doctors, dentists, massage therapists, local ambulance services and more) who agreed to offer a 5–10% discount on their services. However, by 1998 there was enough money in the fund to begin making small grants to members for medical expenses, such as emergency room visits or broken bones. This has grown from a few grants a year to 86 grants in 2009, representing $14,605 in medical bills. Most years I will not need to access the money that I pay in for membership fees, but occasionally I may need to tap into this supplemental community resource that I helped to create. What a refreshing and empowering change from the usual approach of haggling with insurance companies!

In 2006, after two years of organizing efforts, IHA opened a free clinic, which served 861 people in its first year and by 2009 had expanded to offer 2,420 patient visits — an amazing 2.4 % of the population of the entire

A volunteer nurse at Ithaca Free Clinic reviews a patient record.

county![3] The clinic currently is open one afternoon and one evening a week, with pre-employment and school physicals one or two evenings a month, a pain clinic once a week, occupational therapy once a week and a women's health clinic once a month. The emphasis is on serving the uninsured for either conventional medicine or complementary services. For not only does the Ithaca Free Clinic provide primary medical care, employment physicals and visual screening, it also provides therapeutic services and holistic medicine such as acupuncture, chiropractic, massage and more. It is one of the first medically integrated free clinics in the US. All of the practitioners are volunteers from the community who donate their time and skills to help others, including some Ithaca College masters-level students, who provide the weekly occupational therapy clinic.

On top of the Ithaca Health Fund and the Ithaca Free Clinic, IHA also provides access to medical information through an on-site library of health and wellness resources, and in 2008 it even donated $500 to each of two local libraries to provide books on these topics.

Despite the fact that it is a nonprofit organization that just gets by on donations and small grants, the IHA provides a few small grants of its own on an annual basis. Some of the recent recipients were: an organization that provides counseling and practical assistance to homeless youth, the Healthy Food for All CSA program (see Chapter 2), Sustainable Tompkins for its conference on Sustainable Healthcare For All and an Elmira Kids' Health Walk. IHA also offers informative lectures and a quarterly free newsletter.

Bethany Schroeder, president of the Board of the IHA, told me that while a number of other communities around the country have tried to replicate the IHA model, so far it hasn't worked. Unfortunately, similar programs have been shut down by their state insurance departments. The same fate almost occurred when New York State Governor Eliot Spitzer threatened to close the IHA. "We fought his charges and won," Bethany said, "with some changes in terminology in our program." For instance, the IHA issues grants, rather than benefits or reimbursements. They have a limited palette of grants, based on members' expressed needs for preventive or emergency services. "We're unlike insurance in that we use a democratic infrastructure to make improvements to the organization and its services. We don't exclude anyone, so long as he or she resides in New York. We provide one to one advocacy and oversight on every bill a member submits."

Of course, if an affordable national healthcare system is ever put in place, some of IHA's services may no longer be needed, although it is likely that it will always have an important role in the community. "It makes good sense to look at the program as something to augment ordinary insurance plans, which fail to consider the need for preventive, complementary or basic emergency care," Bethany concluded.[4]

Whole Community Project

Another creative response to a chronic societal problem—obesity, and its attendant health problems of diabetes and heart disease—is provided by the Whole Community Project (WCP), an organization that promotes a holistic, family-oriented approach to wellness. The extent of the problem is shocking — not only as it affects adults, but increasingly as it affects children. A recent US study found that one in five young children is now obese, with even higher rates among black and Hispanic kids, and up to a third of American Indian children.[5] It is well-known that high rates of obesity are often correlated with poverty and lack of access to whole foods, and this study showed the severe effects of racism as well. Many urban neighborhoods are *food deserts*, with plenty of liquor stores and McDonald's, but no healthy food choices. When low income people have to work two or three jobs to make ends meet and don't own a car, it can be tough to find the time and the transportation to travel long distances to get healthy groceries. These are deeply ingrained issues with no easy fix. In Tompkins County alone, it is estimated that $12 million in annual costs can be directly related to obesity.[6]

Research during a 2006 Cornell graduate course "Assessing Food and Nutrition in a Social Context" led to the formation of WCP, which is based at CCE–Tompkins and supported by Cornell's Division of Nutritional Sciences. WCP serves as a collaborative resource center which in its first three years has already had a very positive impact. Shira Adriance, the program's coordinator for the first two years, said, "I like to think of the Whole Community Project as the hub of a wheel." She noted that WCP doesn't try to replicate the many projects that are already going on, but rather to increase collaboration and communication among them. "Childhood overweight and obesity is an increasing concern for our community, especially because both can lead to long-term health problems, poor body image and low self-esteem." The goal of WCP is to "celebrate food and movement in our community," and to support the health and well-being of our children and youth. "It will take our whole, diverse community to make a difference," she noted.[7]

Healthy School Food Project

It's shocking to realize that half of 2 to 15-year-olds in the US have early stage heart disease, and some eight-year-olds are already taking cholesterol lowering drugs. As bad as this situation is, it can be turned around with more exercise and a better diet. Since 2004, the New York Coalition for Healthy School Food (NYCHSF), a statewide program based in Ithaca, has worked to improve the health and well-being of New York's students through advocating better nutrition. Since children spend most of their time in school, it is a great place to teach them about a healthy diet.

In a highly successful pilot project at Beverly J. Martin Elementary School in Ithaca, NY, children were served two snacks of fresh fruits and vegetables every day, many of them from local, organic farms. There was a marked improvement in the kids' energy levels. As one young girl reported, "Every time I eat the fruits and vegetables I feel strong and I do better in math." Teachers and the principal alike reported on the excitement the kids felt about their new snack regime and how much it changed home behaviors as well. Amie Hamlin, executive director of NYCHSF, noted that the program only costs $1.00 per student per day, or "less than the cost of a doughnut." It has been funded through the collaboration of local foundations, businesses and community partners, but with the recession, the funding has been in jeopardy. However, energetic activists have teamed with local farmers to supply extra produce from farms and community gardens. The program provides a blueprint for how other schools can help to revolutionize their students' appreciation for healthy, plant-based foods.[8]

WCP helped to pull together a wide-ranging partnership which included school representatives and food service directors from five school districts and community partners such as CCE-Tompkins, Greenstar, GIAC and the NY Coalition for Healthy School Food (NYCHSF). Together, the partners focused attention on how to improve school lunches. The partnership decided to get the kids involved, creating taste tests of new healthy school lunch recipes. Fiesta Tacos and Taco-licious were two creative names that kids proposed for a vegetarian bean taco which they tasted and voted on. Students ranging in age from elementary school to high school cast 260 votes in taste-testing events, and local food service staff modified and retested the recipe based on their feedback before adding it to the district lunch menu.[9]

Despite the great progress made by food service directors in offering healthy alternatives such as whole grains, farm to school programs that bring local produce, salad bars and vegetarian entrees, there is a long way to go, noted Amie Hamlin of NYCHSF and a member of the partnership. "Until we address the whole school food environment, cafeterias have an unfair disadvantage. Class parties, fundraising, vending machines, food used as a reward and school stores all compete with the cafeteria, and even the snack line in the cafeteria competes with the meals. How can we expect our kids to make good choices in an environment that surrounds and tempts them with soda, sports drinks, cookies, ice cream, potato chips and other unhealthy food daily?"[10]

Jemila Sequeira, WCP's current coordinator, has expanded the program beyond the schools. Drawing on her own multicultural background (she is Cherokee, African-American and Chinese and grew up in a housing project in Brooklyn), Jemila has been successful in working with low income people of all races. "These are the ones most affected by diseases that are caused by poor nutrition and lack of access to healthy food," she told me. "These are the voices I want to bring to the table. This is about food justice."

Under Jemila's leadership, WCP has helped to create Gardens-4Humanity community gardens for residents in the poorest neighborhoods in Ithaca. The gardens allow people convenient access to fresh, healthy produce as well as a sense of empowerment. She won a Cornell Civic Fellowship award for her work and now hopes to expand healthy food access through working with churches and temples. She also promotes the Congo Square Market, a series of fun, summer events that combine live music, vendors selling local produce and ethnic foods and crafts in the heart of Southside, a predominantly African-American neighborhood.

Promoting an overall change in values towards making healthy choices in food and activity level is something that needs to be addressed by, you guessed it, the whole community. "The problems, the issues are too large to tackle by ourselves," said Jemila. "We need to recognize our connectedness. The Whole Community Project draws people together on the common basic human right to eat healthy food, and to be active."[11]

A Systemic Look at Healthcare in Tompkins County

Not only does it take a whole community to solve health problems, it also takes a systems-wide analysis of what the problems are and how they might be addressed. Many health problems are inter-twined with the infrastructure of our daily lives — how we get to work, where we live, what we eat and the water we drink. For in-stance obesity, diabetes and environmentally caused cancers could be remedied in many cases by greener living. In the same way that Paul Glover brought visionary ideas to Ithaca's economic and health problems, Gay Nicholson, another visionary, shines an analytical spotlight on healthcare and looks for systemic solutions. In her role as Program Coordinator (at that time) for Sustainable Tompkins, Gay mobilized community partners to put on a very successful re-gional conference, Health and Sustainability, in September 2007. The goal of the conference was to start a conversation about the connections between health, sustainable ways of living and working and economic viability.

"I hope healthcare practitioners will recognize their role in help-ing the community redesign the infrastructure and food systems that would support healthier citizens," Gay said while preparing for the conference. "Another objective is for elected officials and policy makers to understand the linkages between the choices they make around infrastructure such as trails and neighborhood design," she said, referring to reducing sprawl and making neighborhoods walkable.[12]

The conference, held at Ithaca College, was organized by Sustain-able Tompkins and sponsored by Ithaca College School of Health Sciences and Human Performance, with additional assistance from an amazingly diverse array of co-sponsors from the local Park Foun-dation, to Tompkins County Solid Waste, to Excellus BlueCross BlueShield, to the local hospital, a community college nursing pro-gram and a local health club. Health and Sustainability drew hundreds of people from around the Finger Lakes, including healthcare professionals, educators, local officials and planners. The keynote speaker, Dr. Jonathan Patz, a medical researcher from the University of Wisconsin, has briefed the US Congress on the health threats of climate change. He spoke about ways to reduce the risks associated with intensified heatwaves, sprawl development and chemical exposures by challenging us to rethink how we live and work.

Sandra Steingraber, who is often compared to Rachel Carson, is a local environmental researcher and author who was another compelling speaker. Author of *Living Downstream* and *Having Faith*,[13] Dr. Steingraber talked about toxins in the environment, including "windows of vulnerability" that children face. She described how fetuses and babies under six months old don't yet have a barrier between the bloodstream and the brain, making them more susceptible to toxins such as insecticides in food. Dr. Steingraber has done research on pubescent girls who are developing breasts. When breast cells are growing rapidly, they are especially susceptible to environmental and dietary toxins. Because she has directly suffered the effects of cancer herself, her words held extra power.

Other speakers addressed greening medical facilities, improving nutrition and creating healthy community infrastructures. While the conference only lasted a day, the conversation it started continues.

A Smoke-Free Ithaca?

Local government is doing its part to contribute to healthier lifestyles. In addition to enacting a New York statewide ban on indoor smoking in 2003, the City of Ithaca has spent the last two years considering legislation that would ban outdoor smoking in many public areas, including the Commons, outdoor dining areas, outdoor festivals and some parks and playgrounds among other places. It is highly controversial, creating a debate between people who are concerned for public health and those who favor individual rights.

In Ithaca, as in the rest of the US, almost 20% of the population smokes. According to the American Cancer Society, tobacco claims 443,000 lives nationwide per year — more than alcohol, car

accidents, suicide, AIDS, homicide and illegal drugs combined! It is
the most preventable cause of death. However, nicotine is also more
addictive than crack or cocaine. "More than 70% of US smokers say
they want to quit," states the American Cancer Society, "but between 4% to 7% succeed on any given attempt if they try it without
help."[14]

On a Monday afternoon in early April 2009, the New York State
Health Commissioner, Dr. Richard Daines, came to Ithaca to present Public Health Excellence awards to the mayor, the coordinator
of Tobacco Free Tompkins and the Director of the Public Health
Department. Daines eloquently supported Ithaca's anti-smoking efforts. "One of the things that people in public health face is the first
time we float out a new idea, everybody says, 'That's outrageous,
you can't do it. How can you possibly limit advertising of cigarettes?
How can you possibly put warning labels on cigarettes? How can
you use taxes to increase the cost of cigarettes?'" Daines continued,
"That's why I'm so delighted to understand that Ithaca is considering
making this beautiful outdoor space a smoke-free outdoor space."[15]

As of this writing, 37 municipalities in New York state have already adopted ordinances banning smoking in a variety of public
outdoor locations. So, while Ithaca is certainly on the cutting edge,
once again, it is not alone.

Home-grown Heroes for Health

Ithaca is fortunate to have lots of caring people who volunteer for
good causes. Perhaps because of the mythic nature of the name of
our city—home of Homer's Greek hero Odysseus—one of the best
ways to tap into that volunteer energy is to propose a heroic task.
Then people flock to the cause. I know, because I've done it!

One good example is the AIDS Ride for Life, a 100 mile ride
around Cayuga Lake to support AIDS education in the Southern
Tier. This is a critical fundraiser which typically draws 300 to 450 bi-
cyclists a year who together have raised over a million dollars for the
Southern Tier Advocacy Program in the ten years since it started.
On their website, the program promises "you'll be cheered, fed and
celebrated for a ride you'll never forget."[16]

I have done the ride twice — once with my partner Jared and my son Jason, and once with my son Daniel, when each of my sons was in high school. The heroic nature of the ride definitely appealed to me. The first time I registered to ride, I had never biked farther than 20 miles, and 100 seemed almost impossible. I trained for months, gradually taking longer rides, and realizing with a sense of empowerment that I could actually achieve my goal. Not only did the event push my physical limits, it pushed emotional ones as well. Each rider is required to raise $500 for the cause, and this seemed just as hard as climbing all those hills in the summer's heat. But the AIDS Ride for Life also offered me a way to bond with each of my sons when they were coming of age. It seemed appropriate to share something that we all enjoyed — biking in the beautiful Finger Lakes — but to step it up to a major challenge and all for a good cause. When we pedaled in after circling the lake — a full day's ride — there were cheers and clapping. There was even a tent, with students from the Finger Lakes School of Massage waiting to massage the riders. After all the hard work, to feel acknowledged as a hero was blissful!

Another example is Women Swimmin', an annual fundraiser for Hospicare. It all started out with a board member of Hospicare, who went to see her doctor as she was turning 60. She told her doctor, who was also a friend and a swimmer, "I'd really like to do something special for my birthday." The doctor proposed that they swim across Cayuga Lake, about 1.2 miles, and find other women to join them, while raising money for the nonprofit. Now in its fifth year, Women Swimmin' has become a wildly popular event. In 2008 there were 275 swimmers, accompanied by 150 kayaks and canoes, who formed a guiding, protective flotilla around the swimmers. The swimmers leapt into the water on one side of the lake, accompanied by live bagpipe music. The excitement was palpable. Saoirse McClory, one of the event's main organizers, reflected, "This is a very life-enhancing event. It's wonderful to be around all this bubbling, exciting and tender energy. It's about life and making every moment count.… it underscores what Hospicare work is all about." The participants, ranging in age from teens to women in their 70s, heartily agree. Here are a few women's comments:

One of several hundred Women Swimmin' to support Hospicare.

It has become one of my favorite fundraisers each year — the peace of swimming across the lake is a good opportunity to think of those that I have loved and lost, and be thankful for the ones that are in my life still. Hospicare helped my family and many others get through the death of a loved one, and we are all thankful for that.

I swam the first three years, missed last year because of breast cancer, and will train to swim this summer as a major element in regaining wellness. I swim with gratitude for the love of family and friends, with gratitude for healing, and with gratitude and admiration for Hospicare and its Women Swimmin' sisterhood.[17]

This event, just like the AIDS Ride for Life, taps into a deep well of desire for connection and community service. But perhaps more than anything, it becomes a meaningful community ritual which gathers momentum over time, all while raising much needed funds for people who most need the support — people who are ill or dying.

Dying with Integrity

This chapter would not be complete without sharing a couple of vignettes from life at my own community of EcoVillage at Ithaca. When you live in a close-knit community of just 60 households, it's natural to look out for everyone's welfare. Over the last 14 years our group has lived at the EcoVillage together, we've experienced many births (including some home deliveries), a death, two elders with Alzheimer's, some life-threatening illnesses, severe allergies, depressions, broken bones and several bike accidents. Throughout it all, the degree of community caring has been heart-warming. One situation in particular stands out for me.[18]

Pamela Carson, one of our founding members, was in her mid-50s and had just moved into EcoVillage when she was diagnosed with stomach cancer. Stomach cancer is usually a swift killer, cutting down its victims in six months to a year. But Pamela fought long and hard. She had her stomach surgically removed, went through several rounds of chemotherapy and managed to live for three years after she was first diagnosed.

The community stepped in to help Pamela all along the way. In fact she often said, "I'm alive today because I live in this community." When chemotherapy nauseated her and she couldn't eat much (causing drastic weight loss), Susan cooked tasty meals each day to tempt her appetite. Marcie, a professional folksinger, serenaded her during her chemo treatments at the hospital, amazing the nurses! Sandra provided weekly Reiki treatments, and Suzanne gave massages. Many others visited, helped with transportation or shopping or just looked in to make sure she was all right. And I met with her once a week for a delightful hour and a half of creative writing. She was taking a women's writing course at the time and often didn't feel well enough to go to the class, so her instructor sent assignments home. Pamela and I often wrote on some lively topic, then took turns sharing our stories. It was a great way to get to know her better.

And there was a lot to share — she was a remarkable woman. Pamela went from a highly successful career founding a popular Boston restaurant and a major flea market to studying Zen Buddhism in Japan for two years. On her return trip home, she stopped in Nepal and was appalled by the poverty — especially the condition of its many street children. So she adopted two Nepalese boys off the streets of Kathmandu. One of them, Ram Saran Thapa, lived with her at EcoVillage. Her strong sense of justice and caring led her to start a nonprofit, Educate the Children (ETC), which raised money from US donors to sponsor impoverished kids in Nepal. By sending them to boarding school, ETC ensured that they had a roof over their heads and food in their bellies while they also learned to read and write. ETC continues to this day, branching out to teach women literacy, establish microcredit and skills to run their own small businesses.[19]

While Pamela did very well for years, the cancer eventually won. She became weaker and weaker. About a month before Pamela's death, her friends organized a living memorial for her in the Common House. The whole community showed up, although Pamela herself was too ill to attend. People brought their favorite foods and dressed up in elegant clothes for the occasion. Her sister Gail, a former opera singer, sang beautifully. Someone brought a video camera and interviewed people about Pamela's special qualities. After dinner we gathered in a circle to share stories, some lighthearted and some serious.

It was a poignant evening, knowing that we were celebrating memories of Pamela's life while she was still alive. And that, like Huck Finn, our friend could watch her own memorial. Gail took the video home and reported that Pamela enjoyed watching it many times.

By October Pamela was dying, and I went to visit her at her home one last time. She was no longer conscious, and a thin line of spittle ran down her chin. Her breath rasped in and out of a body that looked white and waxy. She looked as if she had aged 20 years. Tears coursed down my cheeks as I held her hand and whispered my last goodbye. Her eyelids flickered, and I hoped that she could still hear me.

How many of us ever see someone as they are dying? Even in her last hours, Pamela was modeling tremendous openness, giving us the gift of witnessing her death. I left and went for a walk on the land, feeling fully alive and in tune with the world. As I walked I was thinking, This is a good day to die. A few hours later Pamela was gone.

But that was not the end of the story. Pamela, organizer that she was, had planned her own elaborate memorial service. She had arranged for the church, pre-printed programs, chosen people to speak and picked the songs she wanted sung. The service was held several weeks after she died. Ram Saran Thapa, looking elegant but uncomfortable in a suit and tie, offered a most moving eulogy. Normally Ram was extremely shy, but he overcame his shyness to speak with eloquence in front of hundreds of people at the church. His face grimaced as he spoke of his childhood, filled with abuse, on the streets of Kathmandu.

Ram had been a beaten, starving and homeless nine-year-old when Pamela first met him, he told us. Pamela took him and his friend to a local restaurant and fed them a good meal. They begged her to come back, and she did. Eventually Pamela adopted him and brought him to the US. It hadn't been easy for him to adjust to his new home or for Pamela to adjust to being a single parent. They had had plenty of ups and downs, but from the way Ram spoke, Pamela had clearly been his saving angel.

Community Wellness

What creates a sense of wellness? I mused, while taking a walk on the EcoVillage land one sunny day in mid-July. Part of it is certainly the absence of pain or illness, but that is only part of the story.

I stopped at the community garden and picked a handful of sugar snap peas from my garden plot, crunchy and sweet, brimming with green aliveness. I paused to pull a few handfuls of sour clover weeds, and hand-fed them to my neighbors' chickens in the pen next to the garden gate. Another neighbor was tending tomato seedlings in the adjacent greenhouse, part of West Haven Farm. We talked about the weather — a record three inches of rain this week — and how that affects the crops.

Several girls, ranging from five to ten years old, passed me on the path. They were laughing and running with plastic containers in their hands, bound for the ripe "black caps," one of many stands of wild, luscious black raspberries that seem to burst with flavor. Meanwhile a bicyclist zoomed by, panniers packed for a day of work up at Cornell. He called hello. He would have to bike down to the valley, then a mile up a steep hill on the other side, but it is a small price to pay for being outside on a beautiful day. Molly, grand-mother of the two laughing girls who ran by, was walking slowly up the path, enjoying the sunshine. She grew up in India, then lived in the Midwest for years and has now purchased a home at EcoVillage to be closer to her son Krishna and his family. She offers free writing classes to residents, and I hope one day to attend.

I continued on my walk. There was a gentle breeze, the birds were singing non-stop and I saw a red-tailed hawk float by above, its tail almost glowing in the sun. On the field below, my eye caught the colors of the many wildflowers. In addition to the pink, compound spheres of milkweed blossoms, there were stands of wild yarrow, white with yellow centers, purple and white crown vetch and many others. When I came to the place the brook crosses the path, I leant over the makeshift bridge to pick the last of the wild cherries. Life is good!

It struck me that all that I'd experienced in the past twenty minutes had been a sense of abundance and connection: a warm connection with friends and neighbors, eating food from the land, enjoying the connection with the birds and the flowers, reveling in nature's stunning peace and beauty. Surely this is wellness at its best — not just individual wellness, but community wellness. I feel so grateful to experience this on a daily basis. Surely I am one of the luckiest women alive!

Whether it is caring for the uninsured through health providers volunteering their time, providing access to local foods for low income and minority groups, holding conferences to build conceptual linkages between sustainable lifestyles and healthcare, adopting strong legislation or taking on heroic physical challenges to raise money, Ithacans are truly exploring innovative approaches to health and wellness for all. In all of these ways, we are building bridges of social and often economic connection — between the haves and the have-nots, between multiple stakeholder groups and between those who are ill or dying and those who enjoy robustly good health. We are also building connections between people and the natural world. For ultimately humans cannot attain wellness if the world we live in is gravely endangered.

9

Addressing
Racism

*The plague of racism is insidious, entering into our minds
as smoothly and quietly and invisibly as floating airborne
microbes enter into our bodies to find lifelong
purchase in our bloodstreams.*

MAYA ANGELOU

*Blacks in the US consistently have dramatically higher
rates of infant mortality, HIV infection, incarceration and
unemployment, as well as lower salaries, life expectancy,
and rates of home ownership. The biggest gap, however,
is in net worth. By the end of the 90's, the average black
family had a net worth one eighth the national average.*

NAOMI KLEIN

Martin Luther King Day, January 19, 2009

The sun was shining on this winter day. We had just endured a week
of Arctic weather so 25°F felt balmy. Starting at the foot of West
Hill, a group of a couple dozen people gathered, and together we
marched to downtown Ithaca, holding a banner, "Working to End
Racism Now! Catch the Winds of Change." Another group came in
from East Hill. Streets were closed off to cars, and there was a wonderful sense of freedom as two hundred people milled in the intersection of Albany and State Streets. We had gathered to celebrate
the dual naming of State Street as Martin Luther King Street. The

151

timing couldn't have been better. This was the day before Barack Obama's inauguration as the first black president of the US.

Local black leader Leslyn McBean addressed the gathering, "Today Ithaca is making history, the day before the nation makes history." She quoted Jesse Jackson, writing in the *New York Times*. "What would Dr. King, who spent much of his life changing conditions so that African Americans could vote without fear of death or intimidation, think of the rise of the nation's 44th president?" Jackson wrote, "I can say without reservation that he would be beaming. I am equally confident that he would not let the euphoria of the moment blind us to the unfinished business that lies ahead. And he would spell out those challenges in biblical terms: feed the hungry, clothe the naked and study war no more."[1]

For years Gino Bush taught a course at Ithaca High School called "The Circle of Recovery," a support group for young men of different races. Some of the boys who had graduated were there by Gino's side. One Iraqi war veteran related how the class had come up with the project to rename State Street to honor Dr. King. "We thought it would take about two weeks," he said, grinning ruefully to laughter from the audience. Six years later, after agonizing struggles and public debate, the students' dream was fulfilled. In a rap song that Leslyn McBean's nephew, Orande McBean chanted to the appreciative audience he called it "a sign of the times." And then the new street sign was ceremoniously unveiled. The crowd was thrilled. There were tears and hugs. It had been a long journey, perhaps symbolic of how much racism is deeply embedded, even in this progressive college town.

On the Road to Freedom

Tompkins County has a checkered history of race relations. On the one hand brave men and women helped slaves escape on the Underground Railway, while on the other hand one can find the sting of racist attitudes both historically and in the present.

The History Center has compiled a wonderful online pamphlet which describes the 19 stops on the Freedom Trail in Tompkins County, an important route on the path from the southern slave states to Canada.[2] The most famous haven was the St. James African Methodist Episcopal (AME) Zion Church, the oldest standing church in the City of Ithaca. One of the pastors, Jermain Lesley Loguen, was himself an escaped slave from Tennessee. He eventually moved to Syracuse and became known as The Railroad King for his work with an organization which helped 1,500 people to freedom.

Once the Fugitive Slave Act passed in 1850, aiding a runaway slave became illegal, and people who violated the law could be fined $1,000 and imprisoned for six months for each escaped slave. It was a dangerous business. Everyone on the Underground Railway had to be extremely careful not to be turned in by neighbors with different views on abolition. One man, Alexander Murdoch, a founder of Hayt's Chapel, a local church which served as a safe haven for runaways, had his home burned down in retaliation for his open views on ending slavery.

The Ugly Face of Racism

Despite this history of courageous activists supporting the Underground Railroad, a few years ago it became glaringly obvious to whites as well as blacks that present-day Ithaca has a race problem when an angry mom brought charges against the Ithaca City School District (ICSD). Amelia Kearney's daughter, who is black, was in seventh grade when she was repeatedly harassed by a group of seven white boys. Called names like "nigger, bitch, whore," she endured daily insults on the bus or at school. When she complained about her book bag being snatched, she was spat upon and punched. Her mother brought the incidents to the school's attention, and several of the boys were suspended for a few days, but it didn't stop the harassment. In fact, Kearney's daughter had to ride home on the bus with the boys the day they were disciplined. Even the associate principal of DeWitt Middle School called the bus "a hell hole." It got uglier. On December 7, 2005, video footage of the rowdy bus confirmed that one boy told her that "I have a gun with your name on it," and the other boys talked about the guns their fathers owned. In school, a boy told her, "We shoot niggers like you in the woods."[3]

Enraged that the ICSD was not adequately protecting her daughter, Amelia Kearney took her claims to the county Human Rights Commission, which referred the case to the New York State Division of Human Rights, which moved to prosecute the district. At this point the ICSD Board of Education took a shocking stand — it challenged New York's human rights law, claiming that the law was not written in such a way as to protect public school students, and therefore could not be applied to the case.

"Over many months, a critical mass of students, families and community members from a variety of races and economic backgrounds spoke effectively with a single voice to articulate many messages about injustice, hypocrisy, equity, due process and common sense," Steve Cariddi wrote in an article in the local paper.[4] These voices were enough to get the ICSD to back down from its position.

Four years after the incidents started, the New York State Division of Human Rights issued a final order in the case, requiring the school district to carry out a long list of reforms and to pay compensation of $200,000 each to Kearney and her daughter, who is now 17. The reforms include extensive training programs for all employees of the district, a new student disciplinary code, a community-based program to address racial tensions, and a staffing plan to ensure the district staff has the diversity, training and tools "to end the racial disharmony evident in this record."[5]

Talking Circles on Race and Racism

The Talking Circles on Race and Racism were started in 2007 by Audrey Cooper, director of the Multicultural Resource Center (MRC), as a way to deepen a community-wide conversation on race. Audrey, whose family is Cherokee on one side and Arab-American from Syria on the other, is keenly aware of the harshness of discrimination.

After racially oriented violence at the high school, she felt a growing conviction that something had to be done. She wanted to provide a safe, intimate space for people of color and white people to have frank discussions about race and racism, so she approached her African-American/Armenian friend Laura Branca of Training for Change Associates. Together with Laura's African-American colleague Kirby Edmonds, they launched an initial pilot course. Audrey related, "It was a pretty dynamic learning experience." When she spoke out in the Talking Circle, she was astounded to find that some white people were afraid of her. "It opened my eyes," Audrey told me, to realize that whites were often afraid of saying the wrong thing and appearing racist. At the same time she felt that the white participants really listened to her on topics that had previously felt taboo to discuss.[6]

More than 165 people have attended the series of five weekly sessions, including ICSD staff, government officials, Cornell students and community members. The feedback, according to MRC and which my personal experience corroborates, "has been overwhelmingly positive, with participants reporting renewed and strengthened relationships, deeper understandings of their peers and colleagues, and a willingness to work for social change and racial equality."[7]

Talking Circle #1, April 2009

Twelve people, half white, and half people of color, meet in a circle in the upstairs room of a local church. I feel a mixture of exhilaration and trepidation. Will it feel uncomfortable? Will I be asked to change? Will I make new friends?

One exercise involves talking in small groups about the first time that we were aware of race in our lives. For me, several things spring to mind: In rural Vermont where I grew up, it was almost all white. However, my best friend was Japanese American, and her father had been in internment camps in California in World War II. As a family they had lived in Europe, and they brought a different lifestyle to our small town. To me, she and her family were special and attractive because of their differences. A few years later, when I was ten years old, my family moved to Peru for two years, and I was the one gringa in my elementary school. It took me a while to learn Spanish, and although most people were very kind, I felt deeply the experience of being a minority. Finally, when I was 14 and 15 years old, I went to an experimental summer camp set up to bring together rural Vermonters with inner city kids from New York City. My eyes flew open to entirely different cultures that Hispanic and black kids brought to Vermont. It was the late 60s, and I loved learning to dance to hip music, to listen to conga drums and began to appreciate "black English." Up to that point, I had thought that black people were just like white people, but with a different skin color. Those two summers helped me to understand that there were deep cultural differences that shaped our experiences. But overall, my early experiences of race were positive and enticing.

Now, as I listen to one African-American man tell the story of his first experience of race, I see how profoundly different our experiences were. He was only six, the fastest runner in his school. Every recess he practiced running, and a group of boys raced with him, trying to catch up. It was fun, and he felt powerful. But one day a shocking thing happened. He tripped and fell, and a group surrounded him. One boy started kicking him. Others joined in, chanting "nigger, nigger." Suddenly he realized that what he thought was an everyday running competition was some-thing else entirely—maybe all this time those boys had been chasing him, waiting for this moment. "That experience shaped my life," he tells us. "I realized that ugly attitudes could kick in at any time."

How could I not have known how hard it was for my black colleagues and friends to just live their lives? The inherent racism in our society is something that I could look at intellectually, but hearing this very per-sonal story of blatant discrimination brings me to tears. I realize that as a white person, I could easily ignore (or choose not to see) institutional racism at every turn.

Audrey noted "The Talking Circles are a great way for folks to begin to really explore social justice through sustainability." Audrey spoke slowly and emphatically. "I think this country also has to admit that it has been founded on racism. Historically it has been stolen from the Native peoples of this country, slaves have built it…there has been so much that has been done, and to deny that racism exists does everyone a disservice."

She paused and looked at me directly, her eyes filled with conviction. "In order for us to move forward and to become a truly sustainable country and community, you have to have the hard conversation of race. And if you can provide people with a safe place to have that conversation, it begins to touch each person in their life differently." She described how the Talking Circles help people see through a different lens. "It's like seeing things for the first time, and seeing how privilege really does make a difference."

Talking Circle #2

We are asked to fill out a chart as homework, with statements such as:
Whether I use checks, credit cards or cash, I can count on my skin color not to work against the appearance of financial reliability.

I am never asked to speak for all the people of my racial group.

I can swear, or dress in secondhand clothes, or not answer letters without having people attribute these choices to the bad morals, the poverty or the illiteracy of my race.

We mark responses on a scale of 1–5, with 5 being "always agree" and 1 "never agree." We have each done this as homework, and it is glaringly obvious that our scores will be drastically different depending on what race we represent. Sure enough, all the whites in the room get scores of 100 or more (the top score is 125). All the people of color in the room (four African-Americans and one Asian-American) get scores of less than 50. Marcia Fort, who just last week was honored on the front page of the local paper, shares her score: only 12. She tells of how, here in enlightened Ithaca, she had been followed as she walked around a store, presumably because the storekeeper thought she might steal something. It is shocking how very different our daily experiences are.

I pose the question, "Why is this? Why does Ithaca have such a problem with racism?" I relate that I had spent 15 years in San Francisco, which seems to be much more relaxed around its multicultural identity. Marcia tells a story of a friend from rural Alabama who had grown up in a town with a public swimming pool. Over the pool hung a sign, "for whites only." Now this sign is covered over with burlap, but it still hangs there, a reminder of the message. "Sometimes Ithaca feels to me like that Alabama town," Marcia sighs. "It's as if people are just waiting for a time when they can take off the burlap and get back to the old way of doing things, when they didn't have to be bothered with race, or gay people or whatever."

Kirby launches into an eloquent response to my question. "I've been thinking about this for decades," he says. "As an anthropologist it is fascinating." In his view, Ithaca has a number of "big irritations" going on, that set people on edge. Upstate New York is mostly rural, farming country, with people who could be characterized as being independent and not wanting change. Then Cornell was plunked down in the middle of it, a liberal university that brings "an invasion" of students into town every fall. Kirby assures us that while he has nothing against students, the effect is like being invaded by a foreign body. The city gets more crowded, noisy and hectic while it doubles in size during the school year. Cornell has not always done well in dealing with racism, Kirby says. This leads to a lot of anger. So between the town/gown split, the rural/urban split and the white/people of color split, there is fertile ground for ongoing, tumultuous conflict. In addition, Ithaca has a small percentage of people of color, unlike a big city, so the conflicts tend to be more bruising.

Kirby Edmonds, Training for Change Associates

Kirby Edmonds, a local African-American leader, brings a truly multicultural perspective to Ithaca. He was born in Texas, but has lived in Germany, Kenya and Beirut among other places. He says, "By the time I was a senior in high school, I had learned a lot about how racism works, in the south, in the northeast, in Africa, and in the Middle East. So I was really angry. It was the year Martin Luther King was killed, and Bobby Kennedy." The next year, Kirby enrolled at Cornell, and was soon engaged in a hotbed of student protests.

While at Cornell, he volunteered at what was then only the second drug hotline in the country. He told me, "That's where I launched my career, because we were training people in an area that scared people to death." What started out as an informal movement of black people helping other blacks soon became professionalized. Over the next decade, as insurance companies got involved, the drug counselors became white, with Masters in Social Work degrees. As qualifications and pay rose, many black colleagues were pushed out of their jobs. Kirby reflected, *"Through very direct experience, I've seen how structural racism works, in ways that seem to be outside the consciousness of the individuals who are involved."*

Utilizing that broad awareness, Kirby founded Training for Change Associates in 1981. He has worked with government bodies both large

Kirby Edmonds, TFC Associates.

and small, not-for-profits, colleges, public schools and unions on a wide variety of topics. He is skilled at putting people at ease while they are tackling difficult issues. And he is a key facilitator of Ithaca's Talking Circles on Race and Racism.

He told me that, *"Talking Circles confront people in a fairly safe way when our perspectives are really different. There is just enough agreement to be accepting and there is not an automatic judgment of the difference in perspective, and that lets people discover what its about. But it also shows that other areas of conversation can be so extremely difficult because the judgment about the difference in perspective is so vast, so immediate, so palpable that it's scary. Why go there?"*

One key strategy Kirby suggests for creating more equality is to get in the habit of asking, *"Who is going to be affected by this decision who is not here in the room?"* He added, *"This is a small shift, but it could make a huge difference."* In addition he feels that we are not facing intractable problems, but rather a failure of imagination. *"I think we need to really master the art of correctly naming the problem—and that influences what problem we are trying to solve."*[8]

I also spoke with Marcia Fort, the dynamic executive director of the Greater Ithaca Activities Center (GIAC), a community center that serves predominantly low income people and people of color. Marcia, who moved to Ithaca from Montgomery, Alabama when she was seven years old, has worked in one capacity or another at GIAC since 1984 — for over 25 years. She was honored by the City with the Annual African-American History Month Award for her tireless advocacy for those whose voices are often not heard or listened to.

I've known Marcia since my two sons attended the GIAC after-school program when I was a single mom. But this is the first time I've been in her busy office. I am struck by the wall of photos behind her. This is clearly a woman who cares about people, and who is deeply rooted in her community. She has a powerful, centered presence, and a warm smile.

To Marcia, Ithaca is special because of its activism, its human services and its progressive outlook. But even here, people sometimes challenge outspokenness. "I've actually heard people say 'Maybe you should find someplace else to live, if you don't like it,' not understanding that people who are activists here love this community. We love it enough to talk about what's wrong with it and to offer solutions around how to make it better."

Because there is so much community involvement in Ithaca, it is hard to acknowledge that we have issues of oppression, Marcia mused. "So yes, this is a welcoming community for people who are lesbian, gay and transgender, but that doesn't mean that there's not homophobia here. And that doesn't mean that we don't have to be mindful and fighting for the rights of LGBT [lesbian, gay, bisexual and transgender] community here. And this is a great place to raise children here. But that doesn't mean that we don't have to be mindful that just like other places, there is child abuse here. We have exploitation of children. We have to be mindful, we have to educate and advocate for kids. And yes this is a diverse community in terms of race, culture and ethnically. The school district has 37 different languages here... That doesn't mean we don't have racism here, and that doesn't mean that people who came here as refugees don't have issues. Sometimes that is difficult, we want to gloss over these kinds of things.

"A few years ago I was at a meeting about a store on the Commons where a number of black people had felt discriminated against in that store," she recalled. "And I remember sitting there was a man who was just furious. He said, 'Don't you realize that people just see you as an angry black bitch?' What was interesting, besides his choice of words, was that I wasn't angry. He was angry. You don't have to be angry to fight for rights. It's interesting how people perceive that. His perception was that I was angry because I was speaking out about a store that people felt they had been discriminated in."

Marcia told me that, "On my good days, my feeling is, 'We can make change in this community'.... I really do honestly feel like we can be a model for the rest of the country. We have all that it takes here, and we're doing some of those things to deal with [the situation]. Not to eradicate racism, not to eradicate classism, that's a whole larger thing, but within our community we can acknowledge that it exists, and we can put structures in place that help people that are experiencing racism, that are experiencing anti-Semitism, that are experiencing classism and homophobia, to get the kind of support and validation and assistance [they need], and to call attention to it."

She reflected, "Sometimes it's intentional, the kind of oppression and intimidation that happens. And sometimes it isn't. And sometimes when you point it out and bring it to someone's attention, that's when change can happen. And particularly if you're saying, 'This is the action that occurred, this is the impact, this is the kind of thing we can do to make a difference.'"[9]

For Marcia, like Audrey and Kirby, the next step is to introduce Talking Circles into the school system. The format would need some changes, she acknowledged, but it could make an enormous difference. And the time that is offset by working it into the school day would be more than made up for by the lack of ugly incidents that result in fights, suspensions and emotional upheaval. So far, the school administration has not shown an interest in introducing this model, but there is hope that may change.

Equity Report Card

Another creative effort to address prejudice is underway by the Village at Ithaca, a small nonprofit organization which is working closely with the Ithaca City School District. The Village at Ithaca has a byline that builds on an African proverb: "It takes an entire village to raise, affirm and educate a child." Their goal is to ensure that a stated goal of the school district ("Eliminating race, class and disability as predictors of success in the Ithaca City School District") gets actualized.

In 2006, the Village at Ithaca and the ICSD undertook a major effort to create a "First Annual Equity Report Card: Holding Ourselves Accountable." The report card included 16 data sets showing performance or participation by race and class in areas such as mathematics, sports, advanced placement courses and staffing levels.[10] It created a benchmark for measuring progress on equity goals, and did so in a transparent way that also suggested possible solutions and invited community participation.

To no one's great surprise, the first Equity Report Card did show gaps by race and economic status. One glaring example was that while 18% of ICSD students were African-American, Latino or Native American, and 10% were Asian for a total of 28%, only 6% of their teachers were people of color. Another example was that students from low income families as well as African-American, Latino and Native American students were not proportionately represented in the more rigorous advanced placement courses.

When the second Annual Equity Report Card was issued in the spring of 2008, Jeff Furman, a local activist and philanthropist who worked on it said in his statement, "We should be pleased that there has been improvement in many areas in this past year. This is encouraging. I also feel encouraged by the growth of policies and practices that show promise for the future." After listing many of the improvements made, Furman continued, "However, there is no getting away from feeling impatient. More than ever, we need both the district and the community to work together. We need our impatience and frustration and we need to be thankful for the small steps. We need to be dissatisfied and we need to be hopeful, particularly in the area of graduation and suspension rates for students of color."[11] It is clear that while progress is being made, it is often painfully slow. However even having the Equity Report Card is a huge step, and a worthwhile achievement that other communities would do well to follow.

School Board Elections: May 2009

The Ithaca City School Board has traditionally been rather conservative — a surprise to me in this progressive community. At the most recent election, three candidates ran unopposed. Two of them were African-American men who have a long history of activism on community issues and education. Eldred Harris is a Cornell-educated lawyer who among other things was a former Director of the Village at Ithaca. Sean Eversley-Bradwell just completed his Ph.D. at Cornell and is a very talented and popular professor in the Center for the Study of Culture, Race and Ethnicity at Ithaca College. He also had the experience of being a local social studies teacher and a member of the Board of the Village at Ithaca.

Jeff Klaus, a fellow professor at Ithaca College, wrote in an e-mail, "Both Sean and Eldred are African American and have been deeply involved in addressing issues of race/racism, diversity, equity, and excellence in Ithaca education for many years. They are very smart, committed, insightful, and analytical, and they are skilled, personable, strong and persuasive communicators. By voting for them we will be saying something important about our community... I encourage you to view voting for them tomorrow as an act of community responsibility, pride and celebration. If Ithaca is ever to come close to living up to our supposedly 'enlightened' status, it will be because we saw fit to 'build' a school board upon which people such as these men are valued members and leaders."[12]

While voting in these two men was a very important step, the School Board has a ways to go to truly represent its constituency, noted outgoing Board member Deborah O'Connor who served for six years. The incoming Board of nine people has only one woman, and has not had any Asian-Americans during her tenure.[13] When it comes to being truly representative, there is always room for improvement.

In conclusion, while Ithaca is known for its progressive views, there seems to be a cultural blind spot for whites around the daily discrimination that people of color experience in this city. Through ongoing efforts, such as the Talking Circles on Race, the Equity Report Card and the work of community leaders like Marcia Fort, Kirby Edmonds and Audrey Cooper to name a few, more people are learning how to effectively bridge racial divides and to begin to address persistent discrimination. But, we as a community have a long way to go!

Ithaca Is Gorges

For in the end, we will conserve only what we love. We will love only what we understand. We will understand only what we are taught.

BABA DIOUM

Clean and abundant water is now the highest priority for human survival. The natural world is the distributor of water, according to the great systems that control our earth and its climate. It belongs to no one person, corporation or nation. Privatization and pollution of water are fundamental violations of our human rights and the rights of the natural world. The balance of life is predicated on sharing the Earth's natural resources.

HAUDENOSAUNEE ENVIRONMENTAL TASK FORCE

It was a day in early autumn — sunny but cool — and my friend Rachael and I decided to go on a bike ride to one of my favorite places in the world. Robert Treman State Park is only a half hour bike ride from our homes at EcoVillage, and after a few miles on a busy state highway, we emerged onto rural roads that glide up and down hills, past trailer parks and farm fields. The vistas were awesome: my eyes traveled from the newly mown golden hayfields in the foreground to gently rolling hills lined by dark green forests, and onward to the blue mountains beyond. We paused on a hilltop to drink it in. Soon we were in the park itself, and we glided past the entry gate — no need to pay a fee since we were on bikes — and past the mill where farmers in centuries past used to bring their grain to be milled into flour. After parking our bikes, we hiked down the path along the rushing brook that has carved the spectacularly beautiful

Enfield Gorge over thousands of years. We rested on an arching stone bridge and admired the view below. The water is clear and sparkling as it hurtles over a six-foot drop into an eddying pool, then hurries into a roiling, narrow channel before leaping over a 12-foot waterfall. Every time I visit this place, it fills me with intense energy as well as a deep upwelling sense of peaceful connection. I am in awe of the beauty of the natural world that is so abundant here. After living for 15 years in drought-parched California, I see so much pure, fresh water as an amazing blessing. And this is just the beginning of the 2.5 mile hike, which includes dozens of small waterfalls as well as the remarkable Lucifer Falls, a stunning 115 feet high.

Lucifer Falls at Treman State Park.

It is no mistake that one of the favorite bumperstickers in this area proclaims, "Ithaca is Gorges." Lucifer Falls is just one of over a hundred waterfalls and gorges within ten miles of downtown Ithaca. These spectacular gorges were created when ice-age glaciers retreated, forming the long, narrow fingers of the Finger Lakes region. As the glaciers scoured out the deep lakes, the tributary streams were left as hanging valleys far above. Over thousands of years, these streams carved out shale and sandstone layers into deep gorges. Fortunately, most of these gorges are preserved as state parks or through local conservation easements. Many of them have well-kept trails which make them accessible to the thousands of visitors who enjoy them annually.

Water is everywhere here, and yet there are still major challenges this region faces with this essential resource. To the north, the Great Lakes are joined together to form the largest body of fresh water in the world, comprising one fifth of the total available fresh water on the planet. They are under increasing pressure of privatization by large corporations who want to secure a part of this natural wealth. And even closer to home, there are immediate threats to Cayuga Lake, the longest of the Finger Lakes, and its tributary streams. The City of Ithaca perches on the southern end of the lake, overlooking a panoramic view of this water.

Energy Boom, Water Quality Bust?

In a time of rapidly rising energy costs, our region has been discovered as a rich source of natural gas, trapped in the Marcellus Shale formation. This is a geological formation 5,000 to 8,000 feet below the surface that runs from central New York state southwest through central Pennsylvania into northwestern West Virginia and southeastern Ohio. It is estimated to contain between 1.9 trillion to 500 trillion cubic feet of natural gas.[1] Even if, as geologists note, only 10% of that gas is recoverable (50 billion cubic feet) that would be enough to supply the entire United States for about two years and have a wellhead value of about one trillion dollars!

The pressure to exploit this resource is enormous, particularly in an economically depressed area such as upstate New York. As a result, according to citizen action group Shaleshock which reviewed public records in March 2009, a shocking 38% of the total land area in Tompkins County is currently leased to oil and gas companies. This varies from a low of 12% of the land in the Town of Ithaca, to 49% of the land next door in the Town of Enfield.[2] Many of the landowners had no idea what future problems they might face when signing over their mineral rights for as little as $100 an acre. As I write this in the summer of 2010, people are waiting while the New York State Department of Environmental Conservation (DEC) decides what kinds of well-drilling regulations to put in place. The New York state legislature is also debating placing a moratorium on the controversial hydro-fracking method of drilling until the EPA finishes a study of its environmental effects.

I've now seen two well-researched presentations about the effects of mining natural gas using the relatively new hydro-fracking process, in which chemically-laced water is forced under high pressure deep into the ground into horizontal wells, fracturing the shale. The effects are appalling! First of all, companies use enormous amounts of fresh water, which they can pump out of public waterways. This is trucked into the well sites, and the heavily polluted water is trucked out for treatment or left in pools of filthy mud on the site. If the pools overflow or if the drilling wells leak, it is easy for groundwater to be contaminated.

In Pennsylvania, which has many natural gas wells and fewer regulations than New York, it is not uncommon to find private water wells that have been heavily contaminated. The Penn State Cooperative Extension estimates that about 8% of private wells have experienced mild to severe impacts.[3] And this was before the advent of horizontal hydro-fracking, which generates 100 times more waste fluid than older, vertical wells! In Texas and other parts of the western US where natural gas drilling is common, many chemicals including carcinogens, neurotoxins and endocrine disrupters have been found. However, the gas companies refuse to divulge their proprietary blend of chemicals, so it is only when contamination of local water sources has occurred that the chemicals can be identified. In New York state, the burden of proving contamination is left to .

the landowner, even though the horizontal well may extend into the rock a mile from the wellhead and contaminate plumes of groundwater that travel downhill. It is also not uncommon for there to be major explosions and fires at the drilling sites. Meanwhile, the local municipalities are often left holding the bills for the emergency services needed and roads damaged by heavy equipment and truck traffic.

Although it can seem like a boon for local economies, with landowners making royalties of 12% or more, the overall region may suffer tremendously. Much of the revenue stream in Tompkins County is generated through tourism, agriculture and the wine industry. Having noisy drilling rigs operating 24 hours a day, seven days a week is hardly conducive to enjoying the scenery or eating local foods grown with water that may be laced with chemicals.

Citizen Activism

It may seem there is little that anyone can do to stop the mad rush for selling out the natural resources of the Finger Lakes for short term profit. The gas companies signed leases with individuals for privately owned land, and many landowners did so before the new horizontal drilling techniques had been established. Municipalities are curtailed by the state, which allows little leeway for them to control gas drilling. On the other hand there are a variety of groups that have sprung up to inform the public.

One is the Community Science Institute, a nonprofit organization located in Ithaca which operates a state-certified water quality testing laboratory. The lab urges people close to a proposed gas well to do a comprehensive set of water quality tests of private wells, springs, ponds and streams prior to drilling, as well as during and after the drilling, and for at least ten years after the well has been plugged and abandoned. Landowners will then have data to challenge oil and gas companies in court if their water has been contaminated.

Another group is Shaleshock Citizens Action Coalition (SCAC),[4] which has put on educational programs for concerned citizens and local government officials. They emphasize coalition building between those who have signed leases and those who have not—not an easy alliance when emotions run so high, but a necessary and practical step in an area in which so many have signed on. In a presentation to the Ithaca Town Board, Shaleshock estimated that over a 20 year extraction period, natural gas wells in this area would bring in $22 billion dollars. However, over the same amount of time, tourism, agriculture, winery, hunting and fishing would bring in $392 billion dollars.[5] Therefore, to the extent that natural gas drilling disrupts the usual revenue stream (which seems quite likely), gas drilling is a very poor choice for the region as a whole.

Building a Movement

Shaleshock and other groups have grown dramatically, elevating a little known issue to something that is on everyone's mind, and that has begun to draw national attention, including a National Public Radio show on the topic. Local government officials got involved and held hearings for people from Tompkins County to voice their opinions. On the night of November 19, 2009, about 1,000 people gathered at the State Theater for a hearing that lasted almost four hours. Usually government hearings are rather dry affairs. This one was totally different. Starting with highly articulate local political leaders and moving on to the public, each person who spoke raised objections to the proposed regulations. While the rationale of different speakers overlapped, many different perspectives were shared—from people with an expertise in watershed management, to local farmers to town officials worried about containing the fracking waste or paying for the damage of heavy truck traffic on country roads. We were united in a strong, angry outcry to the New York State Department of Environmental Conservation (DEC).

Just two weeks later, the State Theater was packed to the gills again. This time it was for a concert called Life is Water, a benefit for Shaleshock. Some of the best local bands played and people danced in the aisles. Gay Nicholson from Sustainable Tompkins introduced the Marcellus Challenge. Acknowledging that we are all still dependent on fossil fuels, including natural gas, as one of our main energy sources, the Marcellus Challenge is a simple online pledge form that allows us to pool and quantify our collective efforts to save energy and phase out fossil fuels. Rather than simply saying, "not in my backyard," the pledge mobilizes people to save energy in very practical ways, from doing a home energy audit to washing clothes in cold water. It also allows ST to track the impact of how much energy people pledge to save.

Meanwhile, the Green Guerrillas competed in a national competition to win prize money for making a documentary about the effects of hydro-fracking. These young people, who are considered at risk because they come from highly vulnerable communities, won finalist status, after mobilizing thousands of votes from the Ithaca area. The Green Guerrillas form a vital link between the predominately white environmental movement and the people of color who often bear the worst brunt of environmental effects — whether from Hurricane Katrina, the poisoning of Native American land through uranium mining or elevated asthma rates caused by air pollution in poor, urban neighborhoods.

As I write this in June 2010, we are all waiting with baited breath to find out whether New York Governor David Paterson will take action to throw out the draft Supplemental Generic Environmental Impact Statement and start over, as many people have recommended. If life is truly water, and we pollute the lifeblood of the Finger Lakes, we will be going down an irrevocable path that has the possibility of poisoning the health and beauty of our home and all the life-forms that live here.

I can't help but think about some prestigious visitors, the Thirteen Indigenous Grandmothers, who visited Ithaca for a few days not long ago. These women, from many different countries and native traditions from all over the world, came together to fulfill a prophecy and usher in a new generation of global healing. They travel widely. At a major forum at Cornell, attended by thousands of people, one of the grandmothers of Mayan descent, Flordemayo, burst into tears as she implored "Take care of the water! Protect the seeds!" Her words haunt me as I find out more about the dangers to our water supply.

Water = Blue Gold

*Pure water is an increasingly precious commodity, and it is needed by
every living thing on earth. Though the planet's surface is 71% water, less
than 3% of this is fresh water. Already our growing population of more
than 6.7 billion people overtaxes the planet's supply of accessible fresh
water, and the UN projects that by 2025 there will be 2.8 billion people
who will face water stress or scarcity. Of all the water on Earth, only a
fraction of 1% is available for drinking, irrigation and industrial use. Of
that, 10% is consumed worldwide for household use, agriculture claims
70%, and industry uses 20%.[6]*

*There are many ways to conserve water, including using low flow
fixtures in homes, drip irrigation on farms and reusing water in industrial
processes. But perhaps the most important lesson is to change our values
and habits and begin to treat water like the precious resource that it is.*

A Watershed Approach

A watershed is the land surrounding a body of water, funneling rain-
fall and runoff into that water. The lowest point in a watershed in-
herits the qualities of all the waters that flow into it, including any
pollution or sediments that it carries. But a watershed encompasses
more than the physical properties of water flowing downhill. It is
also very affected by the human activities that take place within its
boundaries. "In figuring out how a watershed works, land use and
attitudes towards the Cayuga Lake watershed on the part of those
who live, work and play in it are as important as the wetlands, ponds
and streams themselves," explains a publication by the Cayuga Lake
Watershed Network.[7]

Cayuga Lake is part of a very large watershed, called the Oswego River Basin, which handles runoff from all of the Finger Lakes
watersheds in addition to some rivers. The water drains north into
the Seneca River, which flows into the Oswego River, which in turn
goes into Lake Ontario, then travels through the St. Lawrence River
out to the Atlantic. The Cayuga Lake Watershed covers 800 square

miles of land draining into Cayuga Lake and encompasses 49 villages, towns and cities in seven counties. More than 140,000 people live and work in this area. Agriculture, especially livestock and field crops, covers about one third of the watershed, while forests cover another third. The remaining third is a mix of residential, commercial, industrial and public lands. Overall the watershed has beautiful and productive land, rich with wildlife and striking scenery.

Taking care of this water is the responsibility of everyone. To date, Cayuga Lake is relatively healthy, although it does have some water quality issues, including sediments from erosion, some phosphorus and coliform pollution from animal wastes and sewage treatment, as well as some heavy metal contamination and agricultural chemicals. The biggest source of pollution is not a specific identifiable point such as a factory or sewage treatment plant, but rather from nonpoint sources, such as runoff from roads, parking lots, construction sites, huge dairy farms and plowed fields. Because it is harder to pinpoint the source of pollution, it is harder to control and more threatening to water quality. To control nonpoint source pollution, everyone needs to be involved.

One grassroots nonprofit organization that has been key in educating the public and taking leadership on important watershed issues is the Cayuga Lake Watershed Network.[8] Founded in 1998 by concerned citizens, it has accomplished a lot in a short period of time, from mobilizing 400 volunteers a year to help monitor water quality, sponsoring LakeFest (an annual informative and fun celebration of the lake) and conducting seminars about everything from invasive zebra mussels to creating rain gardens (which control runoff through native plantings). It published "Smart Steps for Clean Water," a 24 page consumer friendly publication that eloquently yet simply explains the connection between water and the everyday choices of how we live, including home energy, lawn care, transportation and recreation. It encourages readers to take the online Pledge for Clean Water, as a way to help quantify community participation.[9]

One of the most significant achievements has been the Network's role in the completion of the Cayuga Lake Watershed Protection Plan and partnership with the Cayuga Lake Intermunicipal

Organization (IO), a consortium of municipalities in the watershed. As the IO worked to create a watershed plan, the Network helped to keep the public informed about the process and hosted public meetings and collected comments. It was a great model for how to create a partnership between local government, an advocacy group and concerned citizens.

The next step will be to implement this significant plan. Graduate students at Cornell University are taking one important step by collaborating with the Network to develop a watershed and lake report card that identifies key indicators of health. Meanwhile the Tompkins County Water Resources Council (WRC) and Cornell University staff and faculty developed a comprehensive monitoring plan for the southern end of the lake.

All of these efforts—from citizens' action groups to local government bodies—are working to protect a common legacy. As the Cayuga Lake Watershed Network states, "The lake, streams, and hidden ground water of the Cayuga Lake region are natural treasures for us to protect and enjoy. We cannot afford to wait for a disaster before we act."[10]

Wells College students study Cayuga Lake from the Floating Classroom.

The Floating Classroom

Tiohero Tours' M/V Haendel *is a 45-foot tour boat that is well equipped for water monitoring and other ecological studies. The boat itself is a model of minimizing impact on the lake. It uses biodiesel fuel and a biodegradable paint on the bottom, rather than the traditional toxic copper-based bottom paint that is in widespread use.*

Tiohero Tours offers the Floating Classroom, a program launched in 2002, to provide fun, hands-on experiences for 1,200 students a year. Fifth to ninth graders become citizen scientists, monitoring

the health of the lake by taking water samples and observing the plant
and animal communities in the water.

This Land Is Your Land, This Land Is My Land

Part of the draw of the Cayuga Lake Watershed is not only its sparkling water, but also its landscape of abundantly forested hills and
valleys. Among the 28 parks listed in Tompkins County, four are
state parks that are well-known tourist attractions with their spectacular gorges and waterfalls. The surrounding county includes
41,000 acres of protected natural lands, much of which is available
to the public for hiking, mountain biking and outdoor recreation.
Thirteen percent of county land is now protected natural areas and
forests, and there are plans to increase this to 20% over time.

In Tompkins County, considerable thought has been put into
how to best conserve natural resources while promoting economic
development and how to balance the variety of needs for land use.
After years of study, in 2004 the county planning department produced a comprehensive plan, an impressive study that looked at the
interlocking pieces of housing, transportation and jobs; the environment, neighborhoods and communities. The plan also created
a positive vision of what Tompkins County can become in 20 years.
The focus was very much on creating a vibrant and sustainable
future, in all senses of the word. In the natural areas section, the
overarching principle of the plan is "Natural features that define our
community, and form the foundation of our local and regional ecological systems, should be preserved and enhanced."[11]

One recent innovative land use has been to designate 550 acres
of county-owned forest for Forest Stewardship Council (FSC) certification, allowing the county to sustainably harvest wood. Katie
Borgella, principal planner for the county, has been instrumental
in pushing for the certification, as well as the management plan to
support that certification. "The overarching purpose of the plan
is to provide for the sustainable management for the county forest lands," she said. "But really also to provide a model available for

public review and sharing that information with the public." Timber harvest will provide some income while also serving as a forest management model for other municipalities and private landowners who are thinking green.[12]

On an even larger scale, the Finger Lakes Land Trust (FLLT) is moving closer to completion of a linked network of some 50,000 acres of conserved land around the City of Ithaca. Called the Emerald Necklace Greenbelt Project, it will link nature preserves, designating wildlife areas for quiet recreation and environmental protection. It follows the course of the Finger Lakes Trail, a popular hiking trail. One of the project's recent acquisitions includes frontage along Six Mile Creek, which supplies drinking water to Ithaca and is excellent for bird-watching. Since 1989, FLLT has overseen the protection of 8,800 acres from development by establishing preserves or the purchase of development rights.[13]

Magic in the Woods

It is mid-afternoon, 90°F and sultry. I have just completed a project (writing a book proposal for my publisher) that I had put off for six months, and I reward myself by going for a long walk. As I enter the woods, which is owned by Cornell Plantations and borders our land, I am struck by the blessed coolness on my skin, the chittering of a squirrel and the overall silence. Light filters gently down through the maple and hickory leaves, and I feel in sacred space. As I walk softly on the narrow dirt path, I notice a flash of brilliant, heart-stopping red. My eyes pick out a pileated woodpecker with bright red crest, black wings and white markings, winging its way in front of me. I hold my breath until it disappears. Then, surprise! Another pileated woodpecker appears, following the other one. What a treat...it is only the third time in my life that I have ever seen one of these large, colorful birds. They seem mythical to me, like messengers from the universe, telling me I am on the right path. Walking on, filled with wonder, I watch the two flit through the trees, first one, then the other, guiding my way forward. Then they disappear.

The path is soft and dusty and I continue on, filled with gladness, noticing small purple wood violets by the path. Looking up, I spot white blossoms on a tree, and I leave the path to investigate the clean, crisp dogwood flowers. But what is that? To my side, in a tall dead tree, there is a loud humming noise. Could it be a bee hive—a "honey tree," as Pooh Bear would have said? I look closely for any sign of bees. The noise seems to get louder until the air is thrumming with vibration, but there is no sign of bees. As I watch intently, suddenly the head of mama pileated woodpecker pops out of a large hole. It dawns on me in a flash...that humming sound is her babies! She cocks her red head, looks around and flies away. Soon the humming stops...her babies know better than to attract attention while she is gone.

I make my way back onto the path, and then I see her again. She has landed on a dead tree, cast horizontally over a deep gully. From just 20 feet away, I watch mesmerized as she pecks at the bark. Throwing her whole body into the task, she pecks at the wood fiercely. I wonder, how do woodpecker brains survive the crashing impact of each peck? But she is thinking clearly. Each peck brings her closer to drilling through a slab of bark, and every few moments she stops and pries at the bark in a sideways motion. To my astonishment, she is able to systematically peel off two-foot-long swaths of bark with just a few minutes of work. Then she gorges herself on grubs before starting on the next piece. I watch for 20 minutes or more; then feeling deeply satisfied, I walk back home, stepping softly, softly on the dusty path, careful not to disturb her.

—Journal, June 1, 2007

Cornell Plantations

Cornell University is another major landowner that also values careful stewardship of natural resources. While the University owns over 14,000 acres of land within 20 miles of campus, Cornell Plantations manages about one third of it as biologically diverse ecosystems, including an arboretum, botanical garden and extensive natural areas many of which are open to the public. These gorges, bogs, glens, meadows, old-growth forests and wildflower preserves represent the full range of ecological habitats found in the Finger Lakes region. They are preserved and enhanced both for scientific research and for education of and enjoyment by the general public. Together the holdings represent one of the five largest systems of natural areas associated with public gardens in North America.

"The long-term preservation of our natural heritage requires a unique combination of ever-evolving strategies," said Todd Bittner, Cornell Plantations natural areas director. "Testing new tools and techniques, and sharing our successes and failures with the conservation community, provides an invaluable contribution to the science of conservation." From nurturing and reintroducing rare species, to involving 400 third grade students in botany through an annual Wildflower Explorations program, to contributing to conservation research, the plantations manage to involve thousands of students, faculty and Ithaca residents in shared appreciation and stewardship of the natural world.

The scientific community has been able to use the extensive natural areas to study pressing conservation issues, such as how to best control invasive species or create native landscaping alternatives. One example is a 3,000 square foot demonstration area converted from lawn to native low-growing plants. In addition, natural areas staff recently completed a comprehensive inventory to map the age and vegetation types of Cornell's preserves. They found 32 discrete ecological community types, which will serve as a valuable baseline for future research to evaluate ecosystem changes.

Cornell has a long-term goal of achieving carbon neutrality. It is estimated that Plantations' natural areas absorb enough carbon dioxide to offset about 15% of the carbon emissions generated by faculty and staff commuting to work each year.[14]

Cayuga Waterfront Trail

Closer in to the urban core of Ithaca, the Cayuga Waterfront Trail represents an unusual alliance between the Chamber of Commerce and the City of Ithaca. Rick Manning, a local landscape architect, has been the key leader of initiating the project and keeping it going, despite the rough spots. The trail is a proposed six-mile bike and pedestrian route which will connect many of Ithaca's most popular waterfront destinations, from Cass Park on Cayuga Lake's west shore, down to the West End business district, and on up the east shore to the Ithaca Farmer's Market, Stewart Park and the Tompkins County Visitor's Center. The first phase of the trail, a two-mile loop in Cass Park, was completed in 2003 and is heavily used by walkers, joggers, cyclists, in-line skaters, families with strollers and dog owners.

Phase Three of the Waterfront Trail is planned to finish construction in 2010. This will make it easy for people to get around the waterfront by foot or bicycle, something that many of us have wanted for a long time. The few times I have tried this route on my bike, without a trail, it has involved bumping over railroad tracks and passing abandoned lots with broken glass…not so much fun.

Unfortunately Phase Two of the Waterfront Trail has been a lightning rod for controversy. After six years of debate generated by businesses who did not want the trail to take over a 16 foot sliver of their property, the New York State Department of Transportation stepped in to help acquire the properties by eminent domain. Although the affected businesses are far from happy about it, it looks as if the plans will move forward, with the resounding support of Ithaca's Common Council.

As an avid cyclist myself, I have greatly enjoyed dedicated bike and pedestrian trails in other cities, from Boulder, Colorado to Burlington, Vermont, and in other countries from Toronto, Canada to Copenhagen, Denmark. I love gliding along these trails, enjoying sunshine and greeting the locals who push strollers, zoom by on in-line skates or cruise with fellow cyclists. When these trails pass through urban districts, as Ithaca's trail will, they invariably generate lively foot traffic for local businesses. I can't wait to ride my bike down to the Ithaca Farmer's Market, along a waterfront trail.

Forest City

Ithaca has a history of valuing its trees. In fact, it has long been known as Forest City, according to the City of Ithaca website:

Carol Kammen, a noted Ithaca historian, says Forest City was "one of about 56 now defunct neighborhood post offices." In a quote from *Ithaca and Its Resources*...there is a reference to a train ride from Owego. "As the cars reach the brow of the hill the traveler catches a bird's-eye view of Ithaca and the Cayuga Lake.... Then, as the train moves forward and continues its journey around the hillside another...view is presented.... On the level plain, a half mile below, is seen Ithaca, almost concealed by the tops of trees by which its every street is lined, and to the superabundance of which it is indebted for the title of 'Forest City.'"...

This century-old description of Ithaca holds true today as the traveler enters Ithaca from atop any of its three hills. The traveler sees a canopy of trees looking very much like a natural forest, broken only by its tallest buildings. Arriving downtown, the traveler sees tree-lined streets even in the central business district. Many of Ithaca's trees are large and mature trees and many are young and newly planted. The traveler will see an amazing diversity of tree species ranging from sugar maples to Amur cork trees, from horsechestnuts to Japanese zelkovas. Ithaca's urban forest is alive and well and is there for everyone's enjoyment![15]

At Green Energy at Work: Urban Forestry Tools, Innovations and Challenges, a 2008 statewide forestry conference held at Cornell, Andy Hillman, City Forester of Ithaca, gave a tour of downtown Ithaca, showing off disease-resistant elms, oaks and rubber trees. "Here in Ithaca we can actually quantify the benefits of our urban natural resource management," he noted. "Through our system we can tell that street trees in Ithaca alone are providing the city with $1 million in various ecosystem services."[16]

Well-designed urban forests have multiple benefits. They provide shade and help to cool buildings and parking areas, saving energy. They mitigate the *urban heat island effect* in which urban areas, which are heavily paved, absorb far more heat than surrounding areas. "It could be 90 degrees in town, but 120 if you're standing in the middle of a K-Mart parking lot," Hillman explained. Trees help to cool things down. They also absorb and help to clean rainwater, reduce polluted runoff into local streams and lakes, and provide serenity and beauty to their surroundings.

Hillman also showed conference attendees a parking lot near the flood control channel, which he said people come from all over the world to view. A graduate student of Cornell Horticulture Professor Nina Bassuk helped to discover CU Structural Soil™. This soil allows roots to grow through the soil, while providing enough structural stability for heavy use, such as parked cars. The demonstration lot has CU Structural Soil™, with porous asphalt on top. "We then planted hybrid Elm trees," said Hillman. "Now that they've grown, their roots have plenty of space to expand. The end result is we don't have to give up parking spots for trees and all the water from a rain storm gets stored there as well."[17]

It is interesting to note that in both Cornell Plantations and Ithaca's Community Forest, there are important roles for members of the public to be involved. There is too much work to be done to rely only on a small number of paid staff. Citizen scientists and involved volunteers are a crucial part of carefully maintaining the natural areas.

Preserving Our Natural Legacy

As we've seen in this chapter, Ithaca is blessed with gorgeous natural areas, forests, waterfalls and a deep, glacially-carved lake. Its rich soils and sparkling waters draw farmers and tourists alike. Its spectacular natural heritage is matched with a deep ethic of stewardship, evidenced by vast tracts of land conserved as parks and conservation easements, many of them tied together through the Emerald Necklace. Its waterways are increasingly valued as irreplaceable resources.

There is a truly remarkable degree of collaboration among many entities that has made this possible. State, county, town and city governments have cooperated with academia and citizen advocacy groups to not only preserve the land but also safeguard water quality. All of these groups have worked together to educate and engage the public to be actively involved as stewards of this special place.

Recent additions such as the Cayuga Waterfront Trail build in a delightful element of recreational enjoyment, while boosting local businesses. And the County's Comprehensive Plan offers a clear direction for creating an even greener, more sustainable future.

While this robust, multi-party consensus on the ethic of stewardship is very solid, it can be thrown off balance by major forces seeking to exploit natural resources for profit. Without proper limits in place, natural gas drilling in this region could potentially wreak havoc with both land and water resources. As with many other areas in this book, the dynamic balance between economic, ecological, social and spiritual aspects of sustainability is ever changing. In a society which has valued economic growth at enormous cost to social, ecological and spiritual health, it will take enormous effort to safeguard our resources for future generations of all species.

11

Turning Waste into Gold

If it can't be reduced, reused, repaired, rebuilt, refurbished, refinished, resold, recycled or composted, then it should be restricted, redesigned or removed from production.

BERKELEY, CALIFORNIA, ZERO WASTE RESOLUTION

In fact, if we radically reorient our world view, we can live in a world of little or no waste. Biomimicry—following the designs of nature and the paths of indigenous peoples—can create a nearly waste-free economy. In an ideal world, as in nature, there would be no wastes, only re-purposed resources.

TOM SHELLEY, "WASTING IN THE ENERGY DESCENT:
AN OUTLINE FOR THE FUTURE"

An Integrated Approach to Waste at EcoVillage

It was a day for household chores. I gathered up trash, recycling and my nifty metal compost container (with a carbon-filter lid to reduce odors) and put them in one of the carts we use for hauling loads around our pedestrian neighborhood. Everyone's gardens were blooming with mid-summer flowers, and the bees were humming, especially around the lavender and the bright orange trumpet vines. One of my neighbors had some very healthy sweet potato vines growing in a long mound in her front yard. It was a lovely day, and I stopped and chatted with a couple of friends on my way to the community compost bins. I noticed that there was some *black gold*, or finished compost, waiting to be used. I'd have to come back with a wheelbarrow and get some to enrich my garden. Meanwhile I dumped my contribution of kitchen scraps into the wire mesh enclosed bin and placed brown leaves on top, to help make the compost cook at a high temperature. We have an agreement with the Town of Ithaca to dump leaves here in the fall. It keeps the leaves out of the landfill and offers us a much-needed brown material to mix with the kitchen scraps. As a community we are able to compost all of our kitchen waste (except for meat scraps), and I feel good that it goes right back to our gardens to start the cycle of growing food once again.

The recycling shed was next. Our community is able to recycle cardboard and paper in one set of bins, and glass, metal and most kinds of plastic containers in another set. Bicycles hang on pegs on the wall, and there is a big container for scrap materials that can be used by the Sciencenter, a local science museum that collects unusual materials with which children can build projects. There is a place for Styrofoam packing material, which will be reused by a local packing store, a place for used batteries to be sent back to the factory, a place for bottles with refundable deposits that will be donated to a local charity and even a place for used sneakers, which will be sent back to the Nike factory for making into outdoor athletic fields and playground surfacing. It is very convenient to have one stop recycling!

Then came the dumpster. I'm glad that I only have to take out half a grocery bag of trash every other week, since I'm able to compost and recycle most things. Our community of 60 households uses a common dumpster that is only a quarter of what other US housing developments of this size use. Still, I would like to cut down further.

On my way back from the recycling shed, I decided to visit the reuse room—a closet in the Common House that serves as the repository for donated clothes, shoes and toys. I was delighted to find a fairly new pair of women's hiking boots in my size. I reminded myself to bring up the jeans I've decided to give away, so that someone else can use them.

As I was standing on the Common House porch, I noticed a big basket from West Haven Farm, one of our two on-site organic farms. A label on it proclaimed, "Enjoy!" Inside I found some edible pod peas leftover from the harvest. I happily scooped them up and sampled one for good measure. They were a little limp from being in the sun for the day, but they tasted like summer and my mouth felt green and lush just biting into one. Still munching, I returned my cart to the shed.

Instead of feeling like this trip was a chore, I enjoyed visiting with friends, admiring lush gardens and finding some free hiking boots, all while feeding the earth my leftover scraps and reusing or recycling as much as I could. While living in a community like ours at EcoVillage can make all of this much easier, any of these systems could be set up between a group of neighbors in an apartment building or on a city block.

Garbage Capital

In contrast to treating waste as a resource as described above, our society usually treats waste as a problem. To make it go away, we truck it to mega landfills. One of these is only 40 miles away from Ithaca. Every day 9,000 tons of garbage is trucked into Seneca Meadows Landfill in the town of Seneca Falls (at the northern tip of Cayuga Lake) and ten miles away to the Ontario County Landfill in Stanley, New York. This garbage comes from all over New England, New Jersey and Pennsylvania. It also comes from New York City and over forty New York counties and Canada. "Our beautiful region has become the garbage capital of New York State," bemoans the Finger Lakes Zero Waste Coalition

In addition to the hundreds of 18 wheel trucks that haul trash through the towns (and tear up the roads) and the noxious smell of the landfill, there are also plans afoot to build a waste-to-liquid-fuel gasification pilot plant in Ontario County Landfill. If built, it would be the first commercial facility of its kind in the US, here in the Finger Lakes. It is a testament to how much our society hates waste and hides it away, that I had never even heard of these landfills or the gasification plant until reading information from the Zero Waste Coalition.[1]

Waste Not, Want Not

US citizens generate enormous amounts of trash—4.6 pounds a day per person—much of which could be reused or recycled. Although the US represents only 5% of the world's population, we generate 40% of its waste. In 2006, Americans generated 251 million tons of trash, not including industrial, construction or hazardous waste.

The good news is that our national recycling and composting rates have risen substantially in the last few years. In 2002 the US recycled less than one quarter of its municipal waste. In 2006, we recycled or composted almost one third, or 82 million tons. This is the energy equivalent of saving more than 10 billion tons of gasoline. It brings the trash thrown out down to about three pounds per person a day—although this is still more than what was thrown out in 1960, before recycling programs were set up.[2]

Tompkins County's Ambitious Goals

Luckily, Tompkins County has a different approach than nearby Ontario County. Although it still exports its trash to the Seneca Meadows Landfill, it is taking active steps to greatly reduce the amount that gets dumped. Under the guidance of the Tompkins County Solid Waste Management Division (TCSWMD), there is a countywide commitment to reduce waste by 75% by the year 2015. By the end of 2009, Barbara Eckstrom, TCSWMD manager, told county legislators that Tompkins County has reduced waste by 59% compared to 1992 levels. At a time when national levels of waste output have crept up year by year, this is a startling achievement and one that has taken a lot of strategic planning and careful coordination.[3]

How has Tompkins County managed this successful reduction of municipal solid waste? It has taken the standard adage of "reduce, reuse, and recycle" to a further step with "rebuy," also known as green purchasing. Many of Tompkins County's innovative waste reduction programs have been funded through the one million dollars of income that Tompkins County generates every year through the sale of recyclables, thus forming a positive feedback loop — the more that is recycled, the more money there is to pump back into creating new ways for people to practice the Four Rs.

Black Gold

One of the easiest ways to greatly reduce the waste stream is to compost food and yard wastes. Composting, or creating black gold, has multiple benefits — in addition to diverting material from landfills, compost becomes an excellent soil amendment and helps gardens and lawns to thrive without the use of chemical fertilizers or pesticides. Compost adds nutrients and beneficial organisms to the soil, builds up soil structure and helps to retain moisture in the soil. It also saves money (through reducing cost of trash pickup for the consumer and landfill costs for the county) and saves energy (through cutting out the energy-intensive business of trash hauling).

One successful program aimed at engaging people in home composting is Master Composters, run by Cornell Cooperative Extension of Tompkins County (CCE-TC). The program runs a ten-week training program each year, which trains volunteers in all aspects of composting. Trainees also join experienced Master Composters to do a practical internship to gain hands-on experience. Graduates of the program educate the public about composting through conducting workshops, writing articles and managing demonstration sites. There is even a *Rotline* to call, a phone line which helps home composters with any questions they may have. As Adam Michaelides, the program manager told me, "Volunteers also gather informally to share meals, ideas, and friendship. Master Composters have fun while promoting sound ecological practices."[4] This program is funded by TCSWMD.

Another highly successful program is Cayuga Compost, a local business that works on an institutional scale. Starting out as a cooperative effort between private and public partners to help Tompkins County meet its waste reduction goals, Cayuga Compost provided all the capital equipment and more than 20 years of material handling experience — it actually started as an excavation business which sold sand and gravel. It has now expanded into a growing composting business, which handles all of the county's yard waste. Its byline is "Everyone loves the way Cayuga Compost handles food waste, Mother Nature included." This business collects not only food scraps, but also waste oil, food-soiled paper and waxed cardboard from restaurants, school districts, municipalities, institutional food services, wineries and grocery stores. Using 64-gallon plastic containers that are collected weekly, it is able to compost items like meat scraps and shellfish, pizza boxes and dairy products — things that a home composting system typically would not be able to handle. It even gives its commercial customers a Green Plate Club plaque, so that consumers will know that their business recycles and composts its waste. Cayuga Compost creates black gold from 1,000 tons of Tompkins County waste every week. Once Cayuga Compost collects the scraps, at about half the cost of garbage disposal fees, it creates premium and coarse grade composts, as well as custom mixes for gardeners, landscapers and wineries. Its products are available through a growing network of retailers throughout central New York.[5]

Starting Early

Because Cayuga Compost is able to handle school and cafeteria waste, the Ithaca City School District (ICSD) has been able to jump on the composting bandwagon, with remarkable results. In September 2009, the Child Nutrition Program of the ICSD posted a claim on their website, "In the last four months we reduced the amount of trash going into our waste stream by 42%."[6]

An article in a national publication, *School Nutrition Magazine*, highlighted the ICSD and interviewed Dale McLean, Director of the Child Nutrition Program. The school composting program was partly inspired by a parent who suggested using compostable lunch trays — something McLean was very interested in. The next step was to partner with Cayuga Compost, and with the school board's permission a test site was set up. The pilot project in 2007–2008 was wildly successful. Landfill waste was decreased by 70%! After months of work, and a grant first from a local foundation and the following year from TCSDWD, the program expanded to include all 13 schools in the district. According to McLean, the composting program involves collecting trays, food waste and "basically anything that was once alive" from cafeterias and kitchens. Once sent to Cayuga Compost, it actually takes a year and a half to compost — the long time frame is created by the dense, molded cardboard trays. A committee, with representatives from the director of facilities, the supervisor of district custodians and a science teacher as well as Tompkins County Solid Waste and Cayuga Composting, helped to work out any kinks.

"Our community sees our district as doing something good," McLean said with enthusiasm. Getting close to the goal of removing 50% of the District's waste, or 487,000 pounds from the waste stream in 2008–09, it is clear the program is already making a significant difference. "We've always been inspired to help our environment but, at the same time, we need to be fiscally responsible to our community," McLean said. "Now we have the opportunity to do both."[7]

The Chicken Project

While the Master Composters program and Cayuga Compost handle food wastes on a residential and institutional scale, innovative microprograms have also sprung up. One of these is The Chicken Project, a small-scale attempt to turn urban kitchen scraps into food for chickens. Tom Shelley, a Master Composter and Christianne White, a local farmer, teamed up in the Spring of 2009 to create a pilot project that demonstrates a more sustainable way to produce eggs in the Northeast. As Tom put it, "For anyone who hasn't noticed, grain prices have skyrocketed over the past couple of years."[8] Between the rising grain prices and the increased cost of fossil fuels on all aspects of farm production, it's become much harder for small-scale chicken farmers to compete with factory farms.

Their beginning experiment is a fascinating attempt to solve multiple problems at once. First, it removes organic waste from the urban waste stream. The plan places covered five gallon buckets (donated by Comet Skateboard, a local green business) with about 50 families in downtown Ithaca to collect food scraps. Since 75% of downtown residents are apartment dwellers, it is hard for them to find yard space to compost. The buckets are collected weekly and mixed with leaves, straw or other brown matter to create compost.

Second, the project provides a very low-cost, high protein feed for chickens. Maturing compost is rich in worms, microorganisms and insects, as well as food scraps, and, in addition to some pasturing of the hens, can make up the bulk of the chicken's diet.

Third, it provides some jobs. A local unemployed carpenter was hired to construct the chicken coop, and there is some low-skilled work to collect the food scraps and turn the compost. Tom and Christianne have worked with Recycle Ithaca's Bikes (RIBS) to fabricate a bike trailer to collect the scraps.

Fourth, it returns eggs back to the urban families, and thus closes the urban-rural nutrient cycle. This experiment could be an excellent prototype for other programs around the Northeast.

Go Green Initiative

In addition to vigorously promoting various composting programs, TCSWMD has been proactive by introducing a nationwide environmental education program in all of the county's schools. "The Go Green Initiative unites parents, students, teachers and school administrators in an effort to make real and lasting changes in their campus communities that will protect children and the environment for years to come." Since its inception, the program has grown to encompass schools in all 50 states as well as Canada, Mexico, Asia, Europe and Africa. There are currently over 1.5 million students and teachers in registered Go Green schools.[9]

In the fall of 2008, Tompkins County was recognized with the first national Go Green County of the Year Award by the Go Green Initiative. Linnett Short and Kat McCarthy, two of the TCSWMD staff persons responsible for working with the schools, were interviewed on a national program of Go Green Radio. They were heralded by the program's founder, Jill Buck, for their excellent work. Linnett, who has worked with TCSWMD for 24 years, shared that when they offered to pay half of the composting fees for each area school, schools started coming to them because they could save a substantial amount on trash fees.

In one local success story, Dryden Elementary School typically threw out 20 bags of trash a day. On the very first day of the Go Green Initiative, they reduced that to one bag of trash! In Trumansburg, another small school, the custodians initially grumbled about the changes, but within two weeks they were bringing ideas about more waste reduction to the head custodian. In fact, Trumansburg became a star school, known for being seasoned composters and recyclers. Leo Riley, Operations Manager for TCSWMD, shared that Trumansburg composts 34% of its waste, and along with recycling and reuse has reduced their trash by 66% in 2008. According to Leo, "these are good hard numbers," and they are indicative of what other schools may soon achieve.[10]

Solid Waste Visionary: Barb Eckstrom

As TCSWMD manager, Barb is a modest woman who tends to give lots of credit to her employees, who in turn light up when they talk about their successful programs. But it is clear that Barb's vision and environmental leadership are a key reason that TCSWMD has achieved so much. She told her story at a Green Resource Hub reception at the October 2009 Bioneers Conference of the Finger Lakes—where else but in Ithaca would you have the featured speakers at an evening wine and cheese reception talk about garbage? Barb talked about her horror at what was thrown out in her early days with TCSWMD. "Montgomery Ward would show up with tons of amazing furniture to dump. I was only in my late 20s, and I wanted it all. But I found out, oh, you can't use that stuff. They actually slashed the furniture so that no one else could use it." Cornell threw out wooden desks. Brown Cow yogurt dumped gallons of yogurt down the hill. No one was allowed to scavenge. As the mother of two young kids, Barb couldn't believe the waste.

Barb talked about the adventure of a 20 year solid waste management plan which was started in 1992, based on federal legislation. "We closed leaky landfills. While I was on maternity leave with my second child I started a 'pay as you throw' program—a trash-tag program. We started a bunch of drop-off centers for recycling." As a result of these and the many programs funded by TCSWMD, the county is well on its way to cut solid waste by 75% by 2015—an ambitious goal, but if anyone can do it, Barb and her crew can.[11]

ReBusiness Partners

In 2006, TCSWMD turned its attention from primarily residential waste reduction toward the business sector in an effort to further reduce the county's waste. ReBusiness Partners is an ongoing program to assist local businesses and organizations to reduce waste, increase recycling and to adopt green purchasing practices. In 2009, it won a state award for Recycler of the Year. Kat McCarthy, who runs the program, helps businesses with free technical assistance including a waste assessment with specific recommendations for follow-up actions. Participants also receive free desk-side recycling bins, free signage and public recognition for their efforts to promote a sustainable community. In turn, the participating businesses reduce trash and save energy, natural resources and often money.

There are now 200 businesses that have become ReBusiness Partners. These include retail stores, schools, restaurants, hotels, municipalities and even apartment buildings. "We've noticed increased compost tonnage and higher recycling rates," Kat said. "We've developed a uniform program for all county departments. And people take these habits home with them, which also helps." She continued, "If someone has a question, they know we're not the big bad recycling police. They actually know they're talking to Kat."[12]

Finger Lakes ReUse Center

In 2001, TCSWMD teamed up with Historic Ithaca to create Significant Elements, a warehouse for used building materials, such as doors, hardware, plumbing fixtures, windows and also some furniture. Donations flow in daily, and some materials have to be turned away. This stock is sold at a reduced rate to the public, and every month on Free Friday materials are given away. In its first five years of operation the program had already diverted over 300 tons of materials from the landfill.

In order to take advantage of the program's growing popularity and to exponentially increase the reuse of building materials and furniture, a new nonprofit was started in 2008, whose mission is to "enhance community, economy and environment through reuse." Two years in the planning, the Finger Lakes ReUse Center was developed by an active collaboration between Significant Elements, Ithaca College, TCSWMD, Cornell Cooperative Extension of Tompkins County, Cornell University, Tompkins County Area Development and the Tompkins County Chamber of Commerce. Finger Lakes ReUse is open daily, and in April 2009, a ReUse Revelry was held to celebrate the sale of the first 10,000 items since the store had opened just five months earlier.[13]

No Paper or Plastic, Thanks!

According to the New York Times, *the US goes through 100 billion plastic shopping bags annually. In addition to using 12 million barrels of oil to manufacture, eight billion pounds of plastic bags enter the waste stream every year. As litter, they break down into tiny bits, contaminating soil and water and threatening marine life. In landfills they can take up to 1,000 years to degrade.*

Paper bags aren't a better choice. According to the US EPA, paper manufacturers who use virgin timber consume more fresh water than any other industry and emit significant quantities of dioxin and other hazardous materials. In 1999, 14 million trees were cut to produce the 10 billion paper grocery bags used by Americans.[14]

Ithaca is beginning to take notice. In 2007, the Ithaca Farmer's Market became the second in the country to be a zero waste market. Customers are required to tote out any trash, and composting and recycling bins are handy for depositing food waste. Food vendors also use compostable tableware. In 2008, plastic bags were banned. Greenstar, the popular natural foods cooperative, credits customers with five cents for every shopping bag they bring, as well as selling bright green tote bags

with their logo. Wegman's, a major supermarket, sells reusable bags for
99 cents at each checkout. These handy tote bags soon find many uses
while advertising the store's name.

In 2008, China, a country of 1.3 billion people, adopted a nationwide
ban on plastic bags, labeling them white pollution.[15] *If China, with one*
fifth of the world's population, can do it perhaps it's not too far-fetched
to think the US could also adopt such a ban.

Green Purchasing

As mentioned earlier in this chapter, Tompkins County not only is
committed to the Three Rs — Reduce, Reuse, Recycle — but it has
added a fourth: Rebuy. This is also known as green purchasing. In
2006, TCSWMD teamed up with Sustainable Tompkins to create
the Finger Lakes Buy Green website.[16] According to Kat McCarthy,
it is "a green purchasing resource that's used to help people learn
not just why to buy green, but how, what to look for and what's important about it."[17] The website features useful links, a green glos-
sary of terms and also lists a sampling of environmentally preferable
products that are available at local stores. Products featured are organized into four categories: office, cleaning, yard and garden and
maintenance. While this site originated as a place for individuals to
go, the next obvious step was to organize institutional buyers to use
their combined clout for green purchasing.

The Finger Lakes Environmentally Preferred Procurement Consortium (FLEPPC) includes representatives from Cayuga Medical
Center, the City of Ithaca, Cornell University, Ithaca College, TC3,
TCSWMD, Tompkins County and Tompkins County Chamber of
Commerce among others. Marian Brown, special assistant to the
provost at Ithaca College, is one of the founders of this new consortium. "This is an opportunity to leverage the purchasing volume of
these major institutional partners to really drive the market [price]
down," she noted, "because the only way that you can really affect
pricing on green products is through volume."[18]

FLEPPC started out with purchasing office paper, using the combined buying power to find good deals on paper with a high recycled content. But it has expanded to look at other office supplies such as environmentally sound desk chairs and pens. The organizational reach of so many partners has advantages that are beyond the economic factor. Kat noted "The resources they bring, the skills, the knowledge and expertise multiplies far beyond what one individual or one entity could do."[19]

Cornell's Dump and Run

Every year Cornell participates in a Dump and Run sale. In this national program, at the end of the school year, collection bins are placed in every campus living area and college town building. According to Christina Copeland, student coordinator at Cornell, "We collect items that students no longer want or can't fit in their car or plane ride home. The only things we don't take are socks and underwear, mattresses and pillows; but we definitely get everything else!" She continued, "This year [2008] we collected more than 35 tons of items—clothing, food, furniture, mini-fridges, microwaves, shoes, office supplies, etc." Christina told me that the summer is

Apple Harvest is a Zero Waste Festival.

spent sorting through items in a rented warehouse. Four local non-profit groups provide volunteers to do the sorting, and they track the number of hours they put on the job. Later, they reap the benefits through a huge sale, held during Cornell orientation weekend at the beginning of the following school year. "This year's sale raised $42,758!" Christina informed me enthusiastically. "The program is truly an example of turning waste into gold, since these 35+ tons of items would have gone into a landfill if not for this program."[20]

While there are literally dozens of examples of how Tompkins County uses the Four Rs, they seem to often thread back to Tompkins County Solid Waste. The fact that the county garners a million dollars every year through its recycling program helps tremendously, especially when that money is funneled right back into the local economy to jump-start innovative programs. Just two examples are the role of TCSWMD in helping to fund 50% of business or school composting programs and helping to start up a new business, Cayuga Compost. By starting with strong initiatives such as Go Green in the schools, children learn early how much they can reduce trash and how much fun it can be to compost and recycle. Their parents can catch the enthusiasm for making the most of consumer goods through everything from shopping at the Finger Lakes ReUse Center to having their business assessed by the ReBusiness Partners, to experiencing a zero waste trip to the Farmer's Market. In addition to the many institutional supports for the Four Rs, there is a strong emerging philosophy in Ithaca that it is important to conserve resources — what better way than through turning waste into gold!

12

Local Government and Institutional Change

In Ithaca there is a healthy mix of both bottom-up and top-down approaches to sustainability. Much of this book has concerned itself with grassroots activism, nonprofit and business activity and the role of specific organizations to exert change in a given area. For example in Chapter 2, we saw how influential the roles of the Ithaca Farmer's Market and Greenstar Cooperative Market have been in promoting small-scale farming, organic foods and locavore eating. But in order to affect really large-scale changes, it makes sense that both local government and major institutions need to be involved in setting and practicing policy changes.

What would it look like for city, town and county governments and the largest institutions — in our case, Cornell University, Ithaca College, Tompkins County Community College and the Cayuga Medical Center — to promote long-term planning policies that promote sustainability across all sectors? This chapter addresses that top-down approach. Here, as in other areas of the book, Ithaca is forging ahead in a vigorous way, helped along by visionary leaders at the top, but also pressured from below by an informed and activist constituency.

Cornell's Climate Action Plan

On a cool October day in 2009 when the leaves were at the height of fall color, I attended a community forum held by Cornell University to present their just-released Climate Action Plan (CAP) to local sustainability leaders.[1] While the event was attended by only a few dozen people, it represented an exciting and historic moment.

Two years earlier, Cornell president David Skorton had signed the American College and University Presidents Climate Commitment (ACUPCC), joining 80 other academic institutions around the country (now up to 673) in pledging to move his campus towards climate neutrality. For Cornell this meant not only eliminating net greenhouse gas emissions but also enhancing the university's land-grant mission in support of a socially, economically and environmentally sustainable society. These are enormous commitments and making the pledge represented a big leap of faith by this large university. I credit President Skorton for his deep and forward-looking commitment to sustainability. However, major credit also goes to the agitation of student groups such as Kyoto Now! who first raised the issue, and the support of thousands of students, faculty and staff who advocated for Cornell to sign the agreement.

Dr. David Skorton, president of Cornell University.

Cornell's Climate Action Plan sets the goal of becoming climate neutral by 2050. This is a bold move — especially when contrasted with other plans. Even the most ambitious US government plans have proposed only an 80% cut in emissions by 2050. Cornell is one of the first major universities to undertake such a comprehensive plan. Among the colleges and universities signing the ACUPCC, Cornell and Ithaca College stand out as having "done the work," according to Peter Bardaglio, who serves as senior fellow of Second Nature, which first proposed the ACUPCC. "They were among the 25% of the colleges and universities who completed their CAPs by the October, 2009 deadline."[2]

Cornell's CAP can be described as a dynamic and evolving plan, which sets a direction as much as it sets specific ways to meet its goals. "Ongoing innovation on all fronts is central to the success of the CAP," the plan acknowledges. "The actions we find necessary will change as global conditions change — and will advance with new technological breakthroughs… Implementation will require sustained efforts throughout the university."[3] Not only will there need to be campus engagement from all parties, but new interdisciplinary partnerships will need to be formed, funding will need to be secured and ongoing, active leadership will be necessary. There are actions recommended in five areas:

- green development
- energy conservation
- fuel mix and renewable energy
- transportation
- carbon offsetting actions[4]

Energy Sources — The Biggest Chunk

Cornell's 2008 carbon footprint was 319,000 metric tons of emissions, including carbon dioxide, nitrous oxide and methane — the greenhouse gases associated with fossil-fuel consumption. The biggest contributor was on-site combustion, followed by purchased electricity, commuting and air travel for business. Even without implementing the CAP, Cornell has already cut its projected 2050 emissions by about one third through its Lake Source Cooling, energy conservation and its Combined Heat and Power Plant or CHPP (see Chapter 3). The CHPP came online in January 2010, and as coal is replaced by natural gas, a dramatic 28% drop in total emissions is expected.

But natural gas is still a fossil fuel, so Cornell is researching renewable energy options. Plans are proceeding for the Cornell University Renewable Bioenergy Initiative (CURBI), a demonstration-scale research facility that will showcase several biomass-to-energy technologies, including direct combustion, pyrolysis, syngas production and anaerobic digestion. This College of Agriculture and Life Sciences project will use resources that are readily available from farms, forests and other operations in and around Ithaca to generate energy that is sustainable. The initiative would bring an array of technologies together in a single facility to harvest energy from materials ranging from hazelnut shells to switchgrass to leftover vegetable oil from campus dining facilities.

Other plans call for exploring a hybrid engineered geothermal system (EGS), which could potentially tap geothermal heat at a depth of two to three miles and could be expanded to provide most heat for the campus. Unlike the proposed natural gas drilling in this area, geothermal heat is considered environmentally benign. Since Ithaca sits over the hottest spot in New York state (geologically speaking), it would be relatively easy to tap into existing heat from the earth, by just sending pipes down thousands of feet. Unlike hydro-fracking, no chemicals or pressurized water are needed. Large-scale wind is another option.

In addition to offsetting a whopping 42% of Cornell's carbon emissions through these methods of fuel mix and renewable energy, Cornell expects to save millions of dollars over the next 40 years. In addition, it expects to create local jobs and use local resources, while aiding global and regional research efforts into renewable energy.

Green Development

In 2008, Cornell rolled out its first green building policy, which requires all new construction and renovations of more than $5 million to attain the US Green Building Council's LEED Gold rating. In addition, the Campus Master Plan, completed the same year, calls for a compact, walkable campus and emphasizes environmental stewardship as a core principle.

Carrying this further, the CAP would focus on improved land use, including reducing infrastructure and vehicle miles traveled on campus and naturalizing some landscapes. It would also look at space planning and ensure that building usage is optimized, thus cutting down on the need to build new buildings. In addition it would mandate energy standards for new construction that would require new building design to limit energy usage to 50% of the industry standard.

These activities taken together would reduce carbon emissions by 12% towards the 2050 goal. As Ying Hua, an assistant professor of design and environmental analysis who teaches an award-winning course on collaborative sustainable building practices remarked, "Teams of faculty are now collaborating on smart-grid technology, energy generation and distribution in the built environment and behavior change. I am grateful that the plan [CAP] provides a comprehensive framework for our research to be demonstrated on campus." She went on to say that this enhances the land-grant mission of Cornell to educate the public, while dramatically reducing the university's carbon footprint.[5]

Energy Conservation

Between 1990 and 2008, Cornell managed to keep its energy consumption at a flat rate, despite a growth of 15% in space. By expanding current successful building conservation efforts, by educating the campus community about conservation practices and helping to "build the foundation of a culture of conservation on campus,"[6] and by building in smart-grid features that would allow the campus to be a model demonstration research project, Cornell expects to save 16% of its carbon emissions by 2050.

Green Transportation

A lot of planning has already gone into transportation at Cornell. Recently Cornell completed a strategic plan (Transportation Impact Mitigation Strategies) to promote best practices such as biking, walking, transit use, park-and-rides and other ways to cut down on single occupant vehicle commuting (see Chapter 4). Currently one third of faculty and staff are able to use these methods or carpooling, thus cutting down on some 10 million commuter miles. Cornell also supported the launch of Ithaca Carshare and enabled the inception of a county-wide vanpool program.

In addition to these worthy efforts, the CAP promotes adopting flexible work times and places, promoting teleconferencing rather than plane travel and improving the fuel-efficiency and mix of fleet-owned vehicles. All of these measures together are expected to cut single-occupancy commuter traffic by 50% and reduce carbon emissions by 4%.

Carbon Offsets

When everything above has been achieved (not a small task!), there will still be a need to further reduce Cornell's carbon emissions by 27% to meet its 2050 goal of zero net energy. This is an area that is very tricky—it would be very easy for the institution to be criticized for not doing enough. Carbon offsetting can also readily be exploited. To avoid this, the plan recommends that any carbon offsets acquired by Cornell be "high-quality and verifiable, directly link to the University's core mission, and contribute co-benefits to the community and the environment. Cornell's campus is not a closed system, but an extension of the broader community."[7]

Some ways of doing this are for Cornell to convert idle crop or pasture land to mature forests to provide long-term sequestration of CO_2, producing biochar (low-temperature pyrolysis of biomass material) which can then be sequestered in soils and sponsoring community-based offsets that enhance community welfare.

Cornell Cooperative Extension already reaches thousands of homeowners through Save Energy, Save Dollars workshops and through the Green Buildings Open House (Chapter 3). These programs help families turn their homes into efficient, healthy homes that may even produce energy.

Overall, Cornell is to be congratulated on its ambitious plans for achieving net-zero emissions. As the plan itself states, "Cornell's comprehensive plan for climate neutrality will have an impact well beyond our campus borders. From students, faculty and staff to researchers and the administration, our actions and initiatives to eliminate greenhouse gas emissions will engage, educate and inspire our state, our nation and our world."[8] While these are lofty goals, the proof will be in how the university sticks to its goals in an increasingly energy and finance-constrained world.

Ithaca College Steps Forward

In a neat counterpoint to Cornell's Climate Action Plan, Marian Brown, introduced in Chapter 6, then provided an overview of her institution's CAP. Marian Brown serves as the de facto sustainability coordinator for Ithaca College—a never-ending job in a college that takes its commitment to sustainability seriously.

In 2007 then-college president Peggy Williams signed the Presidents' Climate Commitment. Since then, a CAP planning process has been led by Carl Sgrecci, vice-president of Finance and Administration, a handy ally when it comes to making budget decisions that reflect long-term green goals. Savings from energy conservation measures can be plowed back into creating further opportunities for both energy and financial savings. Ithaca College, Marian pointed out, shares the same lofty goal as Cornell—to reduce carbon emissions to zero by 2050. However, IC, as a much smaller college, produces only one tenth of Cornell's emissions. The per person emissions rate is also much smaller, perhaps because IC is not a research facility. Unlike Cornell's large reductions in emissions through particular strategies, IC plans to "nibble away" at its emissions at a rate of 2.5% yearly, according to Marian.

Ithaca College's CAP will be fulfilled through reducing emissions in several areas. The largest reduction—by about three quarters—will be accomplished through cutting back on buildings' use of heating, cooling and electricity. As noted in the green building chapter, IC has made remarkable headway on building new buildings that are on the cutting edge of energy efficiency. This will be augmented by monitoring energy performance in every building and replacing outdated heating and cooling systems. Another quarter will be through reducing commuting.

Forty years ago, IC moved its campus from downtown Ithaca to the top of South Hill, effectively creating more of a commuting campus. "One third of our students commute, as well as faculty and staff," Marian said. "It's a huge challenge." She shared that the CAP takes a carrot and stick approach. The carrot is providing better access to alternative transportation modes; the stick is higher parking fees.

In reading IC's CAP later, I was struck at how prosaic and efficient its plans are. Mostly it plans to take advantage of things that are common-sense approaches and relatively easy to do. One of the main new ideas is to hire an Energy Manager to make sure that all the energy efficiency measures are implemented. Nothing very sexy here, but monitoring works and saves money. "This report demonstrates that it will actually cost us less to implement this plan than if we took no action at all. Wise investments now will help us to avoid these future costs."[9] This seems like a very mature approach.

Tompkins County's Ambitious Green Plans

Katie Borgella, principal planner for the Tompkins County Planning Department was next to present at the forum. The county has a very forward-looking Comprehensive Plan that was adopted in 2005, and in December of 2008 it adopted an Energy and Greenhouse Gas Emissions amendment that is even more ambitious and won a state-wide award.[10]

The goal is to reduce greenhouse gas emissions in the county by at least 2% of the 2008 level for each of the next 40 years, achieving at least an 80% reduction in greenhouse gas emissions by the year 2050.

This is a goal to knock your socks off. The TC Planning Department is not referring to just county offices here, they are referring to a total reduction by everyone who lives or works in the county — all 100,000 people! As Katie said, "It's one thing to talk about an institution trying to achieve climate neutrality, but trying to do this on a county wide level means working with all of our partners, which means trying to influence local, even individual decision making."[11]

The amendment contains eight policies and 17 possible action items. It covers a very wide scope of issues and shows a remarkable vision for proactive planning. Here are just a few of the action items:
- Work with local municipalities, school districts, businesses, institutions of higher education, and non-profits to develop a 5-year strategy to reduce community GHG emissions by at least 10%...
- Identify and promote utilization of Best Management Practices in agricultural, forestland, and water management to enhance carbon sequestration.

- Develop a strategy to divert 75% of the community waste stream from landfills by 2015.
- Develop a plan to address the specific energy needs of low-income people, including recommendations for improvements to existing energy-related programs and identification of potential pilot projects to address energy needs.[12]

In Tompkins County, almost 40% of the homes were built before 1940; many of these are very poorly insulated, have single-pane windows and rely on aging heating systems. There is a lot that can be done to bring these houses up to a more energy efficient standard. One idea that is being considered is to provide an incentive for homeowners to invest in their property by providing a revolving loan fund for weatherizing these buildings.

In addition to heating losses from buildings, a lot of the county's total energy — 42% — is used by transportation. Therefore some of the plan's measures include nodal development (clustering homes, businesses and services for achieving less sprawl, more transportation efficiency and more walkable communities), alternative forms of transportation and protecting natural resources.

Over the last decade, the county has already taken many strides forward. Starting in 2000, solar panels were installed on the library, the city joined an international sustainability group for local governments in 2001 and adopted a Local Action Plan in 2003 to address climate change. The county carried out a greenhouse gas emissions inventory for 1998 to 2008 and plans to publicize the results. It recently finished Phase I of an energy performance contract and has applied for a grant to cover Phase II. The new county Health Department is being built to LEED Silver standards and will also have solar panels.

Katie mentioned that the Tompkins County Airport has received funding from the Federal Aviation Administration (FAA) to create the nation's first Green Master Plan for an airport. Another impressive achievement is that Tompkins County Solid Waste has been able to divert 62% of all county waste from landfills. There are pilot projects starting that make use of rural, abandoned fields to produce biomass.

After hearing reports from TC3 (the local community college), the city of Ithaca and others, I left the community forum with Katie's final words ringing in my head, "We really all need to work together to make our plans actually happen." I was impressed and humbled by the vast array of expertise, commitment and sheer willpower demonstrated by institutional and local government leaders in the room. At the same time, I knew that all of these leaders (including myself) were to some extent flying blind. None of us knows exactly what will be happening in the coming years, and it is almost impossible to make a 40 year plan in such a rapidly changing world. Perhaps all we can do is make ambitious goals now based on our current understanding, then do our best to carry them out, relying strongly on each other and keeping the flexibility to be able to make use of the latest technologies and social structures as the future unfolds. It is a daunting task!

City of Ithaca—Climate Change Action Steps

In 2001, the City of Ithaca joined the International Council on Local Environmental Initiatives (ICLEI), which works with hundreds of cities around the world to address climate change. In 2005, Mayor Carolyn Peterson was one of the signatories of the newly formed US Mayors Climate Protection Agreement. Both of these commitments led to formulating a plan for reducing greenhouse gas (GHG) emissions.

In July 2006, the City of Ithaca adopted a Local Action Plan, which focuses on energy conservation and greenhouse gas emission reductions relating to the municipal operations which it can directly control. The City set a goal to reduce GHG emissions to 20% below 2001 levels by 2016. In 2009 the City of Ithaca:

- *was recognized by the New York Conference of Mayors for its energy efficiency performance contract and sustainability training program*
- *Common Council adopted the statewide Climate Smart Community resolution*

- *completed its online and classroom based sustainability training program for city employees*
- *developed a sustainability orientation training for new employees*
- *updated its greenhouse gas emission inventory for municipal operations (for 2008)*
- *submitted a draft green fleet policy to Common Council for consideration*[13]

Working Together—Tompkins County Climate Protection Initiative (TCCPI)

In addition to individual efforts by local government and institutions, the Tompkins County Climate Protection Initiative (TCCPI) is a powerful new county-wide coalition funded by the Park Foundation and founded by Peter Bardaglio, senior fellow at Second Nature and former provost of Ithaca College. To learn more, I attended one of the group's meetings in late January 2010. These are held once a month in the beautiful conference room of the Chamber of Commerce, overlooking Cayuga Lake. On that day the lake was frozen, and it was a wintry 10°F outside. Inside, the room was filled with the warmth of determined people, eager to make a difference. The groups represented that day included a mix of local and county governments, local energy-related businesses, the Ithaca City School District, Cornell and Ithaca College and several nonprofits.

The coalition hopes not only to coalesce efforts within Tompkins County, but also to create a replicable model for energy efficiency and climate protection for communities throughout the nation. To do this, TCCPI has identified four major goals:

Peter Bardaglio, founder, Tompkins County Climate Protection Initiative.

1. Facilitate implementation of a common strategy, target, and timetable for achieving significant reductions in greenhouse gas emissions.

2. Creation of a peer-to-peer mentoring network that will provide mutual support among the participants in addressing the problems and challenges involved in meeting the county's target of 80% reductions in greenhouse gas emissions and timetable of 2% per year.

3. Establishment of a consortium that will allow members to explore potential financing mechanisms and purchase the necessary goods and services to achieve greenhouse gas reduction targets at a significant discount.

4. Facilitate development of a process and tools that will allow us to monitor our progress through effective data collection and analysis, promoting transparency, and accountability.[14]

There was a full agenda for the January meeting, starting off with a report on the recent UN Climate Change Conference in Copenhagen by Dominic Frongillo (see Chapter 3). While Dominic reported that the overall feeling at the conference was disappointment that so little progress on an agreement had been made, he was energized by the unprecedented growth of the youth movement, as 100,000 students marched in Copenhagen and delivered the largest petition in world history, with fifteen million signatures, to urge leaders to make a strong and binding climate treaty. When asked how the lessons of the conference applied to Tompkins County, Dominic said, "It really is in many ways state and local governments that push the national governments. It makes the work we do here through local collaboration really important." He paused, "But I also took away that we need to build a movement and build political pressure to get the United States to take action."

The next topic introduced two software tools for residential energy tracking: Green Energy Compass (developed by Ithaca-based business Performance Systems Development, which is using it on a national basis) and Earth Aid. These tools are meant to help consumers identify areas where they could save more energy. Compass is designed more for contractors to help customers, whereas Earth Aid is designed specifically for homeowners. It has been found that these kinds of feedback tools can dramatically change peoples' energy usage behavior, especially if they are informed about how much money they can save and how their energy use is compared to their neighbors. TCCPI members were each asked to take home the forms, and assess their own energy use, as a kind of pilot project. Peter Bardaglio said, "What we're hoping for is some kind of hybrid tool—a way to measure energy consumption that will move us toward more residential energy savings around the county."[15]

The meeting continued with Leslie Schill from the Tompkins County Planning and Public Works presenting a draft Energy Strategy for implementing the Energy and Greenhouse Gas Emissions Element of the County's Comprehensive Plan. An initial goal was to achieve 20% reduction of greenhouse gases by 2020. TCCPI members were asked to provide comments.

Sean Vormwald of Sustainable Transitions was next. He presented a new Finger Lakes Climate Fund developed by Sustainable Tompkins (see Chapter 15) and explained how organizations could purchase carbon offsets for their travel, which would then be reinvested in local residential energy efficiency grants.

During the final part of the meeting, we did a quick round. Each member organization had a chance to talk about their news relating to climate action. It was an impressive list of activities and accomplishments and seemed to strengthen the community resolve: We're all in this together!

The Bigger Picture

Big changes need leaders with big vision. In the same way that individual sectors of society are changing (such as building practices or education), large institutions need to address multiple sectors at once. At the institutional level there is more inertia, but there is also the possibility of making a much larger splash once the waterwheel gets going. In Ithaca there is a wealth of like-minded people who care passionately about both the environment and social justice, and these coalitions can support each other at a leadership level.

By having institutions or local government bodies tap into national movements for change, such as the American College and University Presidents' Climate Commitment or the Cool Mayors initiative, there is a strong incentive to work towards achieving extremely ambitious goals. Once again, just as we saw in the *clustering* of food and green building in previous chapters, there is a very significant momentum that has built up in Tompkins County to work towards reducing greenhouse gases in a concerted way — one that involves not just energy reduction measures, but that strives to work on the social, economic and environmental planes as well.

When all of these players come together and unite their efforts by sharing information, creating shared goals and building relationships across sectors, the momentum towards change is unstoppable!

(13)

Changing Culture, Changing Lives

The cure for anything is salt water—sweat, tears or the sea.

ISAK DINESEN

My friends, do not lose heart. We were made for these times. Ours is not the task of fixing the entire world all at once, but of stretching out to mend the part of the world that is within our reach.

CLARISSA PINKOLA ESTES

Love Knows No Bounds

The Ithaca Montessori school was a beehive of activity. The parking lot was overflowing, people were outside on the benches talking and Cajun music streamed from the open doors. As I entered and purchased a ticket for the evening, a young woman, her face covered by an elaborate mask, came over and with a friendly smile put two glittering strings of Mardi Gras beads around my neck—one green and one gold. This was a benefit for Love Knows No Bounds, a group of Ithacans who have made it their business to offer help and friendship to the impoverished black community of the Seventh Ward in New Orleans, which was devastated by Hurricane Katrina. The support has grown from a tiny group to encompass about 20 organizations and is city wide. In fact, Ithaca became a Sister City to the Seventh Ward on August 1, 2007. Over the years, dozens of volunteers have made trips to New Orleans to help rebuild homes and to deliver badly needed furniture, clothes and other material goods.

Pastor Bruce, the amazingly upbeat minister from St. John's Church in New Orleans, was present with his wife and seven others from his congregation. Pastor Bruce told me, "Before the storm I never heard of Ithaca, now they're treating us like royalty, giving us the red carpet treatment every time we visit." In a rare moment of bitterness he confided, "The government hasn't yet been down to help us there. They treat the Seventh Ward like an illegitimate child."[1]

Pastor Bruce and his wife, Deborah Davenport, enjoy a quiet moment in Ithaca.

Our brief interview was cut short when Pastor Bruce was called inside to do the honors. In a joyful, booming voice, he shared his gratitude for all the help—from Montessori classrooms to Ithaca College faculty and students, from the Greater Ithaca Activities Center (GIAC) to doctors and attorneys, Ithacans have clearly shown their caring. "When the government don't act right," he boomed, "the people act right." People clapped loudly and appreciatively. This has indeed been a grassroots, people-to-people effort. The pastor closed, "If I ever get the Nobel Peace Prize, I'll bring it right here."[2] We all laughed. The love and appreciation flowed freely, just as it should.

When Marcia Fort was leading the Talking Circle on Race and Racism in which I participated (see Chapter 9), she left for a week to go down to New Orleans and work in the Seventh Ward; it was on the same trip that my EcoVillage neighbor, Jim Hodges, took with his Montessori students. Marcia was eloquent about how much she appreciates Love Knows No Bounds, which she watched grow from the beginning.

You've got school kids involved, and religious institutions— Different! Different! You've got city people and rural people, a wonderful mix of people from our community contributing in so many ways. For some people it might be donating money, it has been prayers, it has been families taking time to go down or people hosting people here.

It's these kinds of efforts that help change our culture, help change our world, and we should be so proud of that. And I don't know if there's another city around the country that has as caring a community. Thank God! Blessings to that initial small group of people that decided within their hearts that "we're going to do this" and didn't let it go. Their compassion, their love, their humanity has just spread out so it's become a community project. I'm just really proud of that, I really am.[3]

Vitamin L—20th Anniversary

It was another breezy summer day when I headed up the west side of the lake to the Hangar Theater. Vitamin L (as you may have guessed, the *L* in Vitamin L stands for love), a project of the Center for Transformative Action, was celebrating its 20th anniversary with two back-to back concerts. The Hangar Theater was crowded with several hundred people of all ages, many of whom were proud families of the young singers.

When this interracial group of teens opened their mouths to sing, I was truly amazed. They sounded so professional, and they radiated confidence and goodwill. They took turns as lead singers, with the rest of the group serving as a choral backdrop, complete with hand motions that reminded me of the Supremes. The first song, "Welcome to the Neighborhood," actually brought tears to my eyes. How many times have I or my children felt unwelcome in a new school or a new setting? This song, with its upbeat lyrics, offered a complete contrast to that experience, as a young woman told us "I will show you the park next-door and introduce you to my friends."

The next lead singer introduced a song about walls. He said, "I'm not talking about a wall with bricks or stones or anything, but an invisible wall that shuts other people out. And when we shut these people out we're missing out on a chance of friendship and love." He sang: "There are walls of concrete, walls of steel, but the biggest ones you'll find are the walls that people put up in their hearts

Vitamin L performs in concert.

and in their minds. Walls because of different skin, or the features on a person's face, walls because of their religion, their language or their native place."[4] The interracial harmony between these young people on stage was in direct contrast to the racial tensions with which Ithaca struggles (see Chapter 9). It's good to know that even in the schools, where some of the worst racism occurs, positive values can be taught in a creative and compelling way.

One Vitamin L alumna who is now a teacher, Lily Cavanaugh, reflected on how much Vitamin L influenced her. "Singing these songs taught me moral values and the practical application of those values. I knew the difference between right and wrong, but Vitamin L took that a step further and taught me to think concretely about racism, sexism, and the value of individuality and taking responsibility for my own actions." She continued, "Beyond that, it allowed me to teach those same lessons to my peers and those close in age to myself. Now that I'm a teacher, I infuse character education into my general curriculum, and I attribute this commitment to teaching social justice in part to my involvement with Vitamin L as a team."

Not only has Vitamin L profoundly influenced the lives of children who participate, but it reaches out through performances in the schools to touch a much broader audience. "The members of the group demonstrate teamwork, respect and gratitude during the performance and are wonderful role models for our students," wrote one enthusiastic music teacher. "I just cannot express how much Vitamin L brings our school together! The entire school almost hums with excitement as the concert gets closer. The songs teach such great values and are presented in such a professional manner that we can never seem to get enough."

Even New York State's governor presented Vitamin L a certificate of recognition "for being in the forefront of helping to promote the ideals of Dr. Martin Luther King Junior by promoting peace in our schools and communities."[5]

Save a Forest…Plant Yourself

On a surprisingly balmy Sunday morning in November, I attended a forum at the Unitarian Church about Greensprings, a natural burial ground.[6] I was delighted to finally meet Mary Woodsen, the dedicated founder, whom I'd heard about for years. Greensprings was just a "gleam in the eye" in 2000, she told us, and it took until 2006 to purchase land and get the necessary permits. In the last three years, about 20 burials a year have taken place there. Mary showed us a slideshow of the natural cemetery, which is a beautiful, 100 acres of rolling, hilltop meadows 15 miles south of Ithaca. The land provides a quiet sanctuary for both people and wildlife and over time will be reforested with native trees.

That day I found out some staggering facts about the environmental costs of typical burials: according to the speaker, each year nearly 2.5 million Americans die and are buried in cemeteries. Over 800,000 gallons of embalming fluid, 30 million board feet of top-quality rainforest timber, 100,000 tons of steel and 1.6 million tons of concrete are buried with them. While of course people want to honor their loved ones, to me this seemed like a colossal waste of resources. Moreover to keep up the manicured cemeteries, tons of fertilizers, pesticides and water are applied, and the lawns have to be frequently mowed.

For years, I thought I would prefer to be cremated and have my ashes scattered over my favorite natural area. However, I found out that cremations are environmentally destructive as well. They use so much heat (4 hours at 1800°F) that you could drive 4,800 miles on the energy equivalent for each body that is cremated. Why increase your carbon footprint after you're dead? But the more insidious threat is that for each cremation between 0.8 and 5.9 grams of mercury from dental fillings are released. In Tompkins County, the cremations from just one year released between 1.2 and 6.8 pounds of highly toxic mercury into the atmosphere. Most of this goes into the air, and the rest settles into the ground and water, poisoning all life-forms with which it comes into contact.

Mary pointed out that "Your body is a natural resource, rich with life-sustaining nutrients. Your choice for natural burial is a choice for natural renewal and growth — a way to give back to the earth that sustains us all." She added that in Tompkins County, with about a 3% death rate, 300,000 pounds of nutrients are not returned to the earth each year. Instead, you can make a choice in death that reflects your life's values. By planting your body in a biodegradable casket of local wood or a simple cloth shroud, and by not using embalming fluid, those nutrients continue the cycle of life, nourishing flowers, bees, wildlife and trees.

One question from the audience was "How hard was it to get a permit?" Apparently most Newfield town residents were supportive of the natural cemetery. Mary recalled that at the public hearings, one person said, "I like quiet neighbors." We all laughed. Possible water contamination was brought up, but apparently natural graves are environmentally benign, and even the mercury stays in place.

While the idea appeals to many people, it is still largely unknown, despite the ongoing hard work of Mary, her staff and board members. One of the board members of Greensprings passed out a list of possible tag lines for the organization, as a way to help spread the concept. In addition to "Save a Forest, Plant Yourself," and "Breaking New Ground," my favorite was "Think Outside the Box." You have to love people who have a sense of humor, even when talking about the end of life![7]

Ithaca's Alternative Gift Fair

While I enjoy the extra social events, the promise of spiritual renewal and the sparkle of Christmas lights on fresh snow, for many years I've been turned off by the rampant consumerism that our culture also aggressively promotes in the December holiday season. However, there is an alternative. Along with the Local Lovers Challenge (Chapter 5) which encourages people to purchase locally made gifts, Ithaca has an annual Alternative Gift Fair, which makes it easy to give a charitable donation to a worthy cause in lieu of a more tangible gift.[8] It's the perfect thing for giving to "someone who has everything," which, face it, includes the majority of people in the US. The model for the Alternative Gift Fair started in Tacoma Park, Maryland in 1999, and the idea has spread around the US since then, aided by a national organization, The New American Dream, which has a free guide for how to start a fair in your area.

The Ithaca Alternative Gift Fair was started in 2004 by a couple of young women who were inspired by the idea. The initial fair raised $8,000 to benefit 19 nonprofit organizations. Since then, the all-volunteer-run Fair has grown larger each year as it becomes better known. In 2009 there were a total of 58 participating organizations! The Fair is split between the First Presbyterian Church and the First Baptist Church, which are side by side, nestled at the edge of DeWitt Park in the heart of downtown Ithaca. Hours have expanded, too, so the Fair runs all day. By the time I showed up in the mid-afternoon, I knew it must be successful, since it was really hard to find a parking place nearby.

When I walked into the church, the magic began. For this was not only a simple transaction of money, it was an event that wove together community spirit with the joy of giving in the most satisfying way. The first person I saw was Anke Wessels, executive director of the Center for Transformative Action, which is one of the two main sponsors of the event, along with Tompkins Community Action. Anke gave me a warm smile and handed me a program, listing all the organizations and the gifts they offered.

The next two hours reminded me of a holiday open house, minus the eggnog. I ran into many, many friends and associates. It was a delightful way to spend a Saturday afternoon. I ate too much chocolate, I caught up on people's lives and enjoyed thoughtfully deciding which gifts suited people on my list. I found some wonderful matches: my daughter-in-law from India received a donation in her name to an Ithaca organization which partners with a city in India to provide free medical care and helps street children to go to school. One of my sons received a donation in his name to a partnership between his former alternative high school and the Akwesasne Freedom School, a Native American school which teaches the Mohawk language and life skills. When they were younger, both my sons enjoyed cultural exchange trips with the Akwesasne school, where they built raised garden beds and learned how to make fry bread. My other son received a donation to the Green Guerillas (see Chapter 7).

One hundred dollars lighter and a couple hours later, I felt great! I gave back to my community, made thoughtful gifts to loved ones and renewed ties with dozens of people I love and respect. Later I found that the Alternative Gift Fair raised a stunning $65,000 in $5 to $50 amounts for local nonprofits. Speaking a few days later with Christian Nielsen-Palacios, who was part of the team that organized the Fair, he dreamt of starting similar fairs in Syracuse and other nearby cities. This is such a good idea, I'm sure it will catch on.

SewGreen

SewGreen, which had a table at the Fair, is an innovative enterprise that teaches young people sewing skills, "encouraging sustainability in fabric, fiber, fashion."[9] SewGreen has pulled together a loyal group of diverse local teens and adults who enjoy learning to reuse and conserve fabrics and to design their own clothes. Rather than go on a shopping spree at the mall, these young women (and a few men) take great pride in refashioning old t-shirts or other castoffs into stylish outfits. As the SewGreen website explains, "In a world that chronically squanders resources, it has become important to recast sewing as a sustainable skill and a component of a new thrift." The site continues, "Sewing as practiced by our mothers and grandmothers was traditionally about self-reliance, ingenuity, and a smart use of resources. Today, sewing can recapture these qualities as well as foster creative expression, reduce stress, and create social bonds. Sustainable sewing, such as refashioning new clothes from old ones, encourages fashion independence and — as with past generations — the pleasure of owning fine clothes and linens made at home."[10] In other words, it's cool to make your own clothes!

But SewGreen doesn't stop with sewing classes. They educate about the hazards of fibers such as conventionally grown cotton. I learned that this is the world's most toxin-intensive fiber crop. While conventionally grown cotton occupies just under 3% of the earth's farmland, it accounts for a whopping 25% of all agricultural pesticides and herbicides applied worldwide. Just as an example, it takes about a third of a pound of toxic chemicals to produce the cotton for a typical t-shirt. A pair of blue jeans requires three quarters of a pound. Luckily, acreage for organic cotton is increasing with consumer demand.[11]

On a lighter note, SewGreen offers all kinds of fun and funky contests and events. I enjoyed attending a creative reuse fashion show entitled R-E-S-P-E-C-T (after the Aretha Franklin song) at the Community School of Music and Art. Motown music blasted as the mostly young, hip fashionistas strutted their stuff with pride, wearing their own creations from off the shoulder evening gowns to sexy street clothes. Each of the young (and some older) women exuded an air of the creative artist — some bold, some shy, but all making a statement.

Wendy Skinner, founder of SewGreen, has an interesting background. For many years she worked in marketing and communication. "I always had a secret fashion passion," she confessed, "but I thought it was silly." After hearing local author Sandra Steingraber speak, however, Wendy was inspired to use all of her talents to contribute to a more sustainable world. "I realized that fashion is the perfect magnet for young people," she told me. "It can teach leadership, workplace reliability, self-reliance and inspire self-confidence." Starting out with a few volunteers, SewGreen organized a rummage sale for fabric and a few sewing classes, then rented space for a classroom and recently opened a ReUse store in the DeWitt Mall. The ReUse store provides revenue to help fund some of the other programs. Wendy is particularly proud of a ten-week summer program that employed ten young people from "extremely diverse backgrounds. "We gave them a summer experience they will probably never forget," Wendy smiled. "We taught them to sew, we taught them as much as we know about apparel design. We transformed several of them into teachers. At least three have gone out to get other summer jobs involving sewing."

"When we started my goal was landfill diversion, but it turns out that is very easy to accomplish. But now it is youth development and leadership." When I asked Wendy about whether what she's done in Ithaca could be replicated elsewhere, her eyes lit up. "Sure!" Her advice was: assemble a group of like-minded volunteers, find a space accessible to the whole community, start collecting sewing machines and materials, recruit teachers, at some point provide a resale outlet (like a volunteer-run thrift store), get the community involved as much as possible. Currently there's a lot of interest in sewing and fashion, so this is a good time to get involved.[12]

Soul on Deck

What creates a positive change in our culture? Part of the answer seems to be exposing people to a different set of values than those typically espoused by the mainstream. Rather than throw-away consumerism, some organizations promote reuse of materials, creativity, diversity and service to others in need. Sustainability in practice ideally promotes a strong sense of community and social justice, as well as affordability and the wise use of natural resources. When these values are put into practice, people are able to see practical alternatives to the status quo that are strongly compelling.

In this chapter, we've examined very different initiatives — from Ithaca's partnership with a low income black neighborhood in New Orleans to the uplifting music of a children's singing group, from an alternative way to give holiday gifts to a way of reclaiming clothing as a do-it-yourself enterprise. We've even touched on how to die naturally, and to see one's own body as part of the cycle of giving back to the world.

Each of these initiatives has the potential to revolutionize a part of the culture which we currently take for granted. Rather than assume that people are inherently self-centered, passive consumers who rely on massive institutions to take care of them (for crisis assistance, for schooling, for clothing, for giving gifts, even for dying), these organizations all encourage people to be actively engaged in making other choices. These heart-felt choices can help to shape a positive future. They allow the most important "S" in sustainability to shine forth — Soul. As Clarissa Pinkola Estes wrote, "Soul on deck shines like gold in dark times."[13]

14

Art at the Heart — Ithaca Celebrates!

The Ithaca Festival

It had been a cool but sunny day in late May, with the sweet scent of honeysuckle in bloom and the locust trees dripping long white blossoms. Purple, blue and yellow iris were in their full glory in front yards and street corner plantings. On a Thursday evening at 6 PM all of Ithaca was lining Aurora Street, which was closed to cars. People were chatting and waiting for the upcoming Ithaca Festival parade. It was a diverse crowd of all ages and races — teens talking on their cellphones, white-haired couples in lawn chairs, families with strollers, everyone greeting friends. I felt filled with delight and anticipation. This is one of my favorite times of year, the time when Ithacans emerge in full force after a winter of being cooped up inside, to bring their zest and community spirit into a unique, four-day celebration.

First there were the races — a one-mile men's race, then a women's race, followed by a children's race. While there were clearly seasoned athletes at the front, in true community spirit, we clapped for every runner and perhaps most of all for those who bravely brought up the rear. Several families I know from EcoVillage joined the last race, parents and youngsters running together. I felt proud of them and cheered them on.

Then it was time for the parade itself. First the Family Reading Partnership, a local award-winning nonprofit organization, floated by, highlighting a moving armchair with a parent reading to children snuggled close and a giant green caterpillar from a popular kids' storybook. The Tibetan group included music, prayer flags and traditionally costumed women doing a dance. Ithaca is a haven for Tibetans and has been chosen as the North American home for the Dalai Lama. I spotted the mayor of Ithaca, Carolyn Peterson, walking along the parade route, giving out stickers to the kids. She was dressed in shorts and a t-shirt, and it struck me that some people might not have even known she was the mayor. The local SPCA, known as one of the first in the US for its no-kill policy, featured dozens of dogs, some of whom showed off their tricks for the appreciative audience. There were stilt walkers stalking around on impossibly high, skinny legs. Some had top hats, some wore shorts and one woman even danced around in circles, while a young man on

Stiltwalkers at the popular Ithaca Festival.

stilts rode a bicycle with very high handlebars. There were vans emblazoned with the logos of local radio stations, blaring out rock or country music. There was a very professional sounding band from the local Montessori school. And then there were the classic Volvo ballet and He-Man Chainsaw Marching Band.

The Volvo ballet consisted of four Volvo station wagons, outfitted with ballerina tutus, whose drivers took turns moving the cars gracefully forward, backwards and sideways. They were accompanied by music and several dancing mechanics, both men and women dressed in tutus, wielding huge cardboard wrenches, wove in and out of the cars, landing sometimes for a quick pose on the roof or bounding off the hood. The whole effect is hilarious, and despite having seen this every year, I found myself laughing out loud along with the rest of the crowd. The He-Man Chainsaw Marching Band is another zany Ithaca tradition. Imagine 20 guys (and this year there was also a gal) dressed in work boots and old clothes, carrying chainsaws (minus the chains, for safety) and revving them all at once, accompanied by a loud, metallic drum. It hurts the ears, but it's a funny spoof on he-man machismo.

Two hours and dozens of floats later, the parade was over. The crowd surged into the street, and I joined friends to walk towards the Ithaca Commons. It felt marvelous to take over the streets from cars for the evening. Various police with bullhorns tried to coax us all back onto the sidewalks, but the crowd giddily ignored them, feeling an expansive freedom that could not be roped in, at least for the night.

The parade was just the beginning of the revelry. For the next three days the Festival took over the city. Several blocks of downtown streets near the pedestrian Commons were closed to cars and dedicated instead to food and crafts vendors. There were authentic Middle-Eastern falafels at one stand and spicy Thai food at another. There were homemade smoothies, nachos, hot dogs and corn on the cob. There was Native American fry bread with beans or a sweet version with strawberries and whipped cream. Whatever taste one was craving, it was here, along with jostling crowds and crowded tables in the street.

There were also huge compost and recycling bins. For the first time, all vendors were required to use compostable plates, glasses and cutlery. Tompkins County Solid Waste was aiming for a zero waste event, and volunteers with special t-shirts staffed each station, helping people figure out which bins to use. I felt sad that I accepted a plastic straw, which had to go in the garbage, for my smoothie. But the leftover Thai food, paper plate and napkin and corn-based glass all got to be composted. They must have collected tons of waste, all of which was processed by Cayuga Compost. It was quite an enormous effort to set it all up but well worth it, and the crowd was cooperatively separating out food and paper that might otherwise go into a landfill.

Over the next three days, I enjoyed many different Festival events. There was the haunting music of the high Andes, played by a Peruvian with panpipes on a street corner. I danced to the Carribean reggae music of Kevin Kinsella's band. He got the crowd of hundreds of people to throb with rhythm. Taking a look around the crowd, I feasted on the faces of young and old, black, white, Asian and Hispanic, all enjoying the music. The more enthusiastic people jumped up and down, the more reserved just bounced in place. One little girl danced in a circle around her stroller, her mom following behind.

Saturday night the crowd surged into the State Theater, a beautiful old restored building that seats 1,600 people, for the screening of "The Great White Trail," a silent movie made in Ithaca in 1917. Luckily my friends and I arrived 20 minutes early, but even so there were barely seats left. Although the movie is supposed to be set in the Yukon during the gold rush, the audience laughed delightedly when we recognized the steep mountain ravines to be our very own Treman Gorge just south of town. The film was produced and directed by the Wharton brothers at their Ithaca silent movie studio, part of a short but important era for Ithaca as an East Coast Hollywood. The melodramatic movie was set off by live mood music played on the State Theater's 1907 Steinway grand piano by world-renowned silent film pianist Dr. Philip Carli. At the end we gave Dr. Carli a standing ovation. To me, we were clapping not only for his fine performance, but perhaps even more for the special quality of seeing a silent film made right here in Ithaca. The community was connecting with an important piece of our city's history — it drew us together in a way that watching a modern film with a group of strangers does not. Silent movies require audience participation, I realized. We had to use our imaginations to flesh out the characters, and we listened and responded to the screen more as a collective than as individuals since we could hear and attune to each other's reactions. I hope there will be more screenings in the future.

On Sunday, I set up an EcoVillage table at the Gorges Green Expo, a huge tent at Stewart Park which showcased the work of dozens of nonprofit organizations that are working for a just and sustainable future. Like every other Ithaca Festival I remember, it had been stormy with lots of wind and rain, so my friend and I decided not to bring the solar cooker as we had planned. Needless to say, by the time we arrived at the park, the sun shone brightly! The tent was packed with exhibitors, from local chocolate makers (who gave out tempting samples of fair-trade, organic chocolate) to local green builders, to the Multicultural Resource Center, to New Roots High School to Ithaca Carshare. The groups and the people were mostly familiar to me, like a big extended family. It felt crowded, but it was also a testament to the great variety of sustainability initiatives in this region.

The Gorges Green Expo is just part of the Ithaca Festival's commitment to sustainability. In addition to the composting stations mentioned earlier, the festival's signature t-shirts are 100% organic, the festival is powered by solar and wind power and the performers and most of the vendors are local people. But most of all the celebration creates a refreshing spirit of community. It is a chance for Ithaca to truly shine in all its creative glory.

Light in Winter

Of course, it is easy to celebrate when summer is coming, but what about during the long, dark winter? Luckily, Ithaca also has a premier winter festival, held over a long weekend in mid-January. Light in Winter was the brainchild of Barbara Mink, a local artist, politician, professor, journalist and consummate organizer. It first premiered in 2004 and has grown larger and more sophisticated each year. The festival brings together science and art in surprising ways—a perfect fit for this creative college town. As an *Ithaca Times* reporter put it, "Light in Winter makes the scientific fun and accessible, and considering how many cool events they have planned this year, maybe they should consider a cloning workshop for next year, since you'd need two or three copies of yourself in order to take everything in."[1] Each year has a different theme. In 2008, it was all about exploring identity—who are we, where do we come from and where are we going?—using everything from robots to poets to shed light on the topic. In 2009, the overriding theme was magic: "The magic of exploration, the magic of animals, and the underlying structure of the world, the folds of the universe," said Mink in an interview. "If you think about it, we are surrounded by magic. And part of the fun is figuring it out, and part of it is being fooled."[2]

I decided to take in one of the headliners, Jeff McBride, an internationally known magician who is based in Las Vegas but performs around the world. The State Theater was completely filled as we waited expectantly for the show to begin. I was especially touched to see one of my EcoVillage neighbors, Fred, being wheeled to the front row in his wheelchair. Fred is an amateur magician and knows McBride through magician conferences. Fred enjoyed doing spontaneous magic tricks for anyone who would watch before he was almost completely paralyzed by a terrible infection that also left him deaf. I wondered what it would be like for him to watch this show. Then McBride stepped forward. Using dramatic elements of smoke and light, he astounded the audience with his sleight of hand. Wielding numerous masks, he covered and uncovered his face so fast it was hard to believe that anyone could move with that lightning speed. There was an element of Japanese Kabuki theater in the stylized drama of his show that was also intriguing. When the show was almost over, McBride stepped down to the front row of the audience and engaged a few people as assistants in special magic tricks. He went over to Fred and greeted him. It made me smile—here was a magician who makes magic happen on many levels!

Art at the Heart

Another Ithaca winter art festival, the Holiday Parade of Ice, offers magic of its own. Featuring the largest ice sculpture exhibit in central New York, artists busily carved over 30 sculptures, with several dramatic ones over seven feet tall. I loved watching one artist working on a giant throne. It was amazing to see him standing on huge blocks of ice, which gave off steaming cold vapors, wielding a saw and finding the form within the ice. After he finished I joined a crowd of eager onlookers who took turns posing on the throne while family and friends took snapshots. It made for a cold seat, but it felt strangely peaceful and definitely royal to look out over the Commons from such a high perch.

When summer rolls around again, it is time for Art in the Heart of the City, a delightful annual exhibit of outdoor art focused on sustainability and community. In 2008, the program showcased three women artists whose sculptures used natural or recycled materials. My favorite was "The Three Graces," by artist Kathy Bruce. Using a 15-foot tall construction of bamboo, raffia, straw and soil, she fashioned three female figures. The tallest, at 15 feet high, was striking, with real, living morning glory vines that covered her full-skirted dress. Her head sported lovely green leaves and blue flowers as the summer wore on. A local artist, Kathleen Griffen, created light-filled giant fiberglass butterflies which years later still float gracefully from the ceiling of a parking garage. And Yolanda Daliz created whimsical animals out of reclaimed wood, carved into abstract totems. The base of one sculpture served as a public bike rack.

At the 2009 Art at the Heart of the City ceremony, local artists were introduced, a chocolate cake was cut and Rob Licht, a local artist who once helped us build a passive solar bus shelter at EcoVillage, led a tour of the 18 sculptures scattered around a three block area. One of my favorite pieces was by a New Hampshire artist, Andy Moerlein. His sculpture, "Motherhood, The Ultimate Sustainable Practice," was a dramatic construction of bent wood saplings with a figure of a woman swinging a child into the air. The sculpture was grounded by huge hunks of local slate and was somewhat reminiscent of an Andy Goldsworthy piece. Another piece was by a local muralist whom I've met, Mary Beth Ihnken. Called "Going to Market," her three panel mural depicted the rural landscape, including a windmill and a bicyclist, followed by a busy farm harvest scene and finally a bicyclist who has purchased a handlebar basket full of produce at the bustling Ithaca Farmer's Market.

Permanent Whimsey

These temporary sculptures augment the permanent ones that provide such a delightful eyeful on the Commons and nearby DeWitt Park. While there are many that I enjoy, I have several favorites. A whimsical one, by artist Cherry Rahn, is located on Bank Alley, a section of the Commons dominated by several banks. Entitled "Businessman in Touch with Nature," a life-sized man in a business suit with butterfly wings attached is shown running in full stride. Rather than weighed down by his work, he even looks happy!

Jim Bosjolie

"Businessman in Touch with Nature" by Cherry Rahn, a sculpture on the Ithaca Commons.

Yet another of my favorites is a young man sitting on the grass at DeWitt Park. Like his counterparts, he is life-size. Sculpted by Miguel Antonio Horn, the young man reminds me of my son. He is looking soulfully into the sky and seems to be pondering the meaning of life, or perhaps just enjoying a quiet moment in the sun. Each of these sculptures provides a welcome, momentary distraction from everyday life. Each one seems to say, "Wake up!" to passersby.

The Hangar Theatre

Ithaca is blessed with excellent local theater. In addition to regular productions at Cornell and Ithaca College, there are two small local theater companies, the Kitchen and the Hangar, which provide top-notch entertainment as well as a dazzling array of experimental techniques. One of the area's best bargains is to work as an usher at the Hangar, a local nonprofit organization which puts on five main-stage plays during the summer, as well as five Kiddstuff plays. Jared and I have been ushering there for the last ten years. We show up an hour before the show to hand out programs and help people find their seats. Then we enjoy the show for free!

The Hangar, which opened in 1975 in a renovated airport hangar, has a mission of "providing exceptional theater experiences of high professional quality to enrich, enlighten, educate, and entertain the diverse audience in the Finger Lakes region and beyond."[3] As an organization it takes its role of being available to a diverse audience seriously. At a recent usher orientation, Lisa Bushlow, the executive director, told us how proud she was that the Hangar offers a Pay-What-You-Can night. On the second Wednesday of each show's performance, people who could not otherwise enjoy the theater can claim a ticket for whatever price they can afford.

Strong education and training programs are central parts of the Hangar's mission. After Lisa Bushlow became education director in 1991, the Hangar became recognized throughout New York State and even across the country for its extraordinary, comprehensive, year-round theatre education programs. During the school year, the Hangar brings a range of theatre experiences to students across New York State, with its School Tour Program, Artists-in-the-Schools and Project 4—a program now in every fourth grade class in the Ithaca City, Lansing and Trumansburg School Districts. Throughout the summer, Kiddstuff performances and the Next Generation School of Theatre reach thousands of young people. The Hangar currently serves more than 60,000 adults and children annually.

Good Art Makes Good Business

While art is wonderful for its own sake, it also promotes tourism, a key piece of the economic puzzle in upstate New York. In 1987, the county cleverly decided to tap into the flow of money that tourists bring, by imposing a hotel room occupancy tax on all overnight stays. Although the tax is very small, it brings in over $1.7 million a year, which is then plowed back into tourism promotion, supporting the arts and festivals and creating a self-fulfilling feedback loop. Tourists who are attracted to the beauty and creativity of the Ithaca area also purchase local goods and services and bring in $161 million a year to the Tompkins County economy, according to a statewide Empire State Development study. Tourism brings in about $11.4 million a year in sales tax alone.[4] This is a good example of how the goals of a sustainable culture and a sustainable economy can successfully intertwine.

Homegrown Creativity

On the other end of the spectrum, it seems that creativity often bubbles up spontaneously in healthy people whose basic needs have been met and who have some leisure time. Artistic expression can be enjoyed for its own sake, by young and old, with no economic benefit attached and no desire to achieve a professional status. Unfortunately, this impulse is frequently obscured in a culture dominated by mass media and enthralled with stardom. It is hard to have the patience to learn a new skill if you are only used to people performing at the highest possible level. It is time to reclaim our inherent right to creative self-expression as individuals, and this seems easier to do in a supportive community setting.

One example of creative empowerment is an arts festival that my partner Jared organized with a couple of friends for our community at EcoVillage. Called SparkFest, it made its debut on a sunny Saturday in February 2009. The idea was simple: a gallery was set up for the afternoon at the Common House. A couple of dozen residents showcased their artwork, which ranged from fiber arts to jewelry, from photography to video, from woodworking to painting. The artists, who ranged from 8 years old to 65, arrived early and hovered eagerly nearby their creations. For many of them this was a first time to show off their work, while a few were seasoned artists. After an initial two-hour viewing period, each artist had a chance to present one of their pieces, telling about what inspired them. About

Jim Bosjolie

Young girl tells a story at EcoVillage's SparkFest.

50 people crowded happily together into the common living room to hear the presentations, celebrating the emerging artist in each person.

Meanwhile, culinary artists shared their edible work. One friend, Elan, engaged people in creating their own delicious mouth-sized pieces of art, using rice crackers as a base, with pieces of tangy feta cheese, juicy red pimientos, black olives, avocado and fresh dill as possible layers. The resulting creations brought immediate gratification.

After a dinner break, SparkFest resumed with a celebration of performance artists. The evening brought an embarrassment of riches, from beginning, six-year-old piano players and ballet dancers to well-known EcoVillage musicians who make a living from their art. One fabulous guitar player, Joe Crookston, used to rent a home at EcoVillage. Now a next-door neighbor, he teaches guitar to a handful of young EcoVillage boys, who play amazingly well. Joe received a grant in 2007 to travel throughout the Finger Lakes to collect stories, interview locals and write songs, and he has some hauntingly beautiful pieces. One which touches me deeply is "John Jones," the story of an ex-slave who escaped from Virginia on foot and organized one of the largest stations on the underground railway in Elmira, New York. He helped to free 800 slaves, and his homestead and gravesite are still there. In a change of pace, a couple performed a lively swing dance. The whole event sped by, creating a wonderful, warm feeling.

Jared's initial goals for the event were amply fulfilled and make it easy to replicate this kind of event in other settings. The key concepts of SparkFest were to:

- involve the kids from the beginning
- level the playing field so that the novices are given the same attention as the experts
- focus on collaboration rather than competition
- involve lots of volunteers to help

After such a resounding success, I have no doubt that SparkFest will become an annual tradition.

Sustainable Culture

This chapter barely begins to address the amazing festivals and excellent music, art, theater and dance that are so much a part of the cultural scene in Ithaca. For instance, Ithaca College is renowned for its School of Music, and there are also dozens of well-known local musicians and bands. There are numerous excellent museums and the local theaters draw top-notch actors from around the country. The annual Grassroots Festival in Trumansburg is considered one of the top ten music festivals in the country, and Earth Day is always a wildly creative celebration here.

Whether it is meant for personal expression or for sharing with the public, the art scene is alive and well in Ithaca. Art opens our eyes, surprises and often delights us and makes us think. When it is combined with a social message, such as creating a just and sustainable community, it can help us to imagine the world we want to co-create. Art is truly at the heart of a sustainable culture, and we are beginning to honor and develop that creative impulse as a whole community more with each passing year.

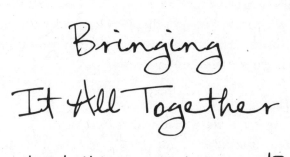

15

Bringing It All Together

What Have We Learned?

We live on one planet, and it is becoming essential to our survival that we begin thinking and acting as one people; this can only realistically begin on the level of community. We have the option right now to choose to prepare our communities for an energy-constrained future. We can choose to do so with humility, with compassion, with creativity—and yes, even with joy. But we must choose, or choices will be made for us.

MICHAEL BROWNLEE, CO-FOUNDER OF
BOULDER VALLEY RELOCALIZATION

Creating a Positive Future

We have learned some lessons in Ithaca, New York and its surrounding communities which I hope will be useful to you. What follows is not comprehensive, but rather some notes from the field as I reflect on the past two decades that I've been engaged in work here and seen numerous grassroots and institutional sustainability initiatives unfold.

Throughout this book, you have been introduced to many initiatives, small and large, that are helping to shape this region. Some of the initiatives have grown from grassroots organizations into important institutions, such as the Ithaca Farmer's Market, or the Alternatives Federal Credit Union. Some have the weight of multi-million

233

dollar endeavors, such as Cornell University's Climate Action Plan or Tompkins County Solid Waste Management, while others are entrepreneurial start-ups such as *Positive News* or the Ithaca Health Alliance. What unites each of these ventures? What makes them successful? And perhaps most important, what can we learn from this upwelling of sustainability approaches?

Visionary Thinking

Each of these initiatives started with a great vision. While each vision may be a little different from each other, like different facets in a jewel they combine into a greater whole. What is this larger vision? I would say it is both simple and complex: we all seek to live in a just and harmonious way with our fellow human beings and with nature. This is simple to say and enormously complex to achieve. Whether it involves relocalizing our food system, reinvesting in the community, eliminating greenhouse gases, creating a more just and equitable culture, sharing positive news stories, taking control of a broken healthcare system or dozens of other possibilities, it is all interwoven. Each of these visions ultimately supports the others.

Burning Souls and Teamwork

Another common element that most of these endeavors share is what I like to call a *burning soul* — that is a person, or occasionally a few people, who are true visionaries. These are people who can look into the future and see a clear picture of what can be created. By articulating this vision, they inspire others to get involved. They are initiators, people without whom the project would not have started. Once the vision is shared, burning souls pour themselves into manifesting it. It is their passion, their commitment, their life energy and often their money (or hard work with little or no pay) that makes the difference between a failed project and one that becomes successful. You have met a couple dozen burning souls in the course of this book, and there are many dozens more who were not profiled due to lack of space and time. In Ithaca we are blessed with the richness of many people who are passionate about creating a better future. Many of them have used their creativity and commitment to begin practical steps towards that future, in the process influencing thousands and sometimes millions of people, as ideas catch hold in the collective imagination.

If a burning soul is crucial to the success of a project, another extremely important element is the working team that surrounds the central person or persons. For a visionary leader alone can not carry out his or her vision without a lot of support. A team of people can provide the multiple skills needed to help a project start. It may seem like a contradiction to have both a strong and visionary leader and an excellent working team, yet it is a way of combining the best of both an entrepreneurial spirit and the solidity of a participatory group. Of course, it can also lead to all kinds of difficult power dynamics if the leader is seen as taking too much credit for the work or if the group doesn't support a new direction the burning soul would like to take. However, this arrangement of a person or persons who play a leadership role, embedded within a group which cooperates to get the work done, is a very powerful model.

As a team develops its capacity it is quite possible, and even desirable, that other members of the team step forward into leadership positions. For leadership can be seen as a role to fill, rather than as the attribute of one individual. While there will always be some people who make outstanding leaders, it is also true that most people have the innate ability to see what needs to be done and to bring their own skills and experience into play. If you have ever watched geese fly in a V formation, you'll know what I mean. The lead goose is at the front for a while, cutting the wind and setting the direction, while the geese behind honk their encouragement. After a while, the lead goose tires and another goose comes forward to fill its place. It is often this true teamwork that is needed to help achieve long-term goals. And building a sustainable society is one of those long-term goals that needs all the leadership and all the teamwork that we can manage!

Systems Thinking
Once a vision takes hold and people begin to mobilize to support it, it is important to look at what role the idea plays in the greater

whole. What forces will support it, what will work against it? How is this vision connected to other initiatives? In what ways can constituencies be influenced?

Consider Sustainable Tompkins' approach to how Tompkins County can address climate change. Ithaca is a small city that is "centrally isolated" in upstate New York, but it is also the home of a major research university with many international faculty and students. And it is a tourist destination. All of these factors combine to bring tens of thousands of travelers to the area. What if each of those people offset the carbon emissions caused by their airline or car travel with a donation to a local cause: weatherizing homes of low income people in the area? In February 2010, Sustainable Tompkins rolled out the Finger Lakes Climate Fund, which offers carbon offsets through just such a program. By tapping into the strong environmental values of the regional population and by using the donations of wealthier residents to assist low income neighbors to lower their high energy bills, it is a win-win proposition.

The Finger Lakes Climate Fund helps to accomplish at least three major goals: cutting down on greenhouse gas emissions (as the county housing stock gets weatherized, it uses less fossil fuel to heat each year), reinvesting dollars in the local community, as well as creating more local jobs (installing insulation and other energy-saving devices). Of course, offsets do not reduce the greenhouse gases caused by air travel, but perhaps the fund will help people to think twice before taking a flight and paying the carbon tax.

When a system is carefully analyzed, there are often high leverage points that can be used to create change for the least amount of effort. Another example, in the economic arena, is a new investment policy by a local environmentally-oriented foundation. Jon Jensen, executive director of the Park Foundation, told me that most foundations only invest 2–3% of their funds in *program-related investment* (PRI) — investments that directly support their mission — whereas Park has 36% of its portfolio in PRI. Because water is a key interest of theirs, he has asked investment officers to look for local, water-related investments. This has the effect of pouring more money into a local cause they support.[1] Likewise, the Alternatives Federal Credit

Union (see Chapter 5) is required to set aside a percentage of its capital that is loaned out. When Park invests $200,000 in AFCU, this allows the credit union to make $2 million in loans, loans that will go directly into building the local econ-

All ages enjoy the Cayuga Waterfront Trail.

Sheryl Sinkow Photography

omy. Once again, through relatively little effort, a huge leverage is exerted which fulfills the goals of both organizations.

Pleasing Partnerships

As organizations grow, developing partnerships with other groups becomes very important. Looking at the vision of creating a sustainable city or region is exciting and often overwhelming. No one group can take it all on. Instead, people can collaborate with each other in both small and big ways.

Often it seems that the wider the gap between different types of organizations the stronger the possible outcomes can be. Just as the boundary between ocean and land teems with the richest sea life, there is tremendous energy in the interface between different partnering organizations.

I am happy to see unusual partnerships often sprout between groups in Ithaca — it seems to be a characteristic of living here. A recent example was between a restaurant and a health clinic. Moosewood, the famous vegetarian restaurant, offered to host a brunch to raise funds for the Ithaca Free Clinic. The brunch, which had two sold-out sittings on a Sunday morning, raised $2,765 for the Clinic, money which was sorely needed. According to Bethany Schroeder, president of the Board of Directors for the Clinic's parent organization, the Ithaca Health Alliance, "Our patient visits are up by 13% [in the last year], and we must make every effort to expand Clinic space in the upcoming year. Supporting the Clinic also shows support for the needs of our neighbors and friends, who have lost their jobs, hours at their jobs, and sometimes their health insurance benefits, too."[2] This is an example of a cooperative restaurant helping out a cooperative health clinic.

Cool Coalitions

If partnerships are remarkable in what they can achieve, alliances of four or more organizations working together can do wonders. This is where the whole really does become greater than its parts. I have mentioned many coalitions in previous chapters. While some of these formed new organizations (such as Ithaca Carshare or Finger Lakes ReUse Center), others accomplish ongoing tasks together (such as Tompkins County Climate Protection Initiative or Ithaca Green Building Alliance).

Many of these coalitions include similar players. We saw in Chapter 6 that Ithaca College places a high priority on community involvement in sustainability initiatives, partly through sending a representative (often Marian Brown) as a liaison to many organizations, but also by having students learn through involvement in projects that benefit community organizations. Likewise, Cornell is most often represented through Cornell Cooperative Extension of Tompkins County, which has programs that relate to most of the topics covered in this book. However, individual departments at Cornell University are at times involved in community coalitions, such as Ithaca Carshare. Center for Transformative Action (CTA), an educational nonprofit organization affiliated with Cornell that nurtures many initiatives for social change and community transformation, has projects that relate to everything from economic equity to sustainable community development and is often represented through one of its projects in these endeavors. EcoVillage, a CTA project, often has volunteers involved in helping to start new coalitions, as does Sustainable Tompkins. Greenstar, which has a community outreach arm, takes a keen interest in sustainability initiatives as well and is a frequent player.

The important thing to notice is that each of these organizations has a mission that includes local community empowerment as a core value, as well as a strong environmental ethic. The strength of many people working together over time, who share a common vision, cannot be underestimated. It reminds me of making bread: the more you knead the dough, the more the strands of wheat protein, called gluten, intertwine, making the dough strong and elastic. It is that strength and elasticity which allows the dough to rise by capturing tiny gas bubbles given off by the growing yeast cells. Similarly, the more these strands of mutual connection between organizations and people are reinforced, the more opportunity there is to capture individual and group initiatives, and rise to become the nourishing bread of community.

Green Cluster Development for a Sustainable Future

I first mentioned cluster development in Chapter 2. Regional economic development can encourage certain businesses or services that become that region's specialty; for instance, California's Silicon Valley is known around the world as a hub of electronic innovation. Together, clustered businesses create high visibility and a seeming paradox of both healthy competition and cooperation. Some other common elements of clusters are: geographic proximity, strong economic ties and social networks among producers, multiple products and distributors and engaged support institutions. I think that one creative way to look at sustainability initiatives is to look at them through this lens.

The Spirit of Local Food

In Chapter 2, we saw a local food and farming system which has already been 30 years in the making. It includes a wide variety of players — from collaborations between local farmers, to the intersection of retailers and suppliers, to a concerted effort to bring access to healthy local food to low income families and fresh produce to school children, to high-end culinary development of wineries and restaurants which emphasize fresh, local ingredients. There is both competition and collaboration between the many players, creating a very healthy food system that benefits everyone.

The net effect addresses the triple bottom line: it saves enormous amounts of energy by shortening the miles that food travels and supports environmentally sound methods of growing food; it bolsters the local economy by supporting local farmers, producers, retailers and chefs (among other livelihoods), as well as keeping food dollars going into local businesses; and it creates a strong sense of community through providing venues (such as the Farmers' Market or Greenstar) where people enjoy shopping partly because it's a social environment — they know they'll run into friends and chat with vendors.

But besides creating social, natural and economic capital, the food cluster provides something even bigger: something more than the sum of its parts, which I'll call *the spirit of local food*. All of these benefits become inextricably woven together, in a new pattern of wholeness that really works on multiple levels. Supporting local food and farming becomes a way of living with the integrity that comes from following one's deepest values, and that way of life feeds the soul. When many people are engaged in this way of life, it creates an ongoing community of shared values that affects the whole region. It begins to bring a system that has been desperately out of balance back into equilibrium. It greens the future, not only for everyone who grows food or who eats, but also for the local water, soil and air and for the long-term livelihoods of everyone who lives here.

A Strong Foundation — Green Building

I mentioned the green building and alternative energy cluster effect in Chapter 3. Ithaca stands out as the Solar Capital of New York State because of its many solar installations. It has a high concentration of both individuals and organizations that have made pioneering steps towards building very energy-efficient buildings, many with passive solar features, green roofs, natural materials and other innovative building techniques. Both Ithaca College and Cornell, as key local institutions that have made strong commitments to green building in the last five years, are actively trying to trim their greenhouse gases to zero emissions by 2050 — a huge goal, and one which informs how they use energy as well as how they build.

The Ithaca Green Building Alliance (IGBA) brings together small businesses and individuals who are engaged in green building practices and provides both support and friendly competition for jobs. Cornell Cooperative Extension of Tompkins County (CCE-TC) together with IGBA hosts a very popular Green Building Open House every year, which has grown to two days of home visits by over 1,000 people. CCE-TC also provides a website with tips and how-to videos for all kinds of home energy repairs. In addition, the Green Resource Hub has a local green business directory that includes many builders and energy providers, and a number of these entrepreneurs have also joined the Hub's Sustainable Enterprise and Entrepreneur Network, which provides even more ways to build social and economic ties.

Taken together, there is both state-wide recognition of the green building interest in this area and a strong county-wide collaboration of individuals, businesses, organizations and institutions which are working together to accomplish similar goals.

Each of the areas mentioned in this book — be it music and art, sustainability education, building a local economy or waste reduction, to name a few — has the potential for remarkable cluster development. You may wish to look for clusters in your region and think about how to further support their development.

Transition Towns

While Green Development Clusters represent a hearty step in the right direction, what does it look like to bring a deliberately planned, community-wide approach to creating a sustainable future? In March of 2009, Tina Clarke, a speaker and trainer with the Transition Towns movement, came to Ithaca to speak to a group of about 20 local sustainability activists. Transition Towns have taken off in Britain and are starting to gain a foothold in the US and other countries as well. According to their website,

Transition US is "a nonprofit organization that provides inspiration, encouragement, support, networking, and training for

Transition Initiatives across the United States.... The Transition movement is part of a vibrant, grassroots movement that seeks to build community resilience in the face of such challenges as peak oil, climate change and the economic crisis.... We believe that we can make the transition to a more sustainable world."[3]

Transition initiatives start building a grassroots community by raising awareness of "the Long Emergency,"[4] one name for the time we are entering in which economic instability, peak oil and climate change all converge. But the message of Transition Towns is basically a positive one. It is meant to awaken citizens to joyfully undertake actions that will create a more resilient community. The consensus of those present at the meeting in Ithaca seemed to be, "Yes, we're already doing that in spades. We just don't use the same terminology."

Ithacans are known for their fierce independence. Since Tompkins County has been on a trajectory to create a more sustainable community for over two decades and the Transition Town movement is relatively young, I sensed a strong resistance from some of the most engaged local activists in formally adopting the name and methods of a Transition Town Initiative. And yet, it seems to me that by aligning with a movement that has gone viral, is rapidly developing around the world and that shares the same values as multiple groups in Ithaca, a lot could be gained.

There have been some follow-up activities exploring the Transition Town concept more in Ithaca since that meeting a year ago. Tina Clarke came back to be a keynote speaker at the CCE-TC Annual Meeting, and we also hosted her for a talk to an enthusiastic audience at EcoVillage, where a study group read and discussed the *Transition Handbook*[5] over a period of months in the fall of 2009. Two of our residents also attended a weekend training session. It will be interesting to see whether formal ties will be established between Ithaca and Transition Town US. In any case, I think it is wise to see that we are all part of the same fabric, working for profound change.

The Revolution May Be Funded

Ithaca has the distinction and good fortune to be home to the Park Foundation, which focuses charitable work on higher education, media and the environment. In 2008, Park gave out $17.5 million dollars in grant money, much of it to national organizations. I interviewed executive director Jon Jensen who began his work at the Park Foundation after moving from Cleveland, Ohio. One of the first things he did was to establish a fund to support local sustainability efforts. This fund has helped to jump-start multiple initiatives, including this book.

According to the Park Foundation website,

> The Sustainable Ithaca grants program is focused on the following topical areas: Green Buildings; Transportation; Smart Growth; Natural Systems; Sustainable Institutions and Green Consumerism; Energy and Climate Change; Toxic Threats; Education; and Communications and Leadership Development.
>
> The goal of this program is to help Ithaca become the most sustainable city of its size in North America. This program is focused on Ithaca, Tompkins County, and the Cayuga Lake watershed. Of special interest are projects and programs that link sustainability to the Foundation's Local Grants program priorities in serving underserved populations.[6]

I asked Jon, as a relative newcomer, about his impressions of Ithaca and the sustainability work going on. He told me, "This is an incredibly unique place. [There are] so many points of light happening here. I found almost as many different nonprofits in Tompkins County, with 100,000 people, as I did in northeast Ohio with 2.5 million. The concentration per capita is amazing. There is huge intellectual content and capacity. Pick any topic and you'll find an expert here." He laughed and went on, thoughtfully, "Here there is a scale of doability, sometimes I call it 'incestuous efficiency.' Here you can get together five people and get anything that you want done. That is a scale you can work at!"[7]

While the community scale makes it easier to affect change, Jon also acknowledged a cultural attitude. "Something's going on here. There is a psychology, a mindset that 'we have to change'... The lines here between top and bottom are very small. There is some insularity here, too. Most people live and work here, so it's more integrated. We're a little self-satisfied in our greenness."

Jon continued, "When I recommended that the Foundation expand our history of local environment grants into a broader scope of sustainability, I think it surprised the Foundation Board, since it was local, not national. I felt there should be funding to develop the eco-spirit that I saw here. Initially this new program cast its net wide. Now we're starting to take a little more initiative and push a little. We're especially trying to develop three areas: a) indicators and measurement, b) local leadership development and c) marketing/communication."

As Jon looked ahead, he reflected on some concerns, "The environmental movement is broad and thin here, just as in many other places. For example, education and social services have a broader base of funding support, but the environmental movement less so. Some of that is compared to other segments of the nonprofit sector, environment is relatively new. I worry about the sustainability of the organizations themselves. So much happens here on a volunteer basis. I'm surprised that, so far, more organizations haven't come to us. What is great is, people here have an idea, and they just start doing it, rather than looking for funding."[8] Although many of the smaller groups may not look for funding and the Sustainable Ithaca grants program is quite new, the Park Foundation has undoubtedly contributed to the success of many of the more established sustainability initiatives, especially through providing funds for staffing innovative programs. We are lucky to have their support.

Specific Tools for Building a Movement

Because I'm a long-time community organizer, I can't close this chapter without suggesting some specific, tried and true tips that have worked well in the Ithaca area. These are in no particular order.

Bring in an Inspiring Outside Speaker

For some reason, people seem to value an expert from another city far more than the local people they know. In addition, there is a lot that can be learned from others who have already done what you are hoping to do. A few examples: When we first started organizing EcoVillage, we brought in six nationally known speakers over the course of a year, people who were architects, community builders or ecological city designers. We funded honoraria for these speakers through the co-sponsorship of various Cornell departments. This had two effects: it allowed us to attract people we could not otherwise afford, and it ensured that professors assigned their students to hear the lecture. While the speakers were present, we also scheduled them for talks at downtown venues and at Ithaca College, we got informal consulting time for our group and we got lots of local media coverage.

In another example, the Partnership for Sustainability Education funded sustainability education consultant Ed Quevedo to come and speak to key stakeholders about his experience in starting Sustainable Sonoma [County], among other topics. This led to great excitement among participants and a partnership between local government, environmental groups, college and university representatives and local businesses to start what became Sustainable Tompkins.

In each case, the outside speaker was brought in to "light the fire" of embers carefully tended by a small group. It was as if hearing about the issue from someone with national credibility gave the local people a chance to set their own dreams alight.

Feasibility Study

While an organization may or may not need a formal business plan, it definitely helps to study an issue before jumping into it. It's important to outline a vision, define a mission and goals, examine what has already been done and what needs to be done, identify stakeholders, analyze strengths and weaknesses and more. Doing this takes diligence, and someone should be funded to be the burning soul to make sure it gets done.

As described in Chapter 6, we conducted a Feasibility Study at EcoVillage at Ithaca, to explore how to put our dreams for an Eco-Village at Ithaca Center for Sustainability Education into a coherent plan. The scope of the vision and the practical possibilities it opened up were very exciting. Two of the initiatives, New Roots School and Groundswell Center for Local Food and Farming, are already up and running less than two years later. The power of creating a strong vision that is tied to reality through a feasibility study, and linked with the passion of a burning soul should not be underestimated!

Study Groups

Getting together like-minded people to learn together can be wonderfully liberating — at least for those who are no longer in school and who may miss intellectual stimulation in their lives. Often these groups have a facilitator rather than a leader, a person who helps to point out resources to read and who helps to guide discussions, but who does not have all the answers.

This was a key strategy that Gay Nicholson used in beginning Sustainable Tompkins. As mentioned in Chapter 6, she organized study circles with invited local leaders and practitioners in five areas. Dozens of people signed up to work on the projects that were presented from the Study Circles, and Sustainable Tompkins began.[9]

Demonstration Projects and Hands-on Learning

Many people learn best through active engagement. It also helps if they see clear examples of what it is possible to create. At New Roots High School, an important part of the pedagogy of sustainability is hands-on activity. The Farm to School program teams New Roots students with West Haven Farm at EcoVillage. Starting in the spring of 2010, teens helped to grow food which they then made into tasty lunches. Students learned practical skills of farming and cooking, the nutritional content of foods and they enjoyed being outside with friends rather than cooped up in the classroom. They could feel proud of their accomplishments, and their fellow students enjoyed delicious, healthy, local foods lunches.

Ithaca College converted a section of lawn in front of the Center for Natural Science building into a field of native plants. Faculty and students from different disciplines studied everything from soil types and nutrient cycling to calculating the reduced carbon footprint resulting from not spraying fertilizers and pesticides and not mowing. The grounds crew learned about taking care of native plants. And the whole experiment was highly visible, at the entrance to the college, with some signage to indicate what was going on.

These kinds of projects not only deeply influence participants, but they also offer a glimpse of a new, positive reality to the public and expand ideas about what is possible.

Mini-Grants

One extremely useful organizing tool has been the use of mini-grants by Partnership in Sustainability Education (PSE). Every year we offer mini-grants of $1,000 to educators at IC or EcoVillage who would like to develop or modify a course to incorporate sustainability into the educational experience. Since the beginning of this program in 2003, nearly 60 grants have been awarded to Ithaca College faculty, staff, students and EcoVillage residents. Educators have reworked traditional course topics from art history to psychology to incorporate a sustainable perspective. The small grants have catalyzed many faculty and students to take sustainability principles seriously, creating an amazing ripple effect.

Mini-grants are such a good way of catalyzing a new level of community involvement, and empowering local leaders, that this successful technique is also being used by Sustainable Tompkins and the Ithaca Health Alliance.

Celebrating Success

Working towards a sustainable future and putting in the hours and effort and entrepreneurial zeal it takes to start a new initiative deserves recognition. That is why Sustainable Tompkins started Signs of Sustainability, an annual celebration of new sustainability initiatives in Tompkins County. Organized by Marian Brown and other volunteers, awards are given in three categories:

- a new sustainable enterprise
- a new group or organization supporting some aspect of sustainable development
- a new sustainable program element or activity rolled out by an existing business or nonprofit

Started in 2006, this program has snowballed into a remarkable community event with more entries every year. In 2009 there were a record 140 Signs of Sustainability recognized! It has actually become hard to find a room large enough to accommodate just the people who win awards, let alone the general public. The ceremony itself is augmented by an ongoing column in *Tompkins Weekly*, which gives a larger audience a chance to be introduced to these exciting initiatives.

I highly recommend celebration as a way of enjoying the fruits of our collective labor! It helps to give each organization some motivation to be publicly recognized, but it also reflects back to the wider community how much is going on. It knits us all together into a whole community.

Making a Choice for a Sustainable Future

I am convinced that at some level we all know that major change is inevitable. All around us we see signs of possible collapse — from the economy, to environmental devastation, to social and cultural breakdown. The signs are hard to ignore. Our Mother Earth and her children are suffering terribly. In the United States, which has 4.5% of the world's population but which uses a quarter of the world's resources, I believe we have an extra moral obligation to turn around our way of life, to learn "to live simply that others may simply live."

But rather than just feeling guilty or overwhelmed by these multiple crises (which we all feel at times), we may also be lucky enough to recognize something else — we do have a choice to learn to live differently, as individuals, as communities and as a culture. There is a wonderful upwelling of energy to make profound changes that are not only necessary, but that also lead to a much higher quality of life. This energy is showing up in the vast citizens' movement around the world that Paul Hawken describes in *Blessed Unrest*, a largely leaderless movement of over a million grassroots organizations, working towards ecological sustainability and social justice. Hawken posits that this movement is acting as the world's immune system, helping to heal its wounds.[10]

In *Choosing a Sustainable Future*, I've filled you in on some of the exciting ways that this energy, this people's movement, has been manifesting around Ithaca, New York. But I hope you will not just read the book. Instead, please see this as an invitation to make a choice in your own life and in your own family, neighborhood or city. There is no right way to begin. Instead it is up to each of us to find what we love to do and then use that talent to help to create a more positive future. As we pool our talents, we can have amazing ripple effects, the results of which may reach further than we can ever know.

Together we are creating a cultural shift which goes far beyond the triple bottom line. For this cultural shift addresses not only "people, planet, prosperity" but also captures that ineffable quality of spirit. Together we can create fresh approaches to terribly complex problems. As Arundhati Roy reminds us, "Another world is not only possible, she is on her way. On a quiet day I can hear her breathing."[11] By our love for the planet and our love for her people, we can be inspired to reach far beyond ourselves and touch that new world.

Endnotes

Preface: Why I Wrote This Book

1. World Commission on Environment and Development. *Our Common Future*. Oxford, 1987, p. 43.

Introduction: Another World Is Possible

1. Jessica Mousseau. "Health, Pollution and Traffic Conditions within Megacities." Associated Content website from Yahoo. [online]. [cited July 11, 2010]. associatedcontent.com/article/29761/health_pollution_and_traffic_conditions.html?cat=27.
2. Helena Norberg-Hodge and Ross Jackson. *Breakaway: From Globalisation to Localisation*. Unpublished manuscript, p. 21. Quoted with permission of the authors.
3. Ibid.
4. Duane Elgin. *Voluntary Simplicity: Toward a Life that is Outwardly Simple, Inwardly Rich*, 2nd ed. Harper, 2010, p. 117.
5. See US Census Bureau. *Current Population Survey*. [online]. [cited July 7, 2010]. census.gov/cps/.
6. Michael Brownlee. "Relocalization and the Regeneration of Community." Speech at Crestone, Colorado conference, June 22, 2007.
7. Richard Louv. *Last Child in the Woods: Saving Our Children From Nature-Deficit Disorder*. Algonquin, 2005.
8. Paul Hawken. *Blessed Unrest: How the Largest Movement in the World Came into Being and Why No One Saw It. Coming*. Viking, 2007.
9. Elgin, p. 23.
10. The United States Conference of Mayors. *Climate Protection Agreement*. [online]. [cited June 18, 2010]. usmayors.org/climateprotection/ agreement.htm.
11. American College and University Presidents' Climate Commitment website. [online]. [cited June 18, 2010]. presidentsclimatecommitment.org/.
12. CNN, quoted on 350.org website. [online]. [cited June 23, 2010]. 350.org/story.
13. MoveOn.org website. [online]. [cited June 18, 2010]. moveon.org.
14. Post Carbon Institute. "Relocalize." [online]. [cited June 18, 2010]. postcarbon.org/relocalize.
15. Transition network website. [online]. [cited June 18, 2010]. transitionnetwork.org/.
16. Visit Ithaca.com website. [online]. [cited July 7, 2010]. visitithaca.com/top-10s.html.

Chapter 1: Learning from the First Nations

1. Excerpted from The Thanksgiving Address, traditional words for the opening and closing of all ceremonial and governmental gatherings held by the Six Nations (Haudenosaunee or Iroquois).
2. Haudenosaunee is the term the Six Nations use for themselves. Although the term *Iroquois* was a name used by the French, among others, it is so much more familiar to the reader, that I will use the terms interchangeably.
3. Heriberto Dixon. *Tutelo Nation*. Written for the program of the September 22, 2007 Tutelo Homecoming Festival.

4. In fact, the Cayuga were neutral in the US Revolutionary War, although some Mohawk mercenary soldiers were hired by the British. Some historians such as Barbara Mann theorize that Washington's campaign was a land-grab to pay soldiers in land.

5. Bruce E. Johansen. "Dating the Iroquois Confederacy." *Akwesasne Notes* Volume 1, #3 and 4. This is an estimate, and some current archaelogical digs suggest that it may have been even earlier.

6. Haudenosaunee — The Longhouse website. [online]. [cited January 8, 2010]. sixnations. org.

7. "Haudenosaunee Culture." Pamphlet #1. Neighbors of the Onondaga Nation (NOON).

8. Ibid.

9. Bruce E. Johansen. *Haudenosaunee Influences on the U.S. Government: A Debt in Governance Style*. Neighbors of the Onondaga Nation (NOON)." [online]. [cited May 14, 2010]. peacecouncil.net/NOON/articles/government.html.

10. Ibid, quoted from the official record of the event.

11. There is some debate among historians about how much influence the Iroquois actually had on the US Constitution. For more discussion of critiques and responses to them, see Bruce E. Johansen. *Debating Democracy: Native American Legacy of Freedom*. Clear Light, 1998.

12. Sally Roesch Wagner. "Iroquois Women Inspire 19th Century Feminists." Neighbors of the Onondaga Nation (NOON). [online]. [cited May 14, 2010]. peacecouncil.net/NOON/articles/Haudwomen.html. For fuller discussion see Sally Roesch Wagner. *Sisters in Spirit: Haudenosaunee (Iroquois) Influence on Early American Feminists*. Native Voices, 2001.

13. Ibid.

14. Richard Wolkomir. "Bringing Ancient Ways to our Farmer's Fields." *Smithsonian* Volume 26 #8 (November 1995), pp. 99–107.

15. David Holmgren. *Permaculture: Principles and Pathways Beyond Sustainability*. Holmgren Design Services, 2002, p. xix.

16. Oren Lyons. Speech at the United Nations Millenium World Peace Summit of Religious and Spiritual Leaders, August 28–31, 2000 in *Neighbor to Neighbor, Nation to Nation*. Neighbors of the Onondaga Nation (NOON).

17. Ibid.

18. Audrey Shenandoah. Speech at the United Nations Millenium World Peace Summit of Religious and Spiritual Leaders, August 28–31, 2000 in *Neighbor to Neighbor, Nation to Nation*. Neighbors of the Onondaga Nation (NOON).

19. Onondaga nation website. "The Complaint in The Onondaga Land Rights Action Opens with the Following Words." [online]. [cited June 22, 2010]. Onondaganation.org/land/complaint.html.

20. Onondaga nation website. "The Onondaga Nation and Environmental Stewardship." [online]. [cited June 22, 2010]. Onondaganation.org/land/stewards.html.

21. Brynn Mannino and Maura Stephens. "Reclaiming Part of a Lost Homeland." *Ithaca College Quarterly*. [online]. [cited November 20, 2007]. ithaca.edu/icq/2006v2/depts/south_hill/cayuga.html.

22. Ibid.

Chapter 2: Growing a Local Food Culture

1. Jan Norman, personal interview, January, 2008.

2. Ibid.

3. Bill McKibben. *Deep Economy: The Wealth of Communities and the Durable Future*. Times, 2005, p. 105.

4. Michael Pollan. "Farmer in Chief." *New York Times*, October 12, 2008.

5. Monika Roth, personal interview, December 12, 2007.

6. Ibid.

7. Jen Bokaer-Smith, local food and farming focus group, January 15, 2008.

8. Norman, interview.

9. Roth, interview.

10. Joe Romano, personal interview, January 10, 2008.

11. Ibid.

12. Joanna Green, local food and farming focus group, March 29, 2007.

13. Kim Severson. "A Finger (Lakes) Food Tour." *New York Times*, August 22, 2008.

14. Green, focus group.

15. Liz Karabanakis, personal interview, January 7, 2008.

16. Roth, interview.

17. Karabanakis, interview.

18. Debbie Teeter, personal interview, December 12, 2007, updated May 20, 2010.

19. "Healthy Food for All." Flyer from Cornell Cooperative Extension of Tompkins County.

20. Krishna Ramanujan. "Cornell Dining triples purchases from local farmers as long-distance food supply system faces rising pressures." *Cornell Chronicle*, November 1, 2006. [online]. [cited May 18, 2010]. news.cornell.edu/stories/Nov06/LocalFoods.kr.html.

21. Dr. Robin Davisson, speech at April 2008 fundraising dinner for Groundswell Center for Local Food and Farming.

Chapter 3: Green Building / Green Energy

1. Tim Knauss. "Solar Power Shines in Ithaca." *Syracuse Post Standard*, April 4, 2007.

2. Steve Nicholson, personal interview, January 27, 2010.

3. Environmental Impacts of US Buildings, based on 2003 figures. Data from: US Department of Energy. *2005 Buildings Energy Databook*, August 2005. [online]. [cited July 8, 2010]. buildingsdatabook.eren.doe.gov/docs\DataBooks\2005_BEDB.pdf.

4. Ibid.

5. Nicholson, interview.

6. Green Buildings Open House (GBOH) brochure, 2008.

7. Guillermo Metz, green building focus group, February 11, 2009.

8. GBOH brochure, 2008.

9. Peter Bardaglio, personal interview, February 20, 2009.

10. GBOH brochure, 2008.

11. Ibid.

12. Taryn Thompson. "Trust Secures Affordable Housing Stock." *Tompkins Weekly*, January 25–31, 2010.

13. GBOH brochure, 2008.

14. Andres Perez-Charneco. "Cornell Upgrades Power Plant." *Tompkins Weekly*, November 5–11, 2007.

15. Tina Wright. "CU Dumps Coal for Gas." *Tompkins Weekly*, January 25–31, 2010.

16. Peter Bardaglio. "Cornell Moves Beyond Coal." *Campus Green Builder*. [online]. [cited May 24, 2010]. campusgreenbuilder.org/node/668.

17. "Sustainability at Cornell: A Short History." *Cornell Chronicle*, August 21–September 1, 2008.

18. Dominic Frongillo, personal interview, March, 2009.

19. Ibid.

20. "In the Community." Enfield Energy website. [online]. [cited February 2, 2010]. enfield-energy.com.

21. Stephen Nicholson. "TREEA supports Connecticut Hill Wind Farm." *Ithaca Journal*, March 7, 2007.

22. Enfield Energy website. [online], [cited February 9, 2009]. enfieldenergy.com.

23. Brent Katzmann, personal interview, February 2009.

Chapter 4: Building a Livable City

1. Unfortunately our car-free adventure lasted just six enjoyable months. When the county downsized its fleet during funding cutbacks, Jared was required to get a car for his job, which requires a lot of home visits. However, another six months later, our new car was smashed in an accident, and we were car-free for several more months before purchasing a half-share in a neighbor's car.

2. Lester Brown. "The Return of the Bicycle." [online]. [cited July 6, 2010]. earthpolicy. greenpress.com/book-bytes/the-return-of-the-bicycle/.

3. Matthew DeBord. "Don't Just Share the Ride, Share the Car." *Los Angeles Times*, reprinted in the *Valley News*, November 18, 2007.

4. "Carsharing is good for the planet." Ithaca Carshare website. [online]. [cited May 21, 2010]. ithacacarshare.org/csh_greenbenefit.html.

5. Dan Chiras and Dave Wann. *Superbia: 31 Ways to Create Sustainable Neighborhoods.* New Society, 2003, p. 15.

6. Foreword by Anna Tibaijuka. *State of the World 2007: Our Urban Future*, Norton/ Worldwatch, 2007, p. xvii.

7. Ram Saran Thapa, quoted by his aunt Gail Carson in an e-mail to EVI, October, 2008.

8. EcoCity World Summit 2008 Conference Guide.

9. Figures from 2000 Census cited in City of Ithaca, New York. *Local Action Plan: to Reduce Greenhouse Gas Emissions for City of Ithaca Government Operations.* February, 2006, p. 4. [online]. [cited May 21, 2010]. ci.ithaca.ny.us/vertical/Sites/{5DCEB23D-5BF8-4AFF-806D-68E7C14DEB0D}/uploads/{3BFA0AD6-086E-4BCD-A8E2-53D85E251924}.PDF.

10. Carol Kammen. "A Hug for the Continuity of Community in Transit." *Ithaca Journal*, February 14, 2009.

11. Tompkins Consolidated Area Transit Inc. "Resolution 2008-14: Approval of Summer Discounted Fare Program." Board of Directors Meeting, August 28, 2008, pp. 4 and 5 [online]. [cited July 12, 2010]. tcatbus.com/files/all/bod_mtg_aug_08_3.pdf; James L.F. Bratton. "TCAT Extends 50-Cent Off-Peak Fare Promotion." *The Lansing Star* online, September 5, 2008. [online]. [cited July 12, 2010]. lansingstar.com/content/ view/3984/289/.

12. "Transportation, Cornell and the Community, Cornell's Proactive Initiative to Manage Its Commuter Traffic." Booklet produced by the Office of Publications and Marketing at Cornell University, September 2008.

13. Cornell University. "Transportation, Cornell and the Community: Cornell's Proactive Initiative to Manage Its Commuter Traffic." p. 4. For more information, see Town of Ithaca-Cornell University t-GEIS Team website. [online]. [cited June 25, 2010]. tgeis-project.org.

14. Krisy Gashler. "Mayor Who Built Commons Dies." *Ithaca Journal*, February 7–8, 2009.

15. Topher Sanders. "LACS gets dirty to keep air clean: Students make bus run on veggie oil." *Neighbors Weekly*, May 14, 2007.

16. Linda Stout. "Bicycle shop brings community together." *Neighbors Weekly*, December 17, 2007; RIBs brochure.

17. "Podcar City: Ithaca." Sustainable Transportation Conference, September, 2008, conference brochure.

18. Danielle Henbest. "Podcar City?" *Ithaca Times*, September 10, 2008.

19. William Kates. "Ithaca, NY wants to be America's 1st Podcar City." Associated Press, October 13, 2008, reported online at *Yahoo News*. [online]. [cited October 15, 2008]. news.yahoo.com/s/ap/20081013/ap_on_bi_ge/podcar_city.

20. "Executive Summary." The Draft Downtown Ithaca 2020 Strategy. [online]. [cited May 27, 2010]. downtownithaca.com/files/all/draft_2020_executive_summary.pdf.

21. *Southwest Urban Neighborhood, Project History.* City of Ithaca website. [online]. [cited March 17, 2009]. ci.ithaca.ny.us.

22. Ibid.
23. David Kay, personal interview, February 2010.
24. New Earth Living website. [online]. [cited May 27, 2010.] newearthliving.net/.
25. Rob Morache, personal interview, March 12, 2009.

Chapter 5: Local, Living Economy

1. SEEN flyer advertising March 2009 event.
2. Tompkins County Health Department. "General Population Description." Community Health Assessment, p.19. [online]. [cited June 1, 2010]. tompkins-co.org/health/cha05/pdf/CHA05-Tomp_ood-GenPop.pdf.
3. Jake Bakkila. "Setting Down A Big Red Footprint." *Ithaca Times*, February 14–20, 2007, a story on Cornell's economic impact study.
4. Tompkins County Living Wage Coalition. *People Who Work and Play by the Rules Should Not be Poor.* Minimum Wage Fact Sheet, February, 2004.
5. Tim Ashmore. "Alternatives' Living Wage up to $11.11." *Ithaca Journal*, April 25–26, 2009.
6. Ibid.
7. "Living Wage 2009 Press Release." AFCU website. [online]. [cited May 23, 2010]. alternatives.org/2009livingwagepressrelease.html.
8. "Individual Development Accounts." AFCU website. [online]. [cited June 1, 2010]. alternatives.org/ida.html.
9. "The Credit Path." AFCU website. [online]. [cited April 16, 2009]. alternatives.org/creditpath.html.
10. Tristram Coffin, focus group on local economy, March 12, 2009.
11. Tina Wright. "Garden Gate Delivery Moves Local Foods." *Ithaca Journal*, March 15, 2009.
12. "Business Services." AFCU website. [online]. [cited June 26, 2010]. alternatives.org/business.html.
13. Tina Wright, "Garden Gate."
14. YunYun Cai. "Ithaca Currency Keeps Money Local." *The Cornell Daily Sun* online, November.16, 2007. [online]. [cited May 23, 2010]. cornellsun.com/print/25453.
15. Steve Burke, focus group on local economy, March 2009.
16. Jan Norman, personal interview, January 8, 2008.
17. Kelly Spillane. "The Green Team," *Ithaca Times*, May 7–13, 2008.
18. Gay Nicholson, personal interview, February 13, 2008.
19. Pat Govang, presentation at "Green Jobs for the Finger Lakes" event, May 6, 2008.
20. "Going Green," PBS video on Challenge Industries website. [online]. [cited April 28, 2009]. aboutchallenge.org.
21. Spillane, "The Green Team."
22. Stacey Shackford. "Seeking Green in a Green Economy." *Ithaca Journal*, November 6, 2008.
23. Spillane, "The Green Team."

Chapter 6: Educating for a Sustainable Future

1. Ithaca College Climate Change Teach-in, February 5, 2009.
2. Association for the Advancement of Sustainability in Higher Education. "AASHE Awards." [online]. [cited February 10, 2009]. aashe.org/programs/awards.php.
3. Sarah Brylinksky, personal interview, March 22, 2009.
4. "Cross-disciplinary Dialogue." The Piedmont Project — About the Project. [online], [cited May 24, 2010]. scienceandsociety.emory.edu/piedmont/project.htm#faculty.
5. The Finger Lakes Project. "Workshop Learning Outcomes." [online]. [cited June 28, 2010]. ithaca.edu/fingerlakes_project/workshop/wksplearninggoals/.
6. Marian Brown, personal interview, February 5, 2010.

7. "Our Mission." Sustainable Tompkins website. [online]. [cited May 24, 2010]. sustainabletompkins.org/about-st/our-mission/.

8. "Tompkins Sustainability Map." Sustainable Tompkins website. [online]. [cited May 24, 2010]. maps.sustainabletompkins.org.

9. "About Us — What We Do — Vision." New Roots Charter School website. [online]. [cited May 24, 2010]. newrootsschool.org/content/view/what-we-do.html.

10. Tina Nilsen-Hodges, personal interview, February 18, 2010.

11. "Core Practices and Benchmarks." Expeditionary Learning website. [online]. [cited May 24, 2010]. elschools.org/aboutus/practices.html.

12. "About Groundswell." Groundswell Center website. [online]. [cited May 25, 2010]. groundswellcenter.org/index.php?option=com_content&view=article&id=46&Itemid=5.

13. Todd McLane, quoted in personal e-mail from Joanna Green, February 10, 2010.

14. Joanna Green, personal interview, February 15, 2010.

15. Cornell's Office of Sustainability website. [online]. [cited July 7, 2010]. cornell.edu/sustainability/.

16. Global Change Project Portal. Museum of the Earth website. [online]. [cited May 25, 2010]. museumoftheearth.org /outreach.php?page=overview/globalchange.

17. Charlie Trautman. "A Change in the Weather." Sciencenter website. [online]. [cited May 25, 2010]. sciencenter.org/monograph/.

Chapter 7: Getting the Word Out—Alternative Media

1. "The Garden" website. [online]. [cited May 25, 2010]. thegardenmovie.com.

2. Finger Lakes Environmental Film Festival, 2009 Program Guide.

3. "Why Positive News?" *Positive News US*, front page, Spring 2010.

4. Becky Daniel. "Ecuador's Historic Vote: Nature Gets Legal Rights." *Positive News US*, Winter 2009, pp. 1 and 13.

5. "Exposing Poverty." *Positive News US*, Winter 2009, p. 1. For more information: pantstopoverty.com.

6. "Reader Appreciation." *Positive News US* website. [online]. [cited May 25, 2010]. positivenewsus.org /about/endorse.html.

7. Personal interview with Ilonka Wloch, June 17, 2009. In a crazy moment of synchronicity, I ran into Ilonka (who now lives in California) by chance, on the paths of EcoVillage at Ithaca, right after deciding to interview her! She was visiting for a few days, unbeknownst to me. "Media works in mysterious ways," she joked.

8. "Young Swede Saves Fins." *Positive News US*, Spring 2009, p. 11.

9. Tompkins Weekly website. [online]. [cited July 7, 2010]. tompkinsweekly.com/.

10. "ITVS Community Cinema." Green Guerrillas website [online] [cited June 2, 2010]. guerrilla-griots.org/communitycinema.html.

11. "Taking Root " film website. [online]. [cited May 25, 2010]. takingrootfilm.com.

12. "Glen Greenwald and Amy Goodman Share Inaugural Izzy Award for Independent Media." Ithaca College, Office of Media Relations news release, March 4, 2009.

13. "Resembling I.F.Stone." Remarks by Jeremy Stone, published by CommonDreams.org on April 1, 2009.

14. "Independent/Progressive Media Internships." Park Center for Independent Media. [online] [cited June 2, 2010]. ithaca.edu/rhp/independentmedia/internships/.

15. Andrew Bernier, e-mail to IC sustainability listserv, fall 2008.

Chapter 8: Health and Wellness for All

1. In Tompkins County, 10.7% of the population did not have health insurance in 2000. This increased to 27.3% in 2005. Figures for 2000: see census.gov/cgi-bin/hhes/sahie/sahie.cgi. Figures for 2005: US Census Bureau. "Small Area Health Insurance Estimates — 2005 Health Insurance Coverage Status for Counties." [online]. [cited July 12, 2010]. smpbff1.dsd.census.gov/TheDataWeb_HotReport/servlet/HotReportEngi

neServlet?reportid=4686aab1f61a5cc93f4eb037c447fe24&emailname=saeb@census.
gov&filename=SAHIE-County07.hrml.

2. Ithaca Health Alliance website. [online]. [cited May 26, 2010]. ithacahealth.org/index.
   html.

3. Bethany Schroeder, personal e-mail, February 26, 2010.

4. Ibid.

5. Associated Press. "One in Five Children in Study Obese." *Ithaca Journal*, April 11, 2009.
   The study analyzed 8,550 nationally representative four-year-olds and was published in
   the *Archives of Pediatrics and Adolescent Medicine*.

6. "Partnership Supports Grassroots Effort to Address Childhood Obesity Factors."
   Cornell Cooperative Extension Annual Report, 2006. Obesity figures for Tompkins
   County quoted in the article are extrapolated from a Center for Disease Control Study,
   and a NYS Department of Health study.

7. Shira Adriance, video interview on Ithaca City Schools website, [online].[cited May 26,
   2010]. icsdbond2007.com/cce.html.

8. Fresh Fruit and Vegetable Snack Program video. NY Coalition for Healthy School Food
   website. [online]. [cited May 26, 2010]. healthyschoolfood.org/video.htm.

9. Sandra Repp and Shira Adriance. "Students Offer Input on Healthy Foods." *Tompkins
   Weekly*, February 18, 2008.

10. Fresh Fruit and Vegetable Snack Program video.

11. Jemila Sequeira, personal interview, December 10, 2009.

12. Linda Stout "Conference to Discuss Green Living." *Ithaca Journal*, August 30, 2007.

13. Sandra Steingraber. *Living Downstream: An Ecologist's Personal Investigation of Cancer
    and the Environment*, 2nd ed. revised and updated. DaCapo, 2010; Sandra Steingraber.
    Having Faith: An Ecologist's Journey to Motherhood. DaCapo, 2001.

14. Jennifer E. Moyer, BSN, RN. "More Reasons to Stop Smoking." *Tompkins Weekly*, July
    13–19, 2009.

15. Krisy Gashler. "State Health Commisioner Lauds Ithaca's Anti-Smoking Efforts." *Ithaca
    Journal*, April 7, 2009.

16. "About the Event." Aids Ride for Life website. [online]. [cited June 29, 2010]. aidsride-
    forlife.org/?page=about.

17. "Why We Swim." Women Swimmin' website. [online]. [cited July 17, 2009]. women-
    swimmin.org/why.mgi.

18. Adapted from "The Cycle of Life," a chapter in Liz Walker. *EcoVillage at Ithaca: Pio-
    neering a Sustainable Culture*. New Society, 2005.

19. Educate the Children International website. [online]. [cited May 27, 2010]. etc-nepal.
    org/.

Chapter 9: Addressing Racism

1. Jesse Jackson Sr. "Dr.King's Last Birthday." Op-Ed Contributor, *New York Times*, January 19, 2009.

2. "The Underground Railway in Tompkins County: Searching for the Path to Freedom."
   The History Center in Tompkins County. [online]. [cited May 28, 2010]. thehistorycen-
   ter.net/PDF/URR%20Packet.pdf.

3. Topher Sanders. "We Could Have Done More to Shield Student, Educator Says." *Ithaca
   Journal*, December 21, 2007.

4. Steve Cariddi. "Human Rights Challenge — Lessons Learned." *Ithaca Journal*, December 11, 2007.

5. Liz Lawyer. "Panel Sides with Kearney in ICSD Case." *Ithaca Journal*, May 12, 2009;
   Sanders. "We Could Have Done More...".

6. Audrey Cooper, personal interview, June 9, 2009.

7. Audrey Cooper, MRC e-mail on "Talking Circles Recruitment," January 14, 2009.

8. Kirby Edmonds, personal interview, May 19, 2009.

9. Marcia Fort, personal interview, May 26, 2009.

10. Village at Ithaca. "Executive Summary." First Annual Equity Report Card: Holding Ourselves Accountable. Fall 2006. [online]. [cited May 31, 2010]. icsd.k12.ny.us/legacy/board/equity/ERC_Exec_summary_12_22f.pdf.
11. Village at Ithaca. "Statement by Jeff Furman." Second Annual Equity Report Card, 2006–2007. [online]. [cited June 9, 2010.]. icsd.k12.ny.us/legacy/board/equity/2ndEquityReportCard.pdf.
12. Jeff Klaus, e-mail to Ithaca College Sustainability listserv, May 13, 2009.
13. Taryn Thompson. "Outgoing School Board Member Reflects on Time in Office." *The Ithaca Times*, May 13–19, 2009.

Chapter 10: Ithaca Is Gorges

1. In 2002, the USGS calculated 1.9 trillion cubic feet of gas was available. In early 2008, Terry Englander, a geoscience professor at Pennsylvania State University and Gary Lash, a geology professor at the State University of New York at Fredonia, surprised everyone with estimates that the Marcellus might contain more than 500 trillion cubic feet of natural gas. See "Marcellus Shale — Appalachian Basin Natural Gas Play." [online]. [cited July 21, 2009]. geology.com/articles/marcellus-shale.shtml.
2. Krisy Gashler. "38% of land area in Tompkins already leased for drilling." *Ithaca Journal*, April 28, 2009.
3. Stephen Penningroth, Ph.D. "Documenting Contamination of Private Water Supplies by Gas Well Drilling in New York State." Community Science Institute. [online]. [cited June 30, 2010]. communityscience.org/documents/Gas wells and water FAQ sheet — Documenting Contamination.pdf.
4. See website: shaleshock.org.
5. Lisa Ann Wright. Shaleshock Power Point presentation. Offered to Ithaca Town Board on July 13, 2009.
6. "Making the Most of Every Drop." *Solutions for a Better World*. National Geographic Supplement, April 2009.
7. "Issues in the Cayuga Lake Watershed." Cayuga Lake Watershed Network, 2004.
8. See website: cayugalake.org.
9. See website: cleanwaterpledge.org.
10. "Smart Steps for Clean Water." Cayuga Lake Watershed Network. [online]. [cited June 30, 1020]. cayugalake.org/images/resources/SmrtStps06.pdf.
11. Tompkins County Planning Department. *Tompkins County Comprehensive Plan: Planning for our Future*, p. 37. [online]. [cited June 2, 2010]. tompkins-co.org/planning/compplan/index.htm.
12. Tim Ashmore. "Management plan promotes stewardship." *Neighbors Weekly*, December 24, 2007.
13. Anthony Hall. "Land Trust Adds to Emerald Necklace." *Tompkins Weekly*, January 7–13, 2008.
14. "Cornell Plantations Natural Areas Program," a publication of Cornell Plantations.
15. City of Ithaca. "Our Master Plan for Ithaca, the 'Forest City.'" City of Ithaca website. [online]. [cited July 31, 2009]. ci.ithaca.ny.us/index.asp?Type=B_BASIC&SEC={3B881805-DA8B-4AE7-B4EB-0BBDFBBB26E5}&DE={B79ACB16-5503-421E-B93D-3E1908234288}.
16. Anne Marie Cummings. "Urban Planning Releaf Comes to Cornell." *Tompkins Weekly*, July 21, 2008.
17. Ibid.

Chapter 11: Turning Waste into Gold

1. Finger Lakes Zero Waste Coalition website. [online]. [cited June 3, 2010]. fingerlakeszerowaste.org.
2. US Environmental Protection Agency. " Municipal Solid Waste Generation, Recycling,

and Disposal in the United States: Facts and Figures for 2006." [online]. [cited September 8, 2009]. epa.gov/epawaste/nonhaz/municipal/pubs/msw06.pdf.

3. Barb Eckstrom, talk at Finger Lakes Bioneers conference, October 16, 2009.
4. Adam Michaelides, e-mail, October 2009.
5. P&S Excavating and Cayuga Compost website. [online]. [cited June 3, 2010]. cayuga-compost.com.
6. Ithaca City School District website. [online]. [cited September 23, 2009]. icsd.k12.ny.us.
7. Rita Nolan. "Pay Dirt." *School Nutrition Magazine,* January 2009.
8. Tom Shelley. "Steep Hollow Farm Sustainable Chicken Project." Unpublished article, September 2008.
9. Go Green Initiative website. [online]. [cited September 25, 2009]. gogreeninitiative. org.
10. Leo Riley, talk at Finger Lakes Bioneers conference, October 16, 2009.
11. Eckstrom, talk.
12. Kat McCarthy, talk at Finger Lakes Bioneers conference, October 16, 2009.
13. Finger Lakes ReUse website. [online]. [cited June 3, 2010]. fingerlakesreuse.org.
14. Editorial. "A Bag Problem Blossoms." *New York Times,* December 3, 2007.
15. "China Says No to Plastic Bags." *Positive News International,* Summer 2008.
16. Finger Lakes Buy Green website. [online]. [cited July 2, 2010]. fingerlakesbuygreen.org.
17. Kelly Spillane. "The Green Team." *Ithaca Times,* May 7–13, 2008.
18. Ibid.
19. Ibid.
20. Christina Copeland, e-mail, December 22, 2008.

Chapter 12: Local Government and Institutional Change

1. For more information, see: Presidents Climate Commitment Implementation Committee. *Climate Action Plan Summary Report.* [online]. [cited June 4, 2010]. sustainablecampus.cornell.edu/docs/cap_report3-22-10-lo res.pdf.
2. Peter Bardaglio, commentary at Cornell CAP release, October, 2009.
3. Cornell *Climate Action Plan Summary Report,* p. 5.
4. Ibid., p. 4.
5. Ibid., p. 7.
6. Ibid., p. 8.
7. Ibid., p. 14.
8. Cornell CAP introduction. [online]. [June 18, 2010]. sustainablecampus.cornell.edu/climate/index.cfm.
9. "Executive Summary." Ithaca College Climate Action Plan, September 15, 2009, p. 5.
10. The New York Upstate Chapter of the American Planning Association awarded its 2009 "Planning Excellence Award for Innovation in Sustainability" to the Tompkins County Planning Department for its Energy and Greenhouse Gas Emissions amendment.
11. Katie Borgella, presentation, Cornell CAP release, October 2009.
12. Tompkins County Comprehensive Plan Energy and Greenhouse Gas Emissions Element 2008 Amendment, p. 6. [online]. [cited June 4, 2010]. tompkins-co.org/planning/compplan/documents/EGGEElementfromPublisher.pdf.
13. "City of Ithaca, Local Action Plan: to reduce greenhouse gas emissions for City government operations" [online].[cited June 16, 2010]. http://www.ci. ithaca.ny.us/index.asp?Type=B_BASIC&SEC={29D0D769-BD56-44D9-BA51-02FA7AFD8969}&DE={BB3ED32C-1F6A-497B-AF8B-BC50BE22E7E1}
14. Tompkins County Climate Protection Initiative. "About Us." [online]. [cited June 7, 2010]. tccpi.org/About_Us.html.
15. Dominic Frongillo and Peter Bardaglio, comments at TCCPI meeting on January 29, 2010.

Chapter 13: Changing Culture, Changing Lives

1. Pastor Bruce, personal interview, August 7, 2009.
2. Pastor Bruce, speech at Love Knows No Bounds benefit, August 7, 2009.
3. Marcia Fort, personal interview, May 26, 2009.
4. Vitamin L concert, "Tear Down the Walls," lyrics by Jan Nigro.
5. Vitamin L publicity materials, August 8, 2009.
6. Greensprings Natural Burial website. [online]. [cited June 7, 2010]. naturalburial.org.
7. Forum at the Unitarian Church of Ithaca, November 8, 2009.
8. Alternative Gift Fair website. [online]. [cited December 5, 2009]. ithacaaltgiftfair.org.
9. SewGreen website. [online]. [cited June 8, 2010]. sew-green.org.
10. Ibid.
11. SewGreen website. "Ethical Shopping." [online]. [cited June 8, 2010]. sew-green.org/sew_shopping.html.
12. Wendy Skinner, personal interview, December 5, 2009.
13. Clarissa Pinkola Estes. "Let Your Soul Light Shine Bright." [online] [cited June 18, 2010]. weboflove.org/070825soullightshinebright.

Chapter 14: Art at the Heart—Ithaca Celebrates!

1. Bryan VanCampen. "Guiding Light." *Ithaca Times*, Winter Guide 2008.
2. Bryan VanCampen. "Shining Light." *Ithaca Times*, Winter Guide 2009.
3. Hangar Theatre website. "Mission." [online]. [cited June 10, 2010]. hangartheatre.org/index.php?page=about.
4. Tim Ashmore. "Official Pursues Room Tax Plan despite drop in hotel stays." *Ithaca Journal*, January 13, 2009.

Chapter 15: Bringing It All Together—What Have We Learned?

1. Jon Jensen, personal interview, December 17, 2009.
2. Bethany Schroeder, event announcement, January 17, 2010.
3. Transition US. "About Us." [online]. [cited June 15, 2010]. transitionus.org/about-us.
4. See James Howard Kunstler. *The Long Emergency: Surviving the End of Oil, Climate Change, and Other Converging Catastrophes of the Twenty-First Century.* Grove, 2006.
5. Rob Hopkins and Richard Heinberg. *The Transition Handbook: From Oil Dependency to Local Resilience.* Chelsea Green 2008.
6. Park Foundation. "Program Areas." [online]. [cited June 15, 2010]. parkfoundation.org/program_areas.php.
7. Jensen, interview.
8. Ibid.
9. For more in-depth discussion, see Gay Nicholson. "Sustainable Tompkins Phase I: a Community Conversation on the Challenge of Sustainable Development." Sustainable Tompkins website. [online]. [cited June 15, 2010]. sustainabletompkins.org/about-st/how-st-got-started/.
10. Paul Hawken. *Blessed Unrest: How the Largest Movement in the World Came into Being and Why No One Saw It Coming.* Viking, 2007.
11. Arundhati Roy. "Confronting Empire." World Social Forum #3, January 27, 2003. [online]. [cited July 6, 2010]. zcommunications.org/confronting-empire-by-arundhati-roy.

Index

About the Author

As the co-founder and executive director of EcoVillage at Ithaca (EVI — ecovillageithaca.org) since 1991, **Liz Walker** has dedicated her full-time work to bring this internationally acclaimed project from vision to reality. Her book, *EcoVillage at Ithaca: Pioneering a Sustainable Culture* (New Soci-ety, 2005), has helped to introduce the concepts of ecovillages and sustainable communities to a broad audience in the US and other countries. Liz travels widely as a speaker and workshop leader and is frequently interviewed by national and international media. She was a founding board member of Gaia Education, which now teaches workshops around the world.

While her primary work has been developing EVI as a living laboratory of sustainable practices, Liz has also been active in the sustainability movement around Ithaca, New York, as a founding member of the Partnership for Sustainability Education between Ithaca College and EVI, which in turn helped to catalyze Sustainable Tompkins and Ithaca Carshare. She serves on the Cayuga Sustainability Council and the Tompkins County Climate Protection Initiative.

Liz lives with her husband at EcoVillage at Ithaca, where she is managing the development of a third cohousing neighborhood, dedicated to affordability, accessibility and cutting edge green design. In her spare time she enjoys biking, dancing, yoga, gardening and cooking. She strives to live a full and balanced life, open to the beauty of living in the moment.

If you have enjoyed *Choosing a Sustainable Future,*
you might also enjoy other

BOOKS TO BUILD A NEW SOCIETY

Our books provide positive solutions for people who want to
make a difference. We specialize in:

**Sustainable Living • Green Building • Peak Oil
Renewable Energy • Environment & Economy
Natural Building & Appropriate Technology
Progressive Leadership • Resistance and Community
Educational & Parenting Resources**

For a full list of NSP titles, please call 1-800-567-6772 *or check out our website* at:

www.newsociety.com

NEW SOCIETY PUBLISHERS
Deep Green for over 30 years